"The writings of Zechariah were a
and apostles because the proph
God's Messiah. Now the scholar
us a tremendous tool to help in
hope."

—**Dr. Mac Brunson**, senior pastor, First Baptist Church, Jacksonville, Florida

"Stephen Rummage's exposition of Zechariah serves as an exemplary display of pastoral exposition, honoring the Word of God with its verse-by-verse exegesis while at the same time applying its eternal principles to contemporary believers. God is certainly honored with such a commentary that brings the original meaning of the text to life and then pours itself into the life of the believer. The end result of this biblical exposition will be the changed lives of those who read it and take the Scripture to heart."

—**Dr. Emir Caner**, president, Truett-McConnell College, Cleveland, Georgia

"Of the many commentaries published each year, few are as well targeted to the needs of pastors as the Christ-Centered Exposition series. This particular volume brings to life the text of four of the Minor Prophets with a major message. The commentary not only provides solid and helpful exegetical insights; it also provides the kind of helpful illustrative and applicational material that is rarely included in other commentaries. This commentary will have great value to any preacher or teacher dealing with these important portions of Scripture."

—**Dr. Michael Duduit**, executive editor, *Preaching* magazine, and dean of the Clamp Divinity School and College of Christian Studies, Anderson University, Anderson, South Carolina

"The 'Minor' Prophets shared 'major' messages that are amazingly relevant today. When rightly explained and applied, these ancient voices provide engaging texts from which to preach and teach in the twenty-first century. In this concise volume, Micah Fries, Stephen Rummage, and Robby Gallaty have opened a treasure chest for every modern-day servant of the Word. Having served as a senior pastor for more than thirty years, I appreciate good commentaries on the biblical text. Accordingly, I highly recommend this work by these gifted, godly men."

—**Dr. Steve Gaines**, senior pastor, Bellevue Baptist Church, Memphis, Tennessee

"Twenty-first-century expositors affirm the sufficiency of every book of the Bible, yet few preach all of them. Somehow the 'Minor Prophets' designation of books like Zephaniah, Haggai, Zechariah, and Malachi suggests that these books are less important than the more familiar books of the Bible. Through his ministry as both a pastor and a preaching professor, Dr. Stephen Rummage exemplifies why any expositor who affirms the sufficiency of the entire Bible must preach every book of the Bible. Rummage's Zechariah commentary in the Christ-Centered Exposition series provides preachers with natural textual divisions, vivid illustrations, and an accurately precise exegesis that will enable them to preach Zechariah in a way that is both text-driven and Christ-centered. This volume will not only convince expositors why they must preach Zechariah from their pulpits but will also demonstrate *how* they should preach Zechariah in their pulpits."

—**Dr. Matt Queen**, L. R. Scarborough Chair of Evangelism ("The Chair of Fire"), associate professor of Evangelism, Southwestern Baptist Theological Seminary, Fort Worth, Texas

"By identifying the main idea of each passage in one sentence, the Christ-Centered Exposition commentary will speed up sermon development and improve clarity in communication. The entire commentary is excellent, and Stephen Rummage in particular is one of the best expositors and communicators in the country, making this volume a must have for any preacher of the gospel of Jesus Christ."

—**Dr. Thomas White**, president and professor of Theology, Cedarville University, Cedarville, Ohio

"Dr. Stephen Rummage is an artist. He paints our Savior, Jesus Christ, in many aspects of His ministry. He describes Him as the King, the Stone, the Slave sold for thirty pieces of silver, the smitten Shepherd, the Branch, and the Glorious Ruler. Zechariah is a commentary of vision. Through Stephen's writng, you will gloriously see a prophet who writes when he is young and when he is old. His two subjects are Jerusalem and Jesus. As one of the minor prophets, Zechariah tells us the Lord is jealous over Jerusalem. His name means 'Jehovah Remembers,' and one of the reasons you will love this book is because when it was written, it came at a time when the remnant was discouraged. As in our day, times were tough. Right people, right place, right time, but downhearted. But God remembers Jerusalem, and He also remembers you. So lift up your head. His kingdom will be established, and our redemption draweth nigh. Even so, 'Come Lord Jesus.' You're going to enjoy this minor prophet and these major messages."

—**Dr. Ken Whitten**, senior pastor, Idlewild Baptist Church, Lutz, Florida

OT / COMMENTARY

AUTHORS Micah Fries, Stephen Rummage, and Robby Gallaty
SERIES EDITORS David Platt, Daniel L. Akin, and Tony Merida

CHRIST-CENTERED Exposition

EXALTING JESUS IN

ZEPHANIAH, HAGGAI, ZECHARIAH, MALACHI

NASHVILLE, TENNESSEE

Christ-Centered Exposition Commentary: Exalting Jesus in Zephaniah, Haggai, Zechariah, Malachi

B&H Publishing Group
Nashville, Tennessee

ISBN 978-0-8054-9648-2

Dewey Decimal Classification:
Subject Heading: BIBLE. O.T.

Printed in the United States of America
2 3 4 5 6 7 8 9 10 • 20 19 18 17 16 15
VP

SERIES DEDICATION

Dedicated to Adrian Rogers and John Piper. They have taught us to love the gospel of Jesus Christ, to preach the Bible as the inerrant Word of God, to pastor the church for which our Savior died, and to have a passion to see all nations gladly worship the Lamb.

—David Platt, Tony Merida, and Danny Akin
March 2013

TABLE OF CONTENTS

Zechariah

Commentary by Stephen Rummage

Malachi

Commentary by Robby Gallaty

ACKNOWLEDGMENTS

I am deeply indebted to a number of people, more than I can adequately acknowledge. Most of all I am grateful for Tracy. Babe, you are God's good gift of grace to me. I love you. I'm also thankful for my daughters Sarah Grace and Kessed Noel, whom I love and who make me happier and more grateful than any one man should be. Finally, I am grateful to the people of Frederick Boulevard Baptist Church whom I was serving when I began writing this, and among whom I learned to love preaching through the Old Testament. Thank you, all of you.

—Micah Fries

I would like to express my deep appreciation for those who have assisted me in completing this book. I am thankful for Hamilton Barber, Jake Pratt, Paul Laso, and Linda Brown for reviewing the manuscript and examining its integrity. I could not have completed the book without your input. I am thankful for the loving supportive congregation of people I have the privilege of preaching to every week at Brainerd Baptist Church. I am grateful for my wife Kandi, who motivates me every day to be a better husband, father, and follower of Christ. Finally, I am eternally thankful for the grace that was extended to me on November 12, 2002. Jesus came looking for me when I wasn't looking for Him.

—Robby Gallaty

I am very grateful to God for several people who helped me bring my commentary on Zechariah to completion. My precious wife, Michele, was a tremendous encourager and wonderful content editor, as always. Thanks also to Perry Kosieniak for valuable editorial insight and assistance. Barbie Frost, my executive assistant, zealously guarded my schedule as I wrote. The congregation of Bell Shoals Baptist Church and listeners to the *Moving Forward* radio program provided a receptive and appreciative audience for my sermons from this book, and they have undergirded my efforts with prayer. To God alone be the glory!

—Stephen Rummage

SERIES INTRODUCTION

Augustine said, "Where Scripture speaks, God speaks." The editors of the Christ-Centered Exposition Commentary series believe that where God speaks, the pastor must speak. God speaks through His written Word. We must speak from that Word. We believe the Bible is God breathed, authoritative, inerrant, sufficient, understandable, necessary, and timeless. We also affirm that the Bible is a Christ-centered book; that is, it contains a unified story of redemptive history of which Jesus is the hero. Because of this Christ-centered trajectory that runs from Genesis 1 through Revelation 22, we believe the Bible has a corresponding global-missions thrust. From beginning to end, we see God's mission as one of making worshipers of Christ from every tribe and tongue worked out through this redemptive drama in Scripture. To that end we must preach the Word.

In addition to these distinct convictions, the Christ-Centered Exposition Commentary series has some distinguishing characteristics. First, this series seeks to display exegetical accuracy. What the Bible says is what we want to say. While not every volume in the series will be a verse-by-verse commentary, we nevertheless desire to handle the text carefully and explain it rightly. Those who teach and preach bear the heavy responsibility of saying what God has said in His Word and declaring what God has done in Christ. We desire to handle God's Word faithfully, knowing that we must give an account for how we have fulfilled this holy calling (Jas 3:1).

Second, the Christ-Centered Exposition Commentary series has pastors in view. While we hope others will read this series, such as parents, teachers, small-group leaders, and student ministers, we desire to provide a commentary busy pastors will use for weekly preparation of biblically faithful and gospel-saturated sermons. This series is not academic in nature. Our aim is to present a readable and pastoral style of commentaries. We believe this aim will serve the church of the Lord Jesus Christ.

Third, we want the Christ-Centered Exposition Commentary series to be known for the inclusion of helpful illustrations and theologically driven applications. Many commentaries offer no help in illustrations, and few offer any kind of help in application. Often those that do offer illustrative material and application unfortunately give little serious attention to the text. While giving ourselves primarily to explanation, we also hope to serve readers by providing inspiring and illuminating illustrations coupled with timely and timeless application.

Finally, as the name suggests, the editors seek to exalt Jesus from every book of the Bible. In saying this, we are not commending wild allegory or fanciful typology. We certainly believe we must be constrained to the meaning intended by the divine Author Himself, the Holy Spirit of God. However, we also believe the Bible has a messianic focus, and our hope is that the individual authors will exalt Christ from particular texts. Luke 24:25-27,44-47 and John 5:39,46 inform both our hermeneutics and our homiletics. Not every author will do this the same way or have the same degree of Christ-centered emphasis. That is fine with us. We believe faithful exposition that is Christ centered is not monolithic. We do believe, however, that we must read the whole Bible as Christian Scripture. Therefore, our aim is both to honor the historical particularity of each biblical passage and to highlight its intrinsic connection to the Redeemer.

The editors are indebted to the contributors of each volume. The reader will detect a unique style from each writer, and we celebrate these unique gifts and traits. While distinctive in their approaches, the authors share a common characteristic in that they are pastoral theologians. They love the church, and they regularly preach and teach God's Word to God's people. Further, many of these contributors are younger voices. We think these new, fresh voices can serve the church well, especially among a rising generation that has the task of proclaiming the Word of Christ and the Christ of the Word to the lost world.

We hope and pray this series will serve the body of Christ well in these ways until our Savior returns in glory. If it does, we will have succeeded in our assignment.

David Platt
Daniel L. Akin
Tony Merida
Series Editors
February 2013

Zephaniah

Introduction

ZEPHANIAH 1:1

Main Idea: The book of Zephaniah is the story of God's powerful judgment and His equally astonishing grace.

Remember "The Boy Who Cried Wolf"? One of the more well known of Aesop's Fables, the story describes the boy who repeatedly called out about impending danger when no danger was present, only to find that when actual danger was present, no one was willing to come to his aid because they no longer believed him when he called. In a small sense Israel, and more specifically, the city of Jerusalem, was guilty of treating the prophet Zephaniah with the same disregard, though Zephaniah was not guilty of deceptively crying out when danger was not present. No, instead the people of Judah had disregarded God for many, many years and found themselves now being called to repentance, only they seem to have had little interest in turning from their sin.

The people of God were in the midst of a long period of rebellion. Zephaniah helps us understand when this occurs by providing for us his lineage. He is the great-great grandson of King Hezekiah. Hezekiah, of course, is known for his illness and request of the Lord for longer life, which God answered by extending his life 15 years. During this time he fathered Manasseh, who would follow him as the next king of Israel. Unfortunately, Manasseh was an evil king who did great spiritual damage in Israel. Following Manasseh was King Amon, who continued Manasseh's legacy and did not honor God with his leadership. As a result Israel continued to be mired in spiritual decline. Manasseh and Amon ruled for a total of 57 years, and Josiah came to power after Amon. Josiah was a different ruler than his two predecessors; he desired to rule in a way that honored God and that called the people to repentance. Zephaniah was a contemporary of Josiah, and it was in the midst of this environment that Zephaniah began to prophesy.

Zephaniah was almost certainly a person of some influence, mostly due to his family heritage. As a direct descendant of Hezekiah, he was probably a man of affluence, some renown, and influence. A contemporary of Jeremiah, Zephaniah would have been one of a few prophetic voices who lent their support to the king's desire for reform. His position in the community would almost certainly have given strength to his voice and granted him a certain audience. However, his position in the community would also have likely exacerbated the opposition when the community realized the content of his call for repentance.

Zephaniah's lineage also helps us to get an idea of when the book was written. His prophecy was written during the reign of Josiah, but before the fall of Nineveh. Helping us pinpoint it a bit more is the fact that it was written before Josiah's reforms, which would have occurred around 621 BC. So, taking into account each of these features, we can be fairly confident that the book was written between 641 and 622 BC.

The dominant themes of the book are pretty clear. This is a book of judgment, a call to repentance, and a declaration of God's gracious work on behalf of His people.

The Day of the Lord Is Coming because of Their Idol Worship

ZEPHANIAH 1:2-18

Main Idea: The judgment of God will be poured out against the whole earth because of people's persistent disobedience.

I. The Whole Earth Will Be Destroyed (1:2-3).
II. God's Own People Will Be Destroyed because of Their Treason and Idolatry (1:4-6).
III. The Day of the Lord Is Upon Them (1:7).
IV. The Grief Will Be Intense Because No One Will Be Exempt from God's Judgment (1:8-11).
V. Those Who Pursue Other Gods Will Lose Everything (1:12-13).
VI. The Day of the Lord Is Unlike Any Other Day in Its Terror (1:14-17).
VII. Their Sin Will Bring About Complete Destruction (1:18).

The Whole Earth Will Be Destroyed

ZEPHANIAH 1:2-3

Talk about a doomsday scenario! Zephaniah kicks off with a bang, and not in a good way. The nation of Judah was guilty of gross negligence in its relationship with God, and as a result Zephaniah warns that judgment is coming. However, this is not your typical warning of judgment. In what is arguably a more intense and extensive warning than anywhere else in Scripture, Zephaniah pleads with the nation, and specifically the inhabitants of Jerusalem, to repent of their sin and to turn back to God. In what can be viewed as one of the more depressing prophetic books, Zephaniah attempts to awaken the people to their disobedience. In an attempt to convey the seriousness of this charge, God, speaking through Zephaniah, threatens not only to judge them, but to wipe them off the face of the earth. Not only will He wipe them off the face of the earth, He makes the claim that He will wipe every living thing off the face of the earth. This is a deep and devastating warning that Judah must heed.

Like every culture and people who have been introduced to God, there is a temptation to diminish God in our minds and to live as if there are no ramifications for our behavior. The people of Judah, like many of us today, found themselves tempted by a host of good things, as we will see later in the passage. The temptation to chase after the good things, though, had caused them to abandon the best thing, namely their pursuit of God. This is not altogether different from our temptations today. In his book *Counterfeit Gods* Dr. Tim Keller speaks about this temptation:

> The human heart takes good things like a successful career, love, material possessions, even family, and turns them into ultimate things. Our hearts deify them as the center of our lives, because, we think, they can give us significance and security, safety and fulfillment, if we attain them. (*Counterfeit Gods*, xiv)

In Zephaniah's day their pursuits appeared to be such things as comfort, wealth, and political influence. Sounds a lot like our contemporary culture, does it not? While we claim allegiance to Jesus, with all that brings, we often attempt to divide our allegiance and chase other things rather than pursue Christ. In these times Jesus' words in Matthew 6 are a reminder to us of the futility of worshipping at the feet of multiple gods: "No one can be a slave of two masters, since either he will hate one and love the other, or be devoted to one and despise the other. You cannot be slaves of God and of money" (Matt 6:24). You and I could insert any number of good things at the end of that verse. Marriage, children, vocation, and rest are all sufficient temptations. In light of those temptations, though, we need to hear and heed Zephaniah's warning to Judah. If we choose to jettison Christ for the pursuit of false gods, we are in danger of judgment. We must choose to follow God or not to follow Him. That choice will have eternal consequences. Like Joshua and the nation of Israel, we must choose to serve Christ, and to serve Him only:

> *But if it doesn't please you to worship Yahweh, choose for yourselves today the one you will worship: the gods your fathers worshiped beyond the Euphrates River or the gods of the Amorites in whose land you are living. As for me and my family, we will worship Yahweh.* (Josh 24:15)

This basic theme will resonate through the rest of the book. Before Judah are two choices. They can choose to honor God, repent of their sin, and experience His blessing, or they can persist in their disobedience and face His judgment, which could include their total destruction.

Making this judgment possible is the anger of God. While we often do not like to speak of God's anger, we cannot study Zephaniah with integrity and not recognize that God is not just a little displeased; no, He is very angry, and His anger has very real and dangerous implications. At the conclusion of the book we will see one of the most beautiful and majestic offers of grace that can be found anywhere in Scripture—both in the Old and New Testaments—but before that offer of grace can be extended, it must be preceded by a clear depiction of God's wrath. It is against the backdrop of God's appropriate wrath that the grace of God is so powerfully displayed.

God's Own People Will Be Destroyed because of Their Treason and Idolatry

ZEPHANIAH 1:4-6

While the declaration of judgment in the first few verses was a bit more general, God begins to zero in, very specifically, on His own people. This, of course, would have shocked and terrified them. God says to Judah that He is ready to stretch out His hand against them. This is a specific reference to judgment. God is going to judge the people that He loves, mainly because they have begun functioning as those who are not His own. The latter part of verse 4 reveals why He is so displeased: their worship of Baal had gone unabated for too long. Not only are they worshipping Baal, but some of them have divided their loyalties between Milcom and Yahweh. Finally, we see a group who has simply rejected the Lord. They have turned their backs on Him and surrendered their allegiance. In the face of this apathy and rejection, God is prepared to act.

When we first read a passage like this, we can be challenged in our view of God. Is He some ogre who is ready to demolish us at the first sign of disobedience? Is He a judgmental overlord who feels no affection and is easily angered? The obvious answer to these questions, from the rest of the storyline of Scripture, is no. God is a God of grace and compassion. In light of that, then, how are we to understand His anger, especially toward His own people? A look to the New Testament might help. In his letter to the Romans Paul pointed out, "Therefore, no condemnation now exists for those in Christ Jesus, because the Spirit's law of life in Christ Jesus has set you free from the law of sin and of death" (Rom 8:1-2). In other words, while Christians may still sin, God's response to their sin has changed. Specifically, God will not punitively discipline His children. The Bible is clear that God does discipline His children: "My son, do not take the Lord's discipline lightly or faint when you are reproved by Him, for the Lord disciplines the one He loves and punishes every son He receives" (Heb 12:5-6). However, while it is true that God disciplines His children, His discipline is corrective. God disciplines the children He loves to correct their behavior, not to punish them for bad behavior. If God were to punish believers for their sin, He would essentially be denying the cross. When Christ died on the cross, He declared, "It is finished," sufficiently announcing to the world that the defeat of death was done. Since it is finished, you and I do not need to assume punishment. We do, however, occasionally need to have our vision and affections adjusted so that we can focus on Christ. It's the corrective discipline that we need.

In much the same way, God's children had abandoned Him. They had thrown themselves at the feet of false gods, and had rejected God and His grace. Still, in His anger He shows them grace by correctively disciplining them so that they will turn from their worship of idols and return to Him. So what appears to be terrifying is indeed terrifying because it's the God of the universe, and He is angry, but it also represents great grace and even hope. Because God does not leave them to die in their sin, He is showing grace by calling them back to Himself.

In the same way, we need to understand that there will be times when God may correct us to return us to Him. Our response, then, should be recognition of His discipline, repentance toward our sin, and embrace of Jesus.

The Day of the Lord Is Upon Them

ZEPHANIAH 1:7

As a child, there were occasions when I would hear my mother say, "Wait until your father gets home." I assume I'm not alone in this experience. The intent behind my mom's declaration was to affirm the impending reckoning that would accompany his imminent coming. As a child I knew to fear that coming because it meant two things. First, it meant that I had done something wrong—something significant enough to warrant my dad's involvement. Second, it meant that discipline was coming. Neither of these was good news for me. In a sense, this is the kind of news that Zephaniah is offering to the people of Judah. In verse 7 he refers to what is coming as the "Day of the Lord." While that phrase might not mean much to us, it should. The *Day of the Lord* is a reference to the coming judgment of God. While we find it mentioned a number of times throughout Scripture, Zephaniah is more uniquely focused on it than any other biblical book.

The Israelites were guilty of disobeying God, and because of their disobedience, God was clarifying through Zephaniah that a reckoning is coming. There is no one, regardless of class, status, or birth order, who can avoid God's judgment. This would have been difficult for Zephaniah's hearers to understand, as those who were part of God's chosen people might have assumed some sense of protection from God's wrath. Instead, God puts them on notice that no one can escape the coming judgment. The intent of the declaration, as we will see at the end of the book, is not to terrify them into cowering before God. It is not to punish them for what they have done. God is not lashing out in uncontrolled anger or sadistically dispensing judgment. This reminder of the coming day of judgment was intended to provoke them to remember their place as His chosen ones and to repent and return to faithful obedience. He compels them in this manner because He understands that life is lived most fully and completely when one is living in harmony with God.

Of course, the natural response to this will either be rejection and the judgment that follows, or obedience and the pleasure of the presence of God that follows. The Day of the Lord is intended, here, to point them to the coming judgment and to compel them to return to God, but the Day of the Lord should not only be understood as a day of judgment. It should also be understood as a day of joy for those who have died to themselves and found themselves alive in Christ Jesus (Luke 9:23).

The Grief Will Be Intense Because No One Will Be Exempt from God's Judgment

ZEPHANIAH 1:8-11

The coming judgment would be gruesome and extraordinarily devastating. This is the message that God is conveying to His people. First, he proclaims the coming Day of the Lord, in verse 7, complete with the unfortunate news that He was preparing His own people, the people of Judah, to be sacrifices, devastated by their enemies, as judgment for their disobedience. Now he takes it further by clarifying this coming judgment. Not only is judgment coming, but in verses 8-11 we learn that the coming judgment will be extensive.

Zephaniah begins with the kings and all those who live in their house. No one should have been more of a leader, both politically and spiritually, than the king and his family. Instead of setting an example, though, there was a lineage of kings who had dishonored God. This lineage of disobedient kings would now feel the full weight of God's judgment. Not only would the kings, the leaders, feel this judgment, but the spiral continues downward now with those who serve the kings. Verse 9 calls out against those who "skip over the threshold" and who "fill their master's house with violence and deceit." The disturbingly sinful behavior of the kings was pervasive among their household and their servants. Verses 10 and 11, however, continue to see the spiral move downward and expand to include all the residents of the city. A resident of Judah might well have expected to see God's judgment and anger extended to their enemies, but to see it extended to those who were the children of God would have been shocking and difficult to reconcile. However, the words of the apostle Peter, in the New Testament, are a strong reminder that no one is exempt from God's judgment: "For the time has come for judgment to begin with God's household, and if it begins with us, what will the outcome be for those who disobey the gospel of God?" (1 Pet 4:17).

Not only that, but those who were part of Judah were learning that there is a high accountability for those who claim the name of God and do not reflect Him in their lives. The prophet wants them to be aware that to embrace God's name and reject God's character is to defame the name of God. To claim to follow Him and then misrepresent Him in behavior was a travesty that must be rectified. A misrepresentation of God's character is but one way in which we break the third commandment. It is easy to think of that command as merely a prohibition against using God's name as a byword in conversation, without realizing that it is much more than that. The name of the Lord, and by extension His character, is to be hallowed and exalted by His children. When we misrepresent the name and character of God, we are not only guilty of engaging in a form of character assassination, we are guilty of preaching a false gospel. Further, we are left longing for more because God has designed us to find our ultimate satisfaction in Him, and our pursuit of other things, as we diminish His name and character, will always leave us lacking. This is what C. S. Lewis was trying to point out to us:

> It would seem that Our Lord finds our desires not too strong, but too weak. We are half-hearted creatures, fooling about with drink and sex and ambition when infinite joy is offered us, like an ignorant child who wants to go on making mud pies in a slum because he cannot imagine what is meant by the offer of a holiday at the sea. We are far too easily pleased. (*Weight*, 26)

When faced with extensive judgment, like we see in these verses, it is easy to think that God's call to abandon our sinful pursuits and chase after Him will cost us everything, and it will. What we often fail to realize, however, is that the loss of everything pales in comparison to what we gain in return. If your life's possessions are worth a thousand dollars, it can be debilitating to think of losing that, unless you realize that you will receive a million dollars in return. In this case you gladly abandon the thousand dollars because you will gain something much more valuable in return. The call to abandon our sin works the same way. We think our sinful life is enjoyable, we think it is fulfilling, but, like Lewis said, we are really just playing around in the mud when so much more is being offered to us.

The people of Jerusalem were widely being judged. They were in danger of losing everything. From the palace to the city gates, everyone was in the path of judgment. Yet, as painful as losing everything might have appeared to them, something much, much greater was available in return—if only they would repent and return to God in obedience.

Those Who Pursue Other Gods Will Lose Everything

ZEPHANIAH 1:12-13

To be an agnostic is to attempt to take no side in a spiritual conversation. An agnostic claims that we cannot know whether God exists or not. They have neither faith nor disbelief. In verses 12 and 13 we find a group of people who were essentially agnostics, and while they surely thought this spiritual position was a strong one to be in, God wanted them to understand that they, too, could not avoid His gaze and His accounting.

Having just clarified the scope of the impending judgment, Zephaniah now turns his attention on the agnostics among them. They lived their lives claiming to neither believe nor disbelieve in the presence of God. However, this lack of belief ultimately put them in the same category as those who would reject God completely. Functionally speaking, they lived for themselves, making themselves the master of their own domain. They could attempt to claim spiritual neutrality, but they were far from neutral. As a result, God would see that their destruction, too, was complete. Notice that God's judgment for these individuals who deluded themselves into thinking that they lived in neutrality, but actually worshipped at the feet of their own comfort and pleasure, was to destroy their gods. In verse 13 Zephaniah prophesies that their houses will be destroyed and their wealth will be taken away. He says that their vineyards and the work of their hands will go to waste and never be enjoyed. God is dismantling their gods all around them.

This is ultimately God's good work to reveal to us the lie of non-worship. We can claim not to know what is right or wrong, and we can claim not to worship, but the truth is that every person will worship, and every person will pursue what they think is right, and every one of us will be accountable for those choices that we make. In Psalm 16 King David explains the folly of chasing after other gods: "The sorrows of those who take another god for themselves will multiply; I will not pour out their drink offerings of blood, and I will not speak their names with my lips" (Ps 16:4). We may think we have rejected God, but we must understand that this will mean that God will reject us. We chase after other gods, seeking satisfaction. Instead we find ourselves drowning in sorrow. We think we are finding a god, and instead we are losing the only God.

So, how do we remedy this evil? First of all, acknowledge that there is but one God, and He is Yahweh. This is, of course, the core of the ancient Shema from Deuteronomy 6: "Listen, Israel: The LORD our God, the LORD is One" (Deut 6:4). This opening line of this ancient recitation reminds us that there is one God. He exists in Trinity, but He is one, and He alone is God. Those who are buried under the weight of their apathy or agnosticism must begin by acknowledging what God's people have been confirming for years: God is.

Secondly, our acknowledgment of God must be accompanied by the sacrifice of our other gods. We must abandon those gods in our pursuit of Him. This will almost always be a challenging and difficult task. Jesus, anticipating how important this would be and how difficult it might prove, said this: "And if your eye causes your downfall, gouge it out. It is better for you to enter the kingdom of God with one eye than to have two eyes and be thrown into hell" (Mark 9:47). This may sound a bit dramatic, but Jesus was making the point that this matters. If we have to take extreme measures, so be it.

Finally, radical severing of the old gods and an embrace of Yahweh runs counter to our typical expectations of lethargy toward God and spiritual activity. It is the exact opposite of that, as a matter of fact. It is spiritual energy. Many times that may be exactly what we need to walk faithfully with God.

The Day of the Lord Is Unlike Any Other Day in Its Terror

ZEPHANIAH 1:14-17

Do you remember a time when you were a child and your mother "had enough"? As a hyperactive child, I can remember quite a few times when my impulsive behavior elicited just such a response from my mom. When mama "had enough," I knew that there was trouble in the offing. This passage resonates with the same type of response from God, only so much worse. In a series of declarations that are among the most discouraging and accusatory in all of Scripture, God's condemnation of His people gets more ominous. God has "had enough," and as He levels these strong accusations against His people, He turns up the heat and begins to deliver stronger and stronger verbal blows. In what should be read like an intensifying crescendo, Zephaniah declares that wrath is coming. As the ferocity builds, so too does God's condemnation, until it explodes with a climax in verse 18. This deafening crescendo of judgment proves its worth by crushing its hearers. While that may seem extreme, it is important to remember that God is crushing His people because He desires them to repent and return to Him. He understands that they love other things more than they love Him, so He systematically begins to eliminate the things that they love, and even their own lives, in an attempt to capture their attention and to see their affections pointed in His direction. His wrath, then, is an act of love, intended to accomplish the best for His children. I appreciate John Piper's thoughts: "The wisdom of God has ordained a way for the love of God to deliver us from the wrath of God without compromising the justice of God" (*Desiring God*, 61). In this attempt to call the nation to repentance, Zephaniah emphasizes a few specific characteristic of God's justice that are intended to heighten the nation's awareness.

1. Imminence

The Day of the Lord is coming, and it is coming soon. This is Zephaniah's cry. The point is that there is no time left to wander between obedience and disobedience. The cry of the prophet is a cry to turn from their sin and return to God, and not to waste time in doing so. It is reminiscent of the Apostle Paul's statement to the Corinthians: "For He says: I heard you in an acceptable time, and I helped you in the day of salvation. Look, now is the acceptable time; now is the day of salvation" (2 Cor 6:2). The imminent coming of God's judgment was intended to provoke an immediate response and to keep the nation from remaining in its present state.

2. Intensity

Not only was God's judgment imminent, but it would be astoundingly intense. The descriptions on display in this passage are not insignificant—the "warrior's cry," "trouble and distress," "clouds of blackness," "their blood will be poured out like dust" and so on. These are not soft or encouraging words—they are not intended to be. God's judgment will be swift, it will be soon, and it will be complete. The pain they experienced would be insuperable.

3. Iniquity

Finally we see the source of their punishment: their sin. "Because they have sinned" Zephaniah declares that they will face this soon-coming, far-reaching judgment. Their impending destruction is their own doing, but the good news is that there is an alternative available. While their sin has kept them from God and brought them face-to-face with God's judgment, some, if not all, of this could be averted if they would simply repent and obey.

Their Sin Will Bring About Complete Destruction

ZEPHANIAH 1:18

The final act of this chapter's devastating judgment is this description of their absolute destruction. It is interesting to consider this text alongside Acts 3. In Acts we find Peter and John going up to the temple where they meet a man who has been lame from birth. The man asks them to provide for him financially, and their reply is to confirm that they do not have "silver or gold" but they do have something worth far more that they can give him, and that is the gift of health. They reach down and restore his health, and he leaves them "walking, leaping, and praising God" (Acts 3:1-10). In this passage we see a people who have "silver and gold" and who think their wealth secures them happiness and protection. Instead, in spite of their wealth, God's judgment is coming, and He will take it all away. Unlike the humility of the lame man in Acts 3, these people are drunk on their own self-confidence, and God is no longer satisfied to allow it to continue. Instead of celebrating God's goodness and their need for Him, these people were ignoring Him, chasing their own satisfaction, and celebrating their self-fulfillment.

Zephaniah begins this verse by reminding the people that their wealth is no barrier to God's judgment. It is apparent, throughout this book, that possessions had consumed the nation. They had become full blown worshippers, bowing at the feet of the god of materialism. Seeking after it for hope, help, protection, and care, they were instead forced to recognize the empty existence that they were experiencing, and to acknowledge a god who was ultimately impotent in the face of the one true God. The words of Jesus again emphasize the importance of getting this right: "No one can be a slave of two masters, since either he will hate one and love the other, or be devoted to one and despise the other. You cannot be slaves of God and of money" (Matt 6:24). Sadly, the people of Judah had decided to chase after money, and their god would now fail them, as Zephaniah reminds them in the beginning of verse 18. So now they find themselves guilty of grievous sin, worshipping a god who has failed them and cannot protect them, and soon with nothing to show for it all. Things are very, very dark indeed.

Not only are they worshipping a false god who cannot serve them in any way, they are now powerless to resist the judgment of the Lord, and His judgment is severe. The text describes Him as "jealous," which indicates His dissatisfaction with their affection for other gods. The text reminds us that His judgment will come with a fire—one that can consume everything that exists. This is "Noah-esque" judgment being declared against the people of God. The end result of His judgment will be complete annihilation, yes, but even worse, the destruction will be so severe that it will be a "horrifying end." The severity of the judgment can cause pause among those who recognize that God is strong in grace, mercy, and love. Why is God's judgment so severe, and how is it consistent with His character?

God's justice is one aspect of His character that we often misunderstand. Justice, simply put, means to do what is right. When we learn that God is just, we can be assured that God will always do what is right. Just as a human judge would be soundly condemned (and rightly so) for freeing a convicted murderer, regardless of how much good the murderer has done, so too God would cease to be just if He simply dismissed our sin. God's justice does not run counter to His love, it runs parallel with His love. This is what makes the cross so majestic. That He condemned His Son to die testifies to God's justice; that He allowed His Son to die in our place testifies to His grace. The cross is the perfect intersection of justice and grace.

This passage, then, reminds us of His justice and compels us to remember the importance of walking faithfully before Him. We desire to know His love, but we have to remember that His love in no way diminishes His justice.

Reflect and Discuss

1. In what ways are you tempted to diminish God in your life by preferring good things over Him?
2. When you hear of God's justice, do you think of Him as an ogre or an uncaring father? If so, is that an accurate picture?
3. Have you ever been tempted to think that you can avoid the penalty for your sin? Why is this not possible?
4. Can you think of a time when the painful conviction of God compelled you to turn away from your sin and to turn to Him?
5. God's call to follow Him is a call to abandon our own lives and receive His. Have you seen examples in your life of how His life is far more fulfilling than your own?
6. Have you ever found yourself vacillating between following God and not following Him? Why is it occasionally difficult to make a decision?
7. In Zephaniah God removes the things that the people love more than Him. Are there any things in your life that you would be devastated to lose? Are you guilty of loving those things more than you love God?
8. Have you ever thought of the wrath of God as a good thing? Why can the wrath of God be good?
9. In Zephaniah the Lord's judgment was imminent. In the New Testament we are taught that the Lord's return is imminent. How does this imminence affect the way you approach life?
10. How does an understanding of God's justice influence the way you understand His love?

Repentance Is Necessary in Response to God's Judgment

ZEPHANIAH 2:1-3

Main Idea: In light of God's judgment, God's people must seek the Lord in humility or face destruction.

I. A Return to Worship Is Necessary to Recall and Repent (2:1).
II. Now Is the Time to Heed the Warning and Turn to the Lord (2:2).
III. Judgment May Be Avoided If God's People Will Seek Him (2:3).
- A. Seek the Lord in humility.
- B. Seek the Lord in obedience.
- C. Seek the Lord in righteousness.

A Return to Worship Is Necessary to Recall and Repent

ZEPHANIAH 2:1

If chapter 1 could be summed up in one word, it would be *judgment*. If the beginning of chapter 2 could be summed up in one word, it would be *repent*. Zephaniah has clearly communicated the impending judgment of God, but now he begins to show God's affection and grace. The means through which God's affection is seen is a call to repentance. Now it might be easy to assume that repentance is not necessarily the most hopeful of concepts, but the truth is that it is magnificently hopeful. It is only through the door of repentance that grace can be experienced. As we acknowledge our disobedience and humble ourselves before Him, we are able to experience grace and God's affection. In this sense repentance is the gateway to grace. "Therefore repent and turn back, so that your sins may be wiped out, that seasons of refreshing may come from the presence of the Lord" (Acts 3:19).

This passage begins with a call to "gather yourselves together," which is a reference to a type of solemn assembly before the Lord. It is a reference to corporate repentance, as God's people gather together for the purpose of corporate confession and repentance. The passage describes them as an "undesirable nation," which underscores the importance of their repentance. They were the children of God, the chosen ones.

Instead of being affirmed in that way, however, they were rejected and "undesirable." God is calling them back, then, to walk in obedience and favor.

This is a good reminder that "undesirable" is a reference to their sinful condition, a result of their own choice. It's a reminder of what they have done to themselves. However, God's call to repentance affirms that He still loves them. This "undesirable" statement is not a statement that God has no affection for His children.

Much like Paul's words to the Roman church, "Therefore, no condemnation now exists for those in Christ Jesus" (Rom 8:1), we can be confident in God's affection for us, even when we fail Him. This does not absolve us from responsibility for the decisions we make, but it can comfort us and remind us of why we should return to Christ. As this verse reminds us, with its call to gather and repent, God is gracious and, in spite of our rebellion, He is calling us to repentance as a sign of His affection for us.

Now Is the Time to Heed the Warning and Turn to the Lord

ZEPHANIAH 2:2

Not only are God's people offered an opportunity to repent, but they are reminded that they should do so now. No more waiting. It is time to respond to God's grace. The passage reminds us that this offer will not last in perpetuity. There is a terminal element to this offer, just like there is a terminal element to our lives. We must respond before the Lord's judgment "overtakes" us. It is coming, like a freight train on the tracks. We can attempt to stand in its way if we like, but we will not win that battle.

As it comes, we must recognize that as powerful as God's love and grace is, it does not diminish His anger and justice. God will do what is right—every time. There is no changing or impeding that reality. Turn now, and follow God; this is the message of Zephaniah.

Judgment May Be Avoided If God's People Will Seek Him

ZEPHANIAH 2:3

Finally, Zephaniah defines repentance for the people. He tells them that they are to seek the Lord with humility, in obedience, and through righteousness. These elements of repentance and obedience are evidence of a life given over to Him.

Seek the Lord in Humility

Zephaniah acknowledges at the beginning of verse 3 that repentance cannot be found until they humble themselves. This is such a key element to walking faithfully with God. There can be no mixture of our confidence in Him and our confidence in ourselves. He not only calls them humble, but he further exhorts them to seek humility. I think the indication of the passage is not simply that they were a prideful, self-confident people (though certainly that seems to be true), but that they, like all of humanity, are constantly prone to turn toward self. Every person, church, and movement is like a car out of alignment, constantly turning inward. Our natural bent is away from humility and toward pride, and pride is the mother of all sin. In order to walk with God, the people of Jerusalem would need to die to themselves and trust in Him, which sounds surprisingly like Jesus' gospel call:

> *Then He said to them all, "If anyone wants to come with Me, he must deny himself, take up his cross daily, and follow Me. For whoever wants to save his life will lose it, but whoever loses his life because of Me will save it.* (Luke 9:23-24)

Seek the Lord in Obedience

Not only must they seek the Lord through humility, but they must also seek Him through active obedience. It is not enough simply to acknowledge (or confess) sin; they must also change their behavior.

They were a people accustomed to advancing self. In response to that, Zephaniah calls them to "carry out what He commands." No matter the sincerity of their intent, if their intentions were not followed with actions, they were of no value.

> *Then Samuel said: Does the Lord take pleasure in burnt offerings and sacrifices as much as in obeying the Lord? Look: to obey is better than sacrifice, to pay attention is better than the fat of rams.* (1 Sam 15:22)

We live in a culture that is confession happy. Whether it be reality TV or talk-radio, tell-all books or water cooler gossip, we live in a culture where confession is often experienced, but we so rarely see changed behavior accompanying it. Confession is good for the soul, but only if it is married to repentance and obedience.

Seek the Lord in Righteousness

Finally, we see one last expectation. God is just, which means that God is right. When God seeks justice, He is seeking what is right. It is necessary for His justice to be on display because holiness is not universal. It is because of the lack of holiness that we so often see God's justice. In light of God's holiness, Zephaniah calls God's people to pursue righteousness. In other words, they are being compelled to become more and more like God. The word *seek* seems to indicate a hunger and a pursuit, two impulses that often are associated with our physical condition but far too rarely with our spiritual condition. In a church full of apathetic believers, hungry pursuit of God and His righteousness has become far too rare in our day.

In Jesus' most famous sermon, the Sermon on the Mount, He would emphasize again for us how central this is, not only to our faith, but to His character: "But seek first the kingdom of God and His righteousness, and all these things will be provided for you" (Matt 6:33). Our pursuit of God's righteousness is part and parcel with our pursuit of God's kingdom.

Verses 1-3 are a breath of fresh air after the devastatingly difficult judgment and condemnation of chapter 1. Yes, God is just and His judgment is coming, but thankfully God is also loving and gracious, and repentance is possible. "But God proves His own love for us in that while we were still sinners, Christ died for us!" (Rom 5:8). Paul's declaration of God's deep and abiding love affirms that God's justice matters, but because of His affection, He has made a way for us in spite of ourselves. This is ultimately the story of the gospel. Verses 1-3 of this passage are a foretaste of the beautiful celebration of God's love that we will see at the conclusion of chapter 3. They are a reminder that God is good, even when it seems like the time is bad. Judgment is coming, but so is grace, so take hold of grace.

Reflect and Discuss

1. Have you ever considered repentance a gateway to grace? How does this change your view of God's call to repent?
2. Are you encouraged that God's affection for you remains even when your sin compels His justice to be exercised in your life?

3. How does the immediacy of the call to repent change the way you view your own personal repentance? What about the others that you invite to repent and to place their faith in Christ?
4. How does the Lord call you back to humility?
5. Do you find yourself more willing to confess than to obey? What should you do in response to that?
6. In what ways do you seek righteousness and also seek the kingdom of God?
7. God loves you deeply in spite of your sin. How do you view God in light of this? How does this knowledge shape your behavior?

The Nations Will Be Judged because of Their Pride

ZEPHANIAH 2:4–3:8

Main Idea: In light of God's judgment, God's people must seek the Lord in humility or face destruction.

I. **The Enemies of God's People Will Be Judged because of Their Pride (2:4-15).**
   A. The land of the Gentiles will become the feed for the animals of God's people (2:6).
   B. The land of the Gentiles will be given to God's people (2:7).
   C. The Gentiles' taunting of God's people has incurred His wrath (2:8).
   D. All the people who have opposed God and His people will bow before Him (2:11).
   E. God will use His own people to destroy the Gentiles (2:9).
   F. The Gentile gods will be proven powerless in the face of Yahweh (2:11).
   G. The pride of the Gentiles will be their undoing (2:10).
   H. The Gentile taunting of God's people is an affront to God Himself (2:10).
   I. Self-confidence betrays a false security that will lead to shame and destruction (2:15).

II. **God's People Will Be Judged because of Their Disobedience (3:1-8).**
   A. God's chosen people are defiled because of their rebellion (3:1).
   B. God's discipline has not compelled His people to obey (3:2).
   C. The disobedience of God's people is due to their lack of trust (3:2).
   D. The political leaders are ruthless and are devouring the people (3:3).
   E. The priests dishonor God and dishonor His word (3:4).
   F. God is faithful when His people are not (3:5).
   G. God's discipline is fruitless (3:6-7).

H. God's justice is coming because of their obstinate disobedience (3:8).

The Enemies of God's People Will Be Judged because of Their Pride

ZEPHANIAH 2:4-15

Faced with God's call to repent, and recognizing the depth of the pending judgment, the prophet Zephaniah now turns his attention to an even more expansive and comprehensive description of the coming judgment. Zephaniah divides this passage up into two sections: God's judgment against the enemies of God's people, and God's judgment against His own people.

One of the greatest natural disasters in recent years has been the massive destruction of the city of New Orleans by Hurricane Katrina. I vividly remember the images on TV of the people living in a devastated Superdome, in the destroyed homes in formerly burgeoning neighborhoods, and in the tent cities set up under overpasses. The destruction was widespread and seemingly never ending. The prophet Zephaniah provides a similar description here as he declares what is coming for the enemies of God's people because of their treatment of the people of Judah. Destruction and devastation appear to be on the horizon for them.

The Land of the Gentiles Will Become the Feed for the Animals of God's People (2:6)

Zephaniah begins with a description of coastal cities, inhabited by Judah's enemies, and describes their destruction in detail. The official declaration by Zephaniah is that "the word of the Lord is against" them. This statement is something of an official pronouncement of pending judgment. They had incurred the wrath of God and would be judged. The specific judgment is that their land would become pastureland for the people of God. Verses 7 and following explain the future possession of God's people. This would have been most offensive to the enemies of God's people. Perceiving themselves to be superior physically, not to mention wealthier, they would have found it absurd that the nation of Judah would overtake them. This is, however, what God decreed because of their insolence and arrogance. In fact, verse 7 gives a foretaste of what was coming for the people of Judah. Yes, they had turned their backs on God, and yes, they were defiantly disobedient, but God was offering them redemption, and it appears, in verse 7, that God believed they would return to Him. He tells us that He would, in fact, return to them. While Judah may not have been significant enough to defeat their enemies on their own, and while they may have currently been in a state of disobedience, God intended for them to return and once again experience His blessings.

The Land of the Gentiles Will Be Given to God's People (2:7)

At the end of verse 7 we see one of the dominant, overarching themes in all of Scripture: restoration. From Genesis to Revelation we see the theme of restoration describing God's work among humanity. Whether it be the restoration of creation or the restoration of God's people, all of it can be traced to God's resurrection of His Son. The resurrection of Jesus marks the pinnacle of God's restoration of all of creation. The rest of Scripture, pointing backward through history and forward into the future, tells the story of God at work among humanity, restoring everything back to the way it was when He created everything and declared, "It is very good." Verse 7 tells us that God will be doing just such a work here among His people, and part of that restoration will be the settling of the enemies of Judah under the authority of Judah. Out of the ashes will rise this restored people, dedicated to God and enjoying life as He intended it. The resurrecting work of God is intended to help humanity flourish.

The Gentiles' Taunting of God's People Has Incurred His Wrath (2:8)

Zephaniah now begins to describe the guilt of the enemies of Judah. At the top of the list is their collective taunting of God's people. This is not your run-of-the-mill taunting that children might experience on the playground. It is most likely evidence of the enemies of God's people taunting them about their God. Their taunting is most likely a blow at the character of God and therefore is much, much worse than simple name-calling. The mocking of the people of Judah may have been much like the psalmist described: "My adversaries taunt me, as if crushing my bones, while all day long they say to me, 'Where is your God?'" (Ps 42:10). Jesus Himself experienced a similar taunting while He was on the cross: "In the same way even the criminals who were crucified with Him kept taunting Him" (Matt 27:44). This taunting had to be defeated. While God gives much grace, at the end of the day those who disparage and attempt to challenge God's character will fail. Not only have they taunted God's people, but they have also "threatened their territory." They not only have disregarded God, but they have attempted to usurp God's authority by encroaching on the territory that God has given to His people. They are guilty of tremendous disobedience and are subject to God's judgment.

All the People Who Have Opposed God and His People Will Bow Before Him (2:11)

Ultimately, inherent in this issue is the fundamental question of the gospel: what will you do with God? In the end, everyone will ultimately respond with the same declaration, "Jesus is Lord," as Scripture reminds us. However, Scripture also affirms that most of those who will ever live will make their declaration through forced submission. Only those who voluntarily declare that Jesus is Lord, in this life, will enjoy the benefits afforded to the children of God. Those who reject Him will not escape the declaration that Jesus is Lord; instead they will find it to be a sobering and terrifying moment as they declare it to be so, but they do so too late, having missed their opportunity to submit before God. Scripture teaches that their just recompense, then, will be eternal judgment. Verse 11 reflects that truth. The attitudes and behavior of the enemies of Judah betrayed a belief that God does not exist or, if He does exist, He is either impotent or absent. They were sorely mistaken.

God Will Use His Own People to Destroy the Gentiles (2:9)

Zephaniah continues his declaration of impending judgment by affirming the total destruction of God's enemies. Verse 9 points out that these enemies would eventually be reminiscent of Sodom and Gomorrah. They would be a "perpetual wasteland," according to the prophet. Their property and land would become the possession of the people of God.

The Gentile Gods Will Be Proven Powerless in the Face of Yahweh (2:11)

Not only will they be crushed, like Sodom and Gomorrah, but verse 11 reminds us that God will become terrifying to them. This God whom they have treated as a false god or an impotent god will be known for who He is: the God of the universe. He will do so by exerting His authority and sovereignty over every other so-called god. Each god who is an object of worship will join with its worshippers and bow at the feet of the one true God. All of this points to a progression that plays out not just in the book of Zephaniah but over and over again throughout human history. Man bows to his pride. Man assumes a position of self-sufficiency. God reveals man for who he is: small, insignificant, and in need of a savior.

The Pride of the Gentiles Will Be Their Undoing (2:10)

Verse 10 points out that they were behaving as enemies of God because they had surrendered to their pride. Their taunting is rooted in their belief that they are the supreme object in the world. Not only are they filled with pride, but their pride has blinded them to truth. This is why Augustine and Bonhoeffer, among others, have claimed pride as the chief of every other sin. G. K. Chesterton once said,

> If I had only one sermon to preach, it would be a sermon against Pride. The more I see of existence, and especially of modern practical and experimental existence, the more I am convinced of the reality of the old religious thesis; that all evil began with some attempt at superiority; some moment when, as we might say, the very skies were cracked across like a mirror, because there was a sneer in Heaven. (*Common Man*, 246)

From Satan's fall out of heaven to our contemporary sins, pride is pervasive and fundamental to every sin we engage in. I am fairly convinced that this is partly why Jesus expanded our understanding of sin in the Sermon on the Mount. Jesus said,

> *You have heard that it was said to our ancestors, Do not murder, and whoever murders will be subject to judgment. But I tell you, everyone who is angry with his brother will be subject to judgment. And whoever says to his brother, "Fool!" will be subject to the Sanhedrin. But whoever says, "You moron!" will be subject to hellfire.* (Matt 5:21-22)

And again we hear Jesus say,

> *You have heard that it was said, Do not commit adultery. But I tell you, everyone who looks at a woman to lust for her has already committed adultery with her in his heart.* (Matt 5:27-28)

Jesus is helping us understand sin and our own hearts by reframing our understanding of sin in these verses. Rather than external behavior, sin first is fostered in the heart and then finds its way out into our behaviors.

The Pharisees, in particular, would have rebelled at this understanding of sin, knowing themselves to be close to perfect at external adherence to the law. Jesus understands that this was not sufficient. We are made unrighteous by what occurs in our hearts, which works its way out into our actions. It is hard to overstate the significance of pride in relationship to the rest of our spiritual condition. Fundamentally, what makes pride so damaging is its inherent blasphemy. It claims that God is not God and that we are. It denies what is the central reality of the universe and creates the justification for every other sin that proceeds from it.

The Gentile Taunting of God's People Is an Affront to God Himself (2:10)

It is because sin is so pervasive and so dangerous that God so vigorously confronts and condemns pride, not just in this passage, but across the whole of Scripture. Consider just a few of these passages.

> *Everyone with a proud heart is detestable to the Lord; be assured, he will not go unpunished.* (Prov 16:5)
>
> *Pride comes before destruction, and an arrogant spirit before a fall.* (Prov 16:18)
>
> *Your presumptuous heart has deceived you, you who live in clefts of the rock in your home on the heights, who say to yourself, "Who can bring me down to the ground?" Though you seem to soar like an eagle and make your nest among the stars, even from there I will bring you down.* (Obad 3-4)
>
> *So, whoever thinks he stands must be careful not to fall.* (1 Cor 10:12)
>
> *He is conceited, understanding nothing, but has a sick interest in disputes and arguments over words. From these come envy, quarreling, slander, evil suspicions.* (1 Tim 6:4)
>
> *But He gives greater grace. Therefore He says: God resists the proud, but gives grace to the humble.* (Jas 4:6)

These are just a few of the copious thoughts that Scripture offers condemning pride and warning us of its dangers. Nevertheless, we dip into the well of pride over and over again. God's aggressive posture against the sin of pride helps us to understand just how dangerous this is. However, this passage does not just stop with their pride. It continues by showing us the next step after our lives have been given over to our pride: the belief that we are enough on our own. In other words, we believe ourselves to be self-sufficient.

Self-Confidence Betrays a False Security That Will Lead to Shame and Destruction (2:15)

When one is steeped in pride, the natural next step is to extrapolate from that our self-sufficiency. This is precisely why God condemns the enemies of Judah. In verse 15 we read, "This is the self-assured city that lives in security, that thinks to herself: I exist and there is no one else." These enemies of God were completely self-confident, to the degree that they no longer acknowledged that anyone else mattered. Of course, this is the natural conclusion when we assume a position of self-confidence. In fact, it is not rare to hear someone today echo that opinion. "It only affects me," or "It's my body," and, among the more famous thoughts, "You worry about yourself, and I will worry about myself." This self-centered, self-confident perspective on life has become somewhat synonymous with our culture. As we have become increasingly self-focused, this ethos has grown louder and louder. Ultimately, self-sufficiency is self-worship. It is a grievous form of idolatry that exalts ourselves to the level of highest order in the universe. Instead of the world revolving around the sun, it revolves around us. Of course, the natural progression of this thought process will ultimately lead to grief and the eventual destruction of our culture. God loves humanity and has a plan to help humanity flourish. At the foundation of His plan is a call to faith in Him, resting on a denial of self. Out of this worship of Him, and through our denial of self, we find a populace able to serve one another and help one another to flourish. When the domino of faith in God is pushed over, the cascading effect is the advance of pride, the increased confidence in self, and the lack of flourishing for those around us. This is precisely what Paul was attempting to address when he wrote to the church at Philippi.

> *Finally, my brothers, rejoice in the Lord. To write to you again about this is no trouble for me and is a protection for you. Watch out for "dogs," watch out for evil workers, watch out for those who mutilate the flesh. For we are the circumcision, the ones who serve by the Spirit of God, boast in Christ Jesus, and do not put confidence in the flesh—although I once also had confidence in the flesh. If anyone else thinks*

> *he has grounds for confidence in the flesh, I have more: circumcised the eighth day; of the nation of Israel, of the tribe of Benjamin, a Hebrew born of Hebrews; regarding the law, a Pharisee; regarding zeal, persecuting the church; regarding the righteousness that is in the law, blameless. But everything that was a gain to me, I have considered to be a loss because of Christ.* (Phil 3:1-7)

Of course, in contemporary society we can learn from the sin of the enemies of God that Zephaniah was addressing. Because of Christ we can turn away from self-confidence and pride and reject the false hope that is contained within. We can take the risk of rejecting self because Christ's life, death, burial, and resurrection have secured for us an alternative future, a far more hopeful future. This was Paul's point when he shared with the church at Galatia:

> *I have been crucified with Christ and I no longer live, but Christ lives in me. The life I now live in the body, I live by faith in the Son of God, who loved me and gave Himself for me.* (Gal 2:19-20)

Those who have trusted in Christ have traded their lives for His. As a result they no longer have to depend on their own pride, and they can reject the temptation to be self-reliant.

Finally, at the end of verse 15, we read that the judgment of God, in response to the pride and self-sufficiency of Judah's enemies, will bring them to nothing, making them a laughingstock among those who pass by them. As we said earlier, this follows this pattern of pride, self-sufficiency, and then God's work to bring humility and compel us to see our dependence. This work, at the end of verse 15, is intended to bring justice and judgment to those who would rebel against God, but it also serves to humble them and allow them to see their need for God. In that sense it is both a work of justice and a work of grace. We see this pattern revealed throughout the rest of Scripture as well. The story of the Rich Young Ruler, from Mark, comes to mind.

> *Then, looking at him, Jesus loved him and said to him, "You lack one thing: Go, sell all you have and give to the poor, and you will have treasure in heaven. Then come, follow Me." But he was stunned at this demand, and he went away grieving, because he had many possessions.* (Mark 10:21-22)

Jesus confronts the man with his self-reliance and lack of dependence on God by calling him to deny the one thing that he trusts—his wealth.

You will note that Jesus does this because "Jesus loved him." Jesus' affection for the man compelled Him to confront him and invite him to turn to Christ. Unfortunately, in this man's case it did not convince him to deny himself and trust in Jesus. In Zephaniah 2 we have no indication that the enemies of God did anything other than oppose God, but that does not negate the good work of God in bringing justice, which also reveals our need and pushes us to trust in Him.

God's People Will Be Judged because of Their Disobedience

ZEPHANIAH 3:1-8

We have now come full circle. As in chapter 1, Zephaniah again turns his prophecy toward the people of Judah. In similar tone and focused on similar targets, Zephaniah levels devastating judgment from God, to His own people, after clearly bringing justice to those who were His enemies. As Zephaniah leveled the charges against Judah's enemies, I can only imagine that Judah stood by and listened with pleasure, only to find that pleasure withering under the return of God's scrutiny.

God's Chosen People Are Defiled because of Their Rebellion (3:1)

Zephaniah opens this chapter with a prophetic condemnation of the people of Judah because of their rebellion and defilement. These two issues are related to one another. Judah was a rebellious people. They knew God's word and had been warned against their disobedience. In spite of that, they continue to revel in their pride and self-confidence, functionally rejecting God and serving themselves instead. This was not unique to this generation of God's chosen people. No, this is a refrain that we hear repeatedly throughout Scripture. "He rescued them many times, but they continued to rebel deliberately and were beaten down by their sin" (Ps 106:43). The psalmist was essentially writing the biography of the people of Israel in that one verse. It applies to more than just the Israelites, however. The truth is that this constant rebellion, met with constant grace, is our story too. Like the people of Judah, we constantly turn away from God, are consistent in our disobedience, and are critically in need of grace. The apostle Paul resonated with this same sentiment: "For I do not understand what I am doing, because I do not practice what I want to do, but I do what I hate" (Rom 7:5). As a result of the fall, all of humanity is damaged and in need of rescue. Apart from the grace of God, we are relentlessly bent toward sin. After coming into contact with God's grace, we are transformed into adopted children of God, but we still retain our sin nature and find ourselves drawn, at times, back into sin. Thankfully, the grace of God makes it possible to be free from sin, but until Jesus returns to make things right, we will probably never be free from the temptation to sin. The people of Judah were susceptible to that same temptation, only they had succumbed to it and were now buried in it. Not only were they rebellious, but God describes their current condition, because of their rebellion, as one of being "defiled." In fact, the word *rebellious* in verse 1 could also be translated "filthy," which would only reinforce their desperate condition as God comes now to mete out justice.

To be rebellious, of course, leads to being defiled. Defilement refers to a loss of status. The people of God had made themselves unfit, unclean, and unholy as a result of their disobedience. God expects holiness, and they were unholy. Of course, this is not a statement that they had previously been holy and this act changed that. No, it is reinforcing that they are an unholy people who, through these actions, had declared themselves to be unholy. Their unholiness, of course, makes them unfit for the kingdom of God, thus justifying God's wrath that was directed toward them. They were desperately in need of salvation. It sounds a lot like our story, does it not? Hopelessly disobedient, running in our own direction, and living unholy lives, we find ourselves condemned before God. "For all have sinned and fall short of the glory of God" (Rom 3:23). Instead of receiving our just rewards, however, the defilement is turned into righteousness as God trades our unrighteousness for the righteousness of Jesus. "He [God] made the One who did not know sin to be sin for us, so that we might become the righteousness of God in Him" (1 Cor 5:21). This change of status, from righteousness to unrighteousness, is readily reversed when we submit, in obedience, to God and follow Him in faith. Our stubborn rebellion is overcome by even more stubborn grace. This is the story of the gospel.

This unfit people have not yet received that kind of grace. They are still in the process of hearing God's judgment. God is winding down His judgment in this book, but the conclusion is among the hardest hitting of all of His condemnations. They are rebellious and they are unholy. As such, they must face God's judgment, unless they repent.

God's Discipline Has Not Compelled His People to Obey (3:2)

Sadly, even though God has extended His discipline, it has not been effective to bring them back into obedience. This is the message that continues in verse 2. In this verse God offers a cascading indictment detailing the specifics of their rebellion. They have been disobedient, they have ignored God's discipline, they have failed to trust God, and they have not drawn near to God. In general, this sounds like the typical pattern for the one who is walking away from God.

The Disobedience of God's People Is Due to Their Lack of Trust (3:2)

However, what makes this judgment more troubling is not simply that they were rebellious, but that when they were confronted with the Lord's discipline, they remained hard-hearted toward Him. In a very real sense they had denied the foundational core of the gospel, which is to trust in God. The Scripture is abundantly clear, from front to back, that faith in God begins with trusting Him. This truth is elementary. For as long as I can remember, my wife has repeated Psalm 56:3 to our two daughters over and over and over again, so much so that they have it memorized and recall it regularly when they are anxious: "When I am afraid, I will trust in You." It is such a simple little truth, and the rest of the truth of Scripture is grounded in this simple little truth. The people of Judah, however, had failed to acknowledge God, let alone trust Him, and as a result they would face His judgment.

Finally, as a result of not trusting God, they did not walk toward Him. Instead they pursued their own desires, leaving Him behind. We see Paul address a similar issue in the New Testament:

> *For though they knew God, they did not glorify Him as God or show gratitude. Instead, their thinking became nonsense, and their senseless minds were darkened. Claiming to be wise, they became fools and exchanged the glory of the immortal God for images resembling mortal man, birds, four-footed animals, and reptiles. Therefore God delivered them over in the cravings of their hearts to sexual impurity, so that their bodies were degraded among themselves.* (Rom 1:21-24)

This rejection of God and His will would lead to His judgment of them.

The Political Leaders Are Ruthless and Are Devouring the People (3:3)

Not only would they thoroughly reject Him, but they have become so completely rebellious that their leadership is devoid of spiritual life in any sense. Zephaniah would go on to describe them as "roaring lions" and "wolves in the night," claiming that they stripped the city bare, leaving nothing behind. In other words, the people were simply following the example of their leadership. The leaders were living for themselves to the degree that they were gladly fleecing their own people, people who had been entrusted to them as a stewardship, and they were now using the people for their own gain. Instead of serving, they were devouring their own people, and their people were then replicating their behavior.

The Priests Dishonor God and Dishonor His Word (3:4)

Not only were the political leaders dishonoring God and leading the people to do so, in what was a much greater tragedy, the religious leaders were doing the same. They are described as "reckless" and "treacherous," not to mention that they "profane the sanctuary" and "they do violence to instruction." Much like the priests in the book of Malachi, these priests had abandoned their calling for their own pursuit of pleasure. Malachi is replete with examples, but one instance stands out:

> *"A son honors his father, and a servant his master. But if I am a father, where is My honor? And if I am a master, where is your fear of Me? says Yahweh of Hosts to you priests, who despise My name."*
> *Yet you ask: "How have we despised Your name?"*
> *"By presenting defiled food on My altar."*
> *You ask: "How have we defiled You?"*
> *When you say: "The LORD's table is contemptible."* (Mal 1:6-7)

In a similar manner to the priests in Zephaniah's day, the priests were condemned by Malachi because they had despised God's name. In other words, in an era when one's name and character were inseparably linked, they had disparaged the character of God. Not only was their behavior a mark on their own character, but as representatives of God among the people, their behavior had practically claimed that God did not exist. They would have agreed with Friedrich Nietzsche: "God is dead" (*Zarathustra,* 122). While these priests were making a show of serving God, their behavior belied any belief in God. This tragedy may not look quite the same in contemporary culture, but no doubt pastoral malpractice continues to this day. The church may not be led by priests, as it was when Zephaniah wrote, but her leaders are just as susceptible today to burnout, doubt, and even self-serving behavior that teeters on the edge of the ethical—occasionally even falling off the edge.

God Is Faithful When His People Are Not (3:5)

After extending judgment to everyone, God reaffirms that even in the midst of this mass rebellion, He remains the same. He is still righteous, He is still holy, His justice is faithful, and still they rejected Him. This consistency proves to be yet another condemnation, contrasting His fidelity with their infidelity. The irony is thick.

God's Discipline Is Fruitless (3:6-7)

Zephaniah concludes this section by describing the discipline God provided, which the people of Judah rejected. He has delivered blow after blow of judgment in an effort to rouse them from their spiritual slumber, but they refuse to respond in obedience. Of particular interest is the dialogue found in verse 7: "I thought: You will certainly fear Me and accept correction" and the verse continues, "However, they became more corrupt in all their actions." These are a radically depraved people. God, in His love and grace, extends discipline to call them back to Him, and yet they reject Him and chase after their own desires.

God's Justice Is Coming because of Their Obstinate Disobedience (3:8)

He follows this up with thundering words that were intended to strike fear in the hearers' hearts. "Wait for Me," He says in verse 8. He is coming; and they will answer for what they have done.

Thankfully, this is not the end of the book. After chapters of devastating critique and withering rebuke, grace now leaps onto the stage, and it could not be more refreshing.

Reflect and Discuss

1. Zephaniah is a difficult book to read. It can be extraordinarily depressing as we read of God's judgment. However, His restoration brings hope. How have you seen God work restoratively in your life?
2. The enemies of God taunted God. In what ways are you tempted to taunt God with your life and with your words?
3. Scripture teaches that every person will someday declare that "Jesus is Lord." Have you believed in Jesus yet? Have you declared that "He is Lord," even in your own life?

4. Chesterton once said, "If I had only one sermon to preach, it would be a sermon against pride." In what ways have you seen your pride make its presence known?
5. Do you understand that sin is, first and foremost, a heart issue? Do you treat your sin as if it is a behavior to correct, or a heart issue to repent of?
6. Do you often struggle with the same sin over and over again? Do you realize that you are not a slave to that sin? Have you confessed and repented of that sin?
7. Have you contemplated that Jesus was covered in your sin so that you could be made righteous? Have you thanked God for that recently?
8. How do you struggle to trust God? Can you confess that right now?
9. In what ways have you seen leaders steer people away from God? Have you been guilty of that? Do you need to confess that?
10. Most of us who know God have someone who looks up to us as a spiritual example. Some have more than others. Are you stewarding the responsibility to point people to Jesus with your life and your words?

God Will Restore His People So That They Will Trust and Obey Him

ZEPHANIAH 3:9-20

Main Idea: God is rich in mercy and will restore His people to a place of prominence and blessing.

I. **God Will Restore His People (3:9-10).**
II. **God Will Preserve the Dignity of His People (3:11a).**
III. **God Will Renew His People (3:11b-12).**
IV. **God Will Give His People Rest (3:13).**
V. **God Will Protect His People (3:14-15).**
VI. **God Will Grace His People (3:16-20).**

God Will Restore His People

ZEPHANIAH 3:9-10

Up to this point, the book of Zephaniah has essentially been one withering critique after another. Arguably the most painful book in the Bible, it has not left us excited and hopeful for more. In what has surely felt like one body blow after another, God has chastised His people, called them to repentance, and threatened them with judgment. In all of this, however, we have maintained that His love and justice are the motivating factors for His behavior. While that can be difficult to see while we are making our way through the first three-plus chapters, it all begins to come into focus now as the book takes what appears to be a decidedly sharp turn, but what is, in fact, consistent with the loving message of judgment that we have heard throughout the rest of the book.

Zephaniah begins verse 9 by declaring that God will "restore pure speech" to His people. This claim of restoring pure speech means much more than just clean language. This is a reference to being purified. It speaks of repentance being accomplished in the hearts of God's people. From rampant rebellion to penitent humility, the people of Judah have been rescued and redeemed. To be purified means to be cleansed. Purification occurs when we are both forgiven and repentant. The old sin is gone and the future behavior is not the same as the past. The result of this purification, then, will be a readiness to call on Yahweh and worship Him with their lives.

Notice two specific ways in which they will respond to His grace. First, they will call on His name. For a people who had previously struggled to trust God, this is a marvelous turnaround. By calling on His name, they are indicating trust in Him. They are affirming His character and His deity, and they are recognizing their need for Him. This is a significant departure from their previous behavior. As a people who trusted in themselves almost exclusively, this represents the kind of change that only God, through His redemptive activity, can accomplish. The call of the gospel reflects this kind of turnaround. Those who used to live for themselves are now dying to themselves precisely because they are trusting in Him. Jesus, in the gospel of Luke, clarified the expectation of the gospel: "Then He said to them all, 'If anyone wants to come with Me, he must deny himself, take up his cross daily, and follow Me'" (Luke 9:23). What we are seeing here, with the people's purification, is their forgiveness and repentance. This opening line is just a glimpse—a taste—of the grace of God that is about to be poured out on His people, and it all begins here with their trust in Him.

Second, not only are they trusting God, they are now committed to serving Him—but not just serving Him, they are committed to doing so with "single purpose." This is, again, far different from the message we heard throughout the rest of the book. These had been a people who were focused on themselves and whose focus was scattered across a host of different ideals and goals. Instead, they are now united in their focus on God and His commands. This, of course, is the natural response to the grace of God being applied in one's life. We are repentant, we believe, and we are transformed. The transformation is so much more than just a concept, it is a reality, as our lives are redirected and our focus is radically changed.

As God is restoring His people, calling them to faith and repentance, He is also collecting His children back, so that they might offer to Him an offering of worship. This is the culmination of the gospel. God pursues His wandering children, bringing them into His adopted family and allowing them to enjoy His presence. This is why the *Westminster Catechism* begins with "The chief end of man is to glorify God and enjoy Him forever." The goal of our redemption is our enjoyment in God. Gathering us together from around the world, God is redeeming a people for Himself. This is the beautiful picture we see resonating across the book of Revelation:

> *After this I looked, and there was a vast multitude from every nation, tribe, people, and language, which no one could number, standing before the throne and before the Lamb. They were robed in white with palm branches in their hands. And they cried out in a loud voice: Salvation belongs to our God, who is seated on the throne, and to the Lamb!* (Rev 7:9)

God Will Preserve the Dignity of His People

ZEPHANIAH 3:11A

Among the most astonishing truths about God and His creation is that God has created humanity in His image. In Latin this is referred to as the *imago Dei.* Unfortunately, that image was stained through Adam and Eve's fall from grace in Genesis 3, and the stain has been passed down from one generation to the next ever since. "Therefore, just as sin entered the world through one man, and death through sin, in this way death spread to all men, because all sinned" (Rom 5:12). This tragic heritage of stained image—sin—has radically impaired humanity. In fact, Scripture says that because of it, all humanity is dead. However, one of the breathtaking truths of the grace of God is that God desires not only to make us alive again, but to restore us as heirs to His kingdom, as adopted children of God. Therefore, His redemption removes not only our death, but also our shame. This is the point Zephaniah is making in the beginning of verse 11.

You and I, and the people of Judah, deserve shame. Through serious and persistent disobedience, we have constantly rejected God and run away from His presence. Yet God, in His grace, has been just as persistent in His pursuit of humanity. All the way back to the Garden of Eden, we find God calling out for Adam, "Where are you?" (Gen 3:9). From that point forward God has been pursuing humanity, in spite of our sin, in an effort to redeem and restore us. That is breathtaking love!

For God to commit to the people of Judah that they would not be put to shame is for God to practice indescribable grace and forgiveness. It is reminiscent of what we find in Hebrews, describing Jesus' orientation to those who have been redeemed: "For the One who sanctifies and those who are sanctified all have one Father. That is why Jesus is not ashamed to call them brothers" (Heb 2:11). The thought that Jesus is "not ashamed" of us is astonishing, and it helps to explain just how thorough God's work of redemption is among us. We were lost, helpless, and rightfully covered in shame, and through the grace of God we are able to be restored and made free from shame. "Because your shame was double, and they cried out, 'Disgrace is their portion,' therefore, they will possess double in their land, and eternal joy will be theirs" (Isa 61:7).

God Will Renew His People

ZEPHANIAH 3:11B-12

Zephaniah continues on this magnificent trajectory of grace at the end of verse 11 and through verse 12. God is going to redeem the people and restore the people, not to mention remove their shame, and now Zephaniah describes one of the ways God will transform the people. Continuing the theme we heard in the previous few verses, God is restoring His people, returning them to the condition Adam and Eve were in in the garden of Eden before they sinned. The people of Judah were a proud people, as the text describes. As they trust in God, though, they are rejecting their trust in self. This rejection leads to the rejection of their pride. God confirms in this passage that He is turning them away from their pride and into something much different.

Instead of a prideful people who seek their own benefit, God is turning them into a humble people who seek Him. As we think through God's grace and our response to it, it's important to note that humility does not result from belittling ourselves. It is instead simply acknowledging the truth about ourselves—namely that we are not good by nature, nor are we able to save ourselves. We are mortal, fallible, and in need of help, and because of God's grace, that help is provided.

Thankfully, as God takes away our pride and replaces it with humility, we find ourselves taking "refuge" in Him. In other words, instead of cowering before God as our judge, we now rest in His care as our provision. The psalmist understood this magnificent gift that God gives His children:

> *The one who lives under the protection of the Most High dwells in the shadow of the Almighty. I will say to the Lord, "My refuge and my fortress, my God, in whom I trust."* (Ps 91:1-2)

Maybe what is most encouraging—if not challenging—about God's status as our refuge is how it positions the followers of God in the world. Consider the words of the psalmist:

> *God is our refuge and strength, a helper who is always found in times of trouble. Therefore we will not be afraid, though the earth trembles and the mountains topple into the depths of the seas, though its waters roar and foam and the mountains quake with its turmoil.* (Ps 46:1-3)

This tremendous statement of trust was generated by their position under the refuge of God. As a result of their position, under God's refuge, they were able to face whatever might come with great confidence, peace, and resolve. In a very real sense this is one of the most prominent distinguishing characteristics of the children of God. Our ability to trust in God when the world crashes around us is radically different from the response of the world. In fact, I have often considered that a theology of pain may be among the most important truths a Christian can comprehend. When we are tempted to fear, we instead place our trust in God. "When I am afraid, I will trust in You" (Ps 56:3).

God Will Give His People Rest

ZEPHANIAH 3:13

Not only does God promise to give His people refuge, He also promises to give them rest. Just as ours is, their culture would have been a busy culture. They would have known stress like we know stress. This reference to rest, however, is intriguing not only because it promises peace in the middle of a lack of peace, but it is even more intriguing as it describes what will lead to that peace. Peace, for the follower of God, will come not just from the removal of chaos (though a day is coming when that will happen), but from the removal of sin in our own lives. Notice the text. There will be no more wrongdoing. There will be no more lies. There will be no more deceitful tongues found among the remnant of Israel. Instead of those things, they will have peace.

This promise underlines what we ought to know but so often miss. So much of our stress and turmoil is a result of sin. As sin is eradicated from our lives, we find ourselves able to rest in the peace of God. God's presence, His holiness, His righteousness, brings us peace. This was particularly the promise that was made regarding the coming Messiah: "But He was pierced because of our transgressions, crushed because of our iniquities; punishment for our peace was on Him, and we are healed by His wounds" (Isa 53:5). His wounds are the gateway to our peace. In the gospel our sin is transferred to Christ while His righteousness is transferred to us. In theological terms we would call this *imputed righteousness.* This is exactly what Paul describes for the Corinthian church: "He made the One who did not know sin to be sin for us, so that we might become the righteousness of God in Him" (2 Cor 5:21). It is this remarkable transfer that enables us to lie down and rest.

Furthermore, His people are able to lie down and rest without fear. This, again, speaks to the eradication of sin—the restoration of all things. God has redeemed us personally from sin and is also redeeming the whole world from sin. He will ultimately set everything right. Both His redemptive work—individually and corporately—and His provision as our security allows us the freedom to lie down with no fear of danger. This is what the psalmist was trying to convey in that most familiar of psalms, Psalm 23:

> *The* Lord *is my shepherd; there is nothing I lack. He lets me lie down in green pastures; He leads me beside quiet waters. He renews my life; He leads me along the right paths for His name's sake. Even when I go through the darkest valley, I fear no danger, for You are with me; Your rod and Your staff—they comfort me.* (vv. 1-5)

That God would love us so much that He would go to the lengths He did in order to secure our redemption, and then would go on to secure the restoration of all things, allowing us to lie down in peace with no fear of danger, speaks to His infinite grace and mercy. However, all of this becomes even more meaningful when you realize that God had to satisfy His own justice in order to extend grace, which means that God Himself would suffer, through His Son, in order that He might accomplish this grand work of redemption among His people and the rest of His creation.

God Will Protect His People

ZEPHANIAH 3:14-15

The Lord has redeemed His people. He has called them to repentance and has provided refuge and rest for the people of Judah. In the face of that, God encourages the people to celebrate. What has predominantly been a book that is both painful and low on hope has dramatically turned a corner. The appropriate response to the redemptive work of God among His people is to throw a party. This is precisely what God is communicating. What's more, this is not just a momentary celebration. The understanding here is that this is their new way of life. This is not just a fleeting, volitional choice to "sing for joy" or "shout loudly." This is a transformation of the heart. Israel was heading toward certain judgment and death, but instead they have inherited the grace of God. There is much to be excited about!

Verse 15 will explain the source of their joy. Their punishment has been removed, their enemies have been turned back, and their king is among them. We have reflected on this over and over throughout this book, but this is the story of the redemptive work of God on display for us to see. This is a picture of the gospel doing its good work in their hearts. It begins with their punishment being removed. This is in such stark contrast to the message we walked through six verses earlier:

> *Therefore, wait for Me—this is the LORD's declaration—until the day I rise up for plunder. For My decision is to gather nations, to assemble kingdoms, in order to pour out My indignation on them, all My burning anger; for the whole earth will be consumed by the fire of My jealousy.* (3:8)

They had earned God's wrath, and rightly were in the crosshairs of His judgment. However, because of His grace they were now freed from that impending punishment.

Not only have they experienced freedom from judgment, but their enemies have been turned back. Of course, the greater image here is the turning back of the greatest enemy. Just as God turned back the enemies of Israel as He accomplished His redemptive work among His people, so too Satan, the great liar and enemy of our soul, will be turned back completely and forever. In fact, in the death of Christ his death was made certain.

> *Now since the children have flesh and blood in common, Jesus also shared in these, so that through His death He might destroy the one holding the power of death—that is, the Devil—and free those who were held in slavery all their lives by the fear of death.* (Heb 2:14-15)

The defeat of the enemy, coupled with the freedom from judgment, is enough to send anyone into an ecstatic celebration. However, these are joined together with one final reason for celebration.

The king has come! This simple little declaration is so powerful. Their king, Yahweh Himself, is among them. Those who had turned their back on God and had wandered far from Him were now gathered back together, and God was among them. This brings to mind Jesus, the Immanuel, the God who is with us: "See, the virgin will become pregnant and give birth to a son, and they will name Him Immanuel, which is translated 'God is with us'" (Matt 1:23). This, then, is the ultimate celebration. Far too often in contemporary evangelicalism we suggest that heaven is the goal of the gospel, which is simply not accurate. The Bible is clear that our sin separated us from God and that the goal of the gospel is reconciliation with God. Heaven is a benefit, not the goal, of the gospel. God is the goal of the gospel. This beautiful statement, that God is with them, is to confirm the greatest gift one can receive, that is, God.

God Will Grace His People

ZEPHANIAH 3:16-20

This chapter, and the book, now closes with what is one of the most stunningly beautiful passages in all of Scripture. In fact, even as I write, I struggle to describe adequately the breathtaking beauty of this passage. The vast majority of this book has been filled with condemning language. By the time the reader gets halfway through chapter 3 it feels as if we have been beaten up, along with Judah, over and over again. This is not to suggest that they did not deserve the judgment, because they did, but this book levels the judgment in ways no other book does. It is swift, it is intense, and it is certain. On the heels of that comes the end of the book, particularly verses 17 and following. God is with them. God is for them. God is celebrating over them. These would seem the most unlikely of thoughts after the vast majority of the book, but these are exactly what God communicates through Zephaniah here.

Confirming what we saw in verse 15, God reiterates that He is among them. In other words, He is with them. This alone is the crown jewel of all the gifts that God can give, but God goes on to bless them with more. God is a "warrior who saves." We see this description referenced in a number of other OT passages, but Job 16 is particularly helpful as we try to understand it: "He breaks through my defenses again and again; He charges at me like a warrior" (Job 16:14). Job is in the middle of one of his complaints when he says this. He is describing how God has behaved toward him. In the verses preceding it he claims that God has essentially assaulted him and left him helpless. In this verse he describes God as a warrior who cannot be stopped. Of course, our reading here in Zephaniah is a radically different picture of God. He is not harming Israel in any way but is instead bringing them grace. He is, however, battling. But His battle is with the enemies of Judah. This hard-charging behavior that Job describes is consistent with God's behavior, only here it is on behalf of His people. His pursuit as a warrior is to save them. What a tremendous picture! It reminds us that our salvation, like the salvation of Israel, is not just a gift of grace (though it is), but is a hard fought victory over the forces of evil. Ephesians 6 is a good reminder here:

> *For our battle is not against flesh and blood, but against the rulers, against the authorities, against the world powers of this darkness, against the spiritual forces of evil in the heavens.* (Eph 6:12)

Salvation is accompanied by a bloody price tag. Forgetting that can make it easy to dismiss or diminish salvation.

He is a warrior, but also, in a great contrast, we see a loving Father who rejoices over the return of His child. Just as He called His children to celebrate, He too joins in the celebration. We are told here that His celebration of us is filled with rejoicing, gladness, love, delight, and joy. It sounds much like a child at Christmas, this generous love of God. What makes this love stand out, aside from its face value, is that it is given to those who have so grievously rejected Him over and over again. The disobedient people of God have repented, so God celebrates with rejoicing. Israel dishonors God by living as if He does not exist but they turn back, so God pours out His love on them. The people of Judah chase after their own happiness, trusting only in themselves, but then become humbled and contrite before God, so God shouts with joy over their return. This is like the climax of a powerful movie. It is also much like the story of the prodigal son: "But while the son was still a long way off, his father saw him and was filled with compassion. He ran, threw his arms around his neck, and kissed him" (Luke 15:20). This is a beautiful picture of affection from a father for his children.

As we consider God's response to Israel, we have to recognize that God's response to us is much the same. His people, made in His image, turned from Him, rebelled, and did not look back. For millennia now they have been running from Him, but some of them have returned. They have recognized their sin and come back to walk with God. Over each one of them God celebrates their return.

As the chapter concludes with verses 18-20, God promises Israel the hope of eternity. He brings them back together. He brings them back to Him. He pursues those who attack His children and vanquishes them. He takes those who have been broken and restores them to health. He takes those who have been shamed and restores their dignity. He gathers them to His kingdom and gives them places of honor and distinction. He then concludes the entire book with these three words: "Yahweh has spoken." These three words affirm that what He has promised will come to fruition. He will make this happen for His people. He will show grace.

Such is the kingdom of God. It is the domain of the king—a place of righteousness, justice, and grace. A place for which those of us who bear His image were intended, but we marred that future with our choice of sin. In response to that, He sets the balance of the universe upright by allowing His own Son to take on His judgment, so that we might once again have a place in His kingdom as co-heirs with Jesus. This is the promise of Zephaniah. For those who will repent—who will hear His voice, and return to Him—to them He promises grace and restoration. So that raises the question, what should we do now? First of all, we should have faith in Him. Beyond that we should repent. Finally, we should live now as we will live then. We who have repented and believed have been adopted into His family. We are His children and we are now residents of His kingdom. Let us rejoice!

Reflect and Discuss

1. Do you find yourself struggling to trust in God? Have you repented recently of your tendency to trust in yourself?
2. In what ways does your trust *in* God lead to changed actions *for* God?
3. God is not ashamed of us, and He is removing our shame. How does that affect the way you view God?
4. In what areas do you still struggle with pride?
5. Do you struggle with stress? God has gone to great lengths to destroy sin, and one of the benefits is that we can "lie down in peace." How do you need to trust God with your life and so experience His peace?
6. Our God is a God who is "among us" meaning that He is with us. Have you considered that being brought together in relationship with God is the purpose of your salvation? Have you thanked Him recently for His presence?

7. God is the conquering warrior who has defeated our enemies. How does this change the way you view your life, particularly when you have struggles?
8. God celebrates over you like a child at Christmas. Do you respond to God differently as you contemplate His love for you?
9. We have an eternal home awaiting us as believers in Christ. How does your anticipated return to paradise shape the way in which you live now?

Haggai

The Call to Repent and Rebuild

HAGGAI 1:1

Main Idea: The book of Haggai is the story of God's people who were focused on their own satisfaction and failed to flourish because of it. Their repentance and obedience would result in God's blessing.

I. The Longing Prophet
II. The Persian Government

The book of Haggai is a bit of an anomaly in the OT canon, particularly among the prophetic books, because Haggai's message gets through and people respond in repentance and obedience. In a sea of prophetic books that decry disobedience only to see the people of God brush off the admonition and continue in their sin, Haggai stands out as an encouraging light, an example of what can happen when God's people listen to God's word delivered through God's prophet and experience God's blessing. We really know very little about the prophet Haggai, though we can surmise a few things from textual evidence.

The Longing Prophet

Haggai was probably an older man, likely in his 70s at least. Haggai 2:3 indicates that Haggai may have seen the original temple, which would have enabled him to understand the significance of God's call to rebuild the temple as well as the value of the temple. Haggai would have understood the importance of the land and the centrality of worship that were vital to the flourishing of God's people. His awareness of this would surely lend weight to God's message, as he would plead with the Israelite people to abandon their apathy and take up, once again, the work of rebuilding the temple. As for the dating of the book, we know that Haggai was part of the returning remnant that was being brought back to Jerusalem after King Darius's decree in 538 BC. After living for years in captivity, the return to their land must have been quite energizing for the Israelite people.

The Persian Government

The Persian government ruled over the people of Israel. After approximately 50,000 Israelites returned home, there was urgent concern for the temple and immediate effort made to rebuild it. The foundation was quickly rebuilt, and the people of Israel rightly celebrated this accomplishment (Ezra 3:8-13). However, in response to their building success, their Samaritan neighbors contrived to slow down their work and were successful in frustrating the progress of the temple. They succeeded, in part, by appealing to the governing authorities (Ezra 4:1-5,24).

The project lay dormant for 16 years, from 536 BC until two years after Darius became King of the Persian Empire. In 520 BC Haggai began to prophesy among the people of God. He pled with them to get over their apathy and to delay their obedience no longer. His pleas were successful and the nation of Israel repented, obeyed God, and began to rebuild the temple.

This book is the story of God's people, and in many ways it's the same story that we see of God's people throughout all of Scripture. God has designed the world to work in a specific way. When the people of God disobey him by sinning, humanity is not able to flourish as God intended. This lack of human flourishing can be made right if the people repent and obey Him. The prophet, then, is God's good gift to the people, calling them to repentance and obedience and sharing with them the hope of God's blessing.

Disregarding God Leads to a Lack of Human Flourishing

HAGGAI 1:2-11

Main Idea: The people of Israel were not seeing the flourishing they expected, and Haggai reminded them that this is due to their apathy and postponed obedience.

I. **The People Had a Problem of Prioritizing Their Comfort over God's Temple (1:2-4).**
   A. Postponed obedience is a consistent condition of the sinful human heart (1:2).
   B. Choosing comfort over obedience is a sign of misplaced priority (1:3-4).

II. **Ignoring God's Temple Led to a Lack of Flourishing (1:5-11).**
   A. Reflecting on their lack of flourishing will point them to God's displeasure (1:5-6).
   B. Repenting will point them to God's pleasure (1:7-11).

The People Had a Problem of Prioritizing Their Comfort over God's Temple

HAGGAI 1:2-4

Postponed Obedience Is a Consistent Condition of the Sinful Human Heart (1:2)

The prophet Haggai was concerned with the Israelite people. They had returned to their home more than 16 years earlier, but they had made very little progress on the rebuilding of the temple. The initial return had caused excitement—in fact one could assume that it was nearly euphoria for many of the Jewish people—and that excitement had initially led them to feverishly rebuild the temple. Ezra tells us that they attacked the building of the foundation, and in fairly quick action they were able to see it rebuilt. The response to the building of the foundation was to throw a party, and at that party many of the older Jews cried and the rest exulted. This was obviously a moving moment.

However, as is so often true with obedience to God's commands, the Jewish people were pressured to abandon their task. Their neighbors, chiefly the Samaritans, apparently feared a renaissance of the power of the Israelite people and so compelled them to abandon their temple rebuilding, going so far as to pressure the controlling government, and their efforts paid off. The Israelite people stopped. They not only stopped, they stopped for more than 16 years. In the interim, however, they moved forward with the rebuilding of the rest of the city. They built homes and businesses, among other things. They established the city once again. It is no stretch to imagine that the city was a hive of activity, as business and pleasure intersected on its streets once more. However, in the midst of life being lived, the most important thing was being forgotten—namely the worship of God. In striking similarity to the behavior of Martha in the account of Jesus at His friend's home (Luke 10:38-42), the Israelite people were busy, but they were ultimately busy with their own things and apathetic to the worship of God. Into this picture comes the voice of Haggai. In verse 2 Haggai recounts the Lord's dismay when he says that the people of Israel had no interest in rebuilding the temple: "These people say: The time has not come for the house of the LORD to be rebuilt." "The time has not come" is code for "I have better things to do." This is not new for the Israelites of Haggai's time, nor is it foreign in our day. Overlooking the things of God in favor of our own things is fairly commonplace. It is the same thing that we see in play in Genesis 3 when the serpent convinces Eve to disregard God's words and believe that her own wisdom is sufficient:

> *Then the woman saw that the tree was good for food and delightful to look at, and that it was desirable for obtaining wisdom. So she took some of its fruit and ate it; she also gave some to her husband, who was with her, and he ate it.* (Gen 3:6)

This willingness to postpone obedience or disregard it altogether has been the marker of the human race ever since Eve's initial transgression. At the root of this sin is the nastiness of pride: the belief that our wisdom and preferences are greater than His. This is why G. K. Chesterton once said, "If I had only one sermon to preach it would be a sermon against pride" (*Common Man*, 246).

What Haggai desired for the people of Israel was a changed heart that would lead to changed behavior. He desired to see them prioritize God and His commands over and above all other concerns. This is precisely what Jesus sought to instill in Martha when she was so busy working for Jesus that she forgot that the greatest importance is to worship Him. The Lord told her, "Martha, Martha, you are worried and upset about many things, but one thing is necessary. Mary has made the right choice, and it will not be taken away from her" (Luke 10:41-42). This passage reminds us that God's greatest desire for us is that we honor Him and obey His commands. Much like little children who constantly question their parents at night in an attempt to postpone their sleep, Christians are tempted to exhaust our energies on other issues and areas in an attempt to postpone obedience. This postponing is rooted in theology and history, as we understand clearly that humanity is inherently sinful and has been since the garden of Eden.

Choosing Comfort over Obedience Is a Sign of Misplaced Priority (1:3-4)

Haggai continues by offering a striking condemnation of the Israelite people. Keep in mind that at this point they were fairly established after their return from exile. They had built homes and businesses and were settled in their regular routines. In spite of that, they had abandoned their commitment to the temple of God. Haggai, therefore, raises his voice in opposition. He begins by decrying their "paneled houses." Haggai specifically uses a word for *paneled* that implies "well appointed" or "comfortable." In other words, they were not only settled in their homes, they had been to their equivalent of Pier One, had acquired all sorts of beautiful accoutrements for their homes, and were living comfortably. While Haggai is not condemning their comfortable living, he is condemning this living at the expense of obedience to God's commands. He specifically contrasts their "paneled houses" with the temple, which "lies in ruins." These are strong words and are intended to clarify the radical disparity between their own standard of living and the condition of the house of God. They were living in comfort while God's house remained unbuilt and God's will remained undone.

This kind of disparity is not uncommon among God's people. It is similar to what the prophet Malachi prophesied about in the final book of the Old Testament:

> *A son honors his father, and a servant his master. But if I am a father, where is My honor? And if I am a master, where is your fear of Me? says Yahweh of Hosts to you priests, who despise My name. Yet you ask: "How have we despised Your name?"*
> *"By presenting defiled food on My altar."*

> *You ask: "How have we defiled You?"*
> *When you say: "The LORD's table is contemptible.* (Mal 1:6-7)

Like the priests of Malachi's day, the Israelites were substantively more interested in what they could gain than they were in obeying God's commands. The chief objection to obeying God's commands was the cost involved in doing so. During Jesus' life, He would again clarify for us that the cost of following Him was significant: "Then He said to them all, 'If anyone wants to come with Me, he must deny himself, take up his cross daily, and follow Me'" (Luke 9:23).

Although the Israelite people had an obedience issue, Haggai understood that this was an issue of the heart. If their hearts were warmed toward God, their behavior would follow. They were disobedient because they had chosen to love themselves more than they loved Him. Ultimately this is an example of idol worship, with themselves at the center of their worship. They were, in subtle ways, mimicking the kind of worship that the American writer, David Foster Wallace, once described in a commencement speech at Kenyon College:

> Everybody worships. The only choice we get is what to worship. And the compelling reason for maybe choosing some sort of god . . . to worship . . . is that pretty much anything else you worship will eat you alive. If you worship money and things, if they are where you tap real meaning in life, then you will never have enough, never feel you have enough. It's the truth. Worship your own body and beauty and sexual allure, and you will always feel ugly. And when time and age start showing, you will die a million deaths before [your loved ones] finally plant you. . . . Worship power, and you will end up feeling weak and afraid, and you will need ever more power over others to numb you to your own fear. Worship your intellect, being seen as smart, you will end up feeling stupid, a fraud, always on the verge of being found out. Look, the insidious thing about these forms of worship is not that they are evil or sinful; it is that they're unconscious. They are default settings. ("This Is Water")

The danger for the Israelite people was not that they had abandoned the building of the temple, it was that they had abandoned God. Their comfort rose in importance, their fear of the Samaritans, among others, was greater than their fear of God, and they succumbed to the pressure of self-preservation. Sadly, as Haggai would go on to point out, their attempts at self-preservation, or human flourishing, would backfire. What they believed to be critical to the advancement of their comfort actually served to accomplish the opposite. They desired to flourish and instead they were failing, all because they had rejected God as the primary object of their worship.

Ignoring God's Temple Led to a Lack of Flourishing

HAGGAI 1:5-11

Reflecting on Their Lack of Flourishing Will Point Them to God's Displeasure (1:5-6)

Haggai follows up his condemnation of their abandonment of God by pointing out that their behavior was ultimately a failed experiment. They had stopped building the temple because of pressure from outside their community and idol worship inside the community. They thought that this path would lead them to satisfaction and happiness. They were tired of the resistance and attracted to a future that seemed more appealing. Haggai points out that they were wrong. Instead of satisfaction and happiness, they were experiencing a lack of flourishing, a lack of satisfaction.

Haggai begins in verse 5 by calling them to **consider their lives**: "Think carefully about your ways." He wanted them to engage in some self-examination. This same word that he uses in verse 5 he will again use in 2:15 and 2:18 to establish this point: they will be able to trace their flourishing to their obedience to God's commands. It matters that they consider that connection. Now, this is not some early version of a prosperity gospel. It is not a promise that if they scratched God's back, He will scratch theirs. Instead it is a basic principle that God has designed the world so that it functions best when we are aligned with His commands and His purposes. Human flourishing generally occurs when we honor God and follow His commands. The Israelites had not honored God, nor had they obeyed His commands. Haggai wanted to draw a clear and decisive connection between their lack of obedience and their obvious lack of flourishing, so three separate times he invited them to consider where they found themselves in light of their obedience or disobedience.

This is an important lesson for us in our own lives. Far too often we fail to consider where we are or where we have been. Taking stock of our lives is challenging and can at times be painful, yet this is exactly why it is so important. When we consider own lives, we are challenged to consider whether or not we have been—or are—walking in obedience to God's purposes and His commands.

Haggai goes on in verse 6 to **clarify their lack**. He says they planted but did not harvest like they anticipated. This lack of harvest was leading to a lack of satisfaction and provision. He goes on and on with other illustrations like drink, clothes, and income. All these things were less than they expected, and the shortfall was a result of their delayed obedience. The unfortunate reality is that God generally desires us to flourish and to be a blessing to the city in which we live. The prophet Jeremiah declared,

> *Build houses and live in them. Plant gardens and eat their produce. Take wives and have sons and daughters. Take wives for your sons and give your daughters to men in marriage so that they may bear sons and daughters. Multiply there; do not decrease. Seek the welfare of the city I have deported you to. Pray to the Lord on its behalf, for when it has prosperity, you will prosper.* (Jer 29:5-7)

Jeremiah's declaration is a reminder that God's design is for His people to prosper and for us to seek the prosperity of the place in which we live. God wants the Israelite people to prosper, but their delayed obedience had led to their lack of flourishing.

Haggai's point in these verses is that our actions have consequences. It sounds a lot like the wisdom our parents offer us as children, but it is an excellent point. Our actions never happen in isolation and always lead to consequences. Sometimes those consequences are encouraging and life-giving, and sometimes those consequences are painful and challenging. In particular, and for the purposes of this passage, the Israelites' sin had consequences. The prophet Isaiah has said, "But your iniquities have built barriers between you and your God, and your sins have made Him hide His face from you so that He does not listen" (Isa 59:2). This is a reminder that while all of our behavior has consequences, our sin has serious and even deadly consequences because it creates separation between us and God. When we disregard God so that we can please ourselves, we place ourselves in the precarious situation of being outside of God's intended order and therefore susceptible to a lack of flourishing, but we also place ourselves in the crosshairs of God's wrath and therefore in danger of God's judgment. In the case of the Israelites in Haggai's day, they were desperately in need of obedience.

Of course, this passage reminds us that we are incapable of providing the obedience that God requires. God is perfectly holy, and as such He requires perfect holiness from us. When we are unable to comply, we must either face God's wrath or appeal to a mediator. In order to escape the wrath of God, we need someone who is able to redeem us. Of course, this is pointing us forward to Jesus. Every generation, both those before and those after these Israelites, would face the same problem—a lack of flourishing and the presence of God's wrath. We all are in need of a redeemer. The author of Hebrews reminds us, "it is appointed for people to die once—and after this, judgment" (Heb 9:27). Unless intervention is applied, we all are in danger. Thank God that He has provided the needed intervention: "He made the One who did not know sin to be sin for us, so that we might become the righteousness of God in Him" (2 Cor 5:21). This passage serves to point us to Jesus as it reminds us that we, like the Israelites, are guilty of disobedience and are under the wrath of God, but because of Christ's sacrifice in our place, redemption is available.

Repenting Will Point Them to God's Pleasure (1:7-11)

In response to the people's delayed obedience, and ultimately to their idol worship, Haggai now moves on to begin charting the way forward for the Israelites. As he did in verse 5, Haggai once again reminds them to "think carefully." He is asking them to consider their response. Previously they considered their behavior and what they had to show for it. Now Haggai is calling them to consider their response. So, what is this response that Haggai is calling them to? Repentance. Repentance, as you are aware, is defined in a number of different ways by a number of different people. For our purposes here we will define it as a turning of the heart that leads to a turning of the behavior. Haggai is calling the Israelite people to decisively turn their hearts Godward, and when their hearts have turned away from their sin—their delayed obedience—and turned toward God, their behavior would also be pleasing to God.

Throughout Scripture we see this pattern: heart change leads to behavioral change. God expects our behavior to change, but He is clear that behavior is simply a reflection of the heart. When our hearts change, our behavior follows. We are reminded in Proverbs, "Guard your heart above all else, for it is the source of life" (Prov 23:4). Looking to the New Testament we see Jesus Himself, during the Sermon on the Mount, teaching that the action of murder and the action of adultery are both indicative of sinful hearts long before the behavior itself actually occurs (Matt 5:21-30). Haggai understands that rebuilding the temple is a heart issue. He desires to see their behavior change, but he understands that behavior follows desire. The Israelites, as we said earlier, had a desire problem. They needed to repent, and their repentance needed to identify their misplaced affection. When their idolatrous affection was confessed and rejected, right behavior would follow. Verse 8 describes the behavior that would follow in incredibly simple terms: "'Go up into the hills, bring down lumber, and build the house. Then I will be pleased with it and be glorified,' says the LORD." This repentance would be complete when they built the house of God, the temple. They could not walk rightly before God until they repented, as Haggai called them to "think rightly" and "build the house." This repentance is first internal and heart-focused, and second external and hands-focused.

Our repentance must be the same. Sadly, far too often we find it easy simply to acknowledge wrongdoing and hope that we can just behave our way out of a situation. I say this is sad because to those around us it can appear to work. We can conform our behavior, pleasing those around us, yet still be far from God. Our hearts must be the starting place, or our behavior is essentially meaningless action.

Finally, in verses 9 through 11, Haggai points out that they do have the opportunity to reject repentance. They can choose to continue walking as they have already been, but if they do they will continue to experience God working against them, keeping them from flourishing. The choice is simple, then. They can repent, follow God's way, and flourish as they find themselves in harmony with the world as God intended it; or they can reject repentance and risk God's wrath as He actively works against them, keeping them from flourishing.

Reflect and Discuss

1. Can you think of a time that God, through His Word, a sermon, or another source, called you to obedience and yet you postponed obedience?
2. What motivates your heart to desire to postpone obedience?
3. Can you think of items in your life that are too valuable to give up, even if God required it of you?
4. If you have had times of spiritual lethargy, have you noticed how easy it is to convince others you are doing fine with religious behavior, even while you are walking further and further from God?

5. How can you resist simply engaging in religious behavior and maintain spiritual vitality?
6. What evidence do you see in Scripture or in creation of God's general design for the world to flourish?
7. In what ways can you see a disregard for God's plan leading to a lack of flourishing?
8. Is there an example in your life of your disobedience leading to a lack of flourishing?
9. Have you surrendered your life to God, having recognized your own disobedience and Christ's sacrifice in your place?

Fear of God Leads to Repentance

HAGGAI 1:12-15

Main Idea: The people of Israel heard the word of the Lord, repented together, and obeyed God. As they obeyed God, He affirmed His presence among them.

I. God's Word Led to Fear of the Lord and Repentance (1:12).
  - A. God's word brings forth obedience (1:12).
  - B. God's word brings forth fear of the Lord (1:12).

II. The Repentance of the People Led to the Restoration of the Temple (1:13-15).
  - A. The messenger of the Lord delivered the message of the Lord (1:13).
  - B. The Lord promises His presence to His people to stir them to obedience (1:13).
  - C. The Lord stirs the spirits of the leaders and the people to encourage them and equip them to obey (1:14).

God's Word Led to Fear of the Lord and Repentance

HAGGAI 1:12

God's Word Brings Forth Obedience (1:12)

God had spoken through Haggai, and the people heard God's voice and responded obediently. Here in verse 12 we see that the high priest was the first to respond. As the high priest responded, so too the people responded. All of this, then, was precipitated by one significant event: the proclamation of God's words. We see two distinct phrases in this verse that explain the significance of God's words in the lives of the Jewish people. First, and most clearly, the text tells us that the people "obeyed the voice of the LORD their God." God spoke, and they listened. However, it was not as if God audibly spoke to them from heaven. So how did God speak, and how did they hear? The verse goes on to point out that God spoke through his prophet Haggai. Continuing on in the verse, we are reminded that the people obeyed God's voice, and second, they obeyed Haggai's voice, his words, "because the LORD had sent him." All things considered, verse 12 indicates three very important realities about God's word and our obedience.

First, **God's word is powerful and effective**. Scripture reminds us,

> *the word of God is living and effective and sharper than any double-edged sword, penetrating as far as the separation of soul and spirit, joints and marrow. It is able to judge the ideas and thoughts of the heart.* (Heb 4:12)

God's words are designed, by God, to quickly and effectively cut through the clutter and the chaos in our hearts and simply to define His will for us in a manner that compels us to obey. In a time when it seems that fewer and fewer pastors, church leaders, and Christians trust in the Word of God to adequately speak God's truth to our hearts, this passage is a strong and compelling call back to the sufficiency of Scripture. God's Word is enough to compel obedience to God's will. This passage reminds us to trust in God's Word and to center our pursuits, as leaders of the church, around His Word. R. C. Sproul has rightly said, regarding God's Word and its authority in our lives,

> It is fashionable in some academic circles to exercise scholarly criticism of the Bible. In so doing, scholars place themselves above the Bible and seek to correct it. If indeed the Bible is the Word of God, nothing could be more arrogant. It is God who corrects us; we don't correct Him. We do not stand over God but under Him. (*Five Things*, 21)

Not only does this passage teach us that we must trust the power of God's words, but it also teaches us that **God often chooses to deliver His words through a preacher**. Not only do the Israelite people respond to God's voice, but they respond to Haggai's voice, because he spoke as a representative of the Lord, sent by God. We have to be careful here to understand that every word that Haggai spoke was not inspired. There is a movement in contemporary church culture to acknowledge the pastor/preacher as if they are somehow supernaturally inspired, and therefore to challenge them is to challenge God Himself. This is a dangerous precedent, and it sets the pastor/preacher up for failure. However, it would be equally dangerous for us to assume that the pastor/preacher is just another person, standing up front, delivering a speech. Haggai was a prophet, delivering God's words, under God's power and because of

God's authority. This message should not have been casually dismissed, and thankfully the Israelite people did not make that tragic mistake. God's words are powerful, but God has ordained the preaching of His Word by faithful preachers as the primary means in which His message is to be delivered to the world. This is among the greatest reasons why Paul felt so compelled to challenge his son in the faith, Timothy, about the importance of preaching God's Word:

> *I solemnly charge you before God and Christ Jesus, who is going to judge the living and the dead, and because of His appearing and His kingdom: Proclaim the message; persist in it whether convenient or not; rebuke, correct, and encourage with great patience and teaching.* (1 Tim 4:1-2)

God's words are authoritative, but God's chosen method for delivering His words is most often through a preacher.

The final lesson in verse 12 that we can learn regarding the words of God is **the power of leadership in respect to repentance**. It is no small thing that, when confronted by God's words, the Israelite people repented, but only after the high priest, their spiritual leader, first modeled repentance. Good leadership leads by example, in humility, and in obedience to God's words. It is hard to overstate how significant this is. It is powerful to note that, in response to the high priest's obedience, the "entire" remnant of the Israelite people repented. I think it may be quite possible that, among many of our churches today, sin is not taken seriously because the church has never seen her leaders publicly taking sin seriously. It may be that the church is just waiting for the leadership to acknowledge the deadly danger of sin, to recognize that this sin sometime exists in their own lives, and to repent and walk away from sin toward righteousness.

God's Word Brings Forth Fear of the Lord (1:12)

In response to God's words being preached, the Israelite people repented. They did not merely change their behavior, though; this passage points out that they were completely reoriented around the nature and character of God. Verse 12 ends with a declaration that the people "feared the LORD." This statement is a powerful one, and one which is a little bit difficult to fully understand in English. The original word used here does not have an exact equivalent in the English language. It conveys a couple of ideas about fear, neither of which convey terror, but instead they combine to provide a picture of affection and worship driven by an acute awareness of God's character.

First, this fear conveys a sense of **submission to the authority of God** in response to God's character as God. In other words, the people become intimately aware of who God is—His holiness and His awesome power, among other things—and they are compelled to bow in obedience and submission. In a very real sense, this mirrors the picture we see of Isaiah in the throne room of God in Isaiah 6. As Isaiah saw the Lord "high and lifted up" and became deeply aware of who God is, his response was,

> *Then I said: Woe is me for I am ruined because I am a man of unclean lips and live among a people of unclean lips, and because my eyes have seen the King, the LORD of Hosts.* (Isa 6:5)

Awareness of God should always drive us to our knees in confession and humility, compelling us to obey. After David committed his sin of adultery with Bathsheba and was confronted about his sin by the prophet Nathan, David composed one of the most moving passages in all of Scripture, a statement of confession and submission, in Psalm 51. Specifically David said, "The sacrifice pleasing to God is a broken spirit. God, You will not despise a broken and humbled heart" (Ps 51:17). David understood that the appropriate response to God is a heart that is surrendered to Him and a life that is bowed down before Him. Of course, this raises the question, "Why is the church so full of people who do not seem to have a life bowed down in obedience before God?" Might it be possible that this is true because so many who call themselves believers in Christ rarely, if ever, come into the presence of God to be confronted with the reality of how great our God is? I fear so.

Not only does the word *fear* convey the idea of submission in response to God's character, but it also communicates a sense of **awe because of God's power and might**. The Israelite people were repenting and preparing to walk in obedience partly because they were driven to worship God as they became more distinctly aware of His might. The psalmist once said,

> *God, hear my cry; pay attention to my prayer. I call to You from the ends of the earth when my heart is without strength. Lead me to a rock that is high above me, for You have been a refuge for me, a strong tower in the face of the enemy. I will live in Your tent forever and take refuge under the shelter of Your wings.* (Ps 61:1-4)

The idea that God is majestic, powerful, and able to save is a key element to rightly understanding who God is and to rightly worshiping Him. The Israelites' disobedience would have been, at least in part, driven by their forgetfulness of who God is, how awe-inspiring He is, and how He is able to save. Like the psalmist in Psalm 61, the Israelites were in need of repentance and saving. They needed to remember again that God is sufficient, that He is all powerful, and that He is mighty to save. Haggai's proclamation of the words of God served that specific purpose. The Israelites were called back to rest under the authority of His strength and, like the psalmist in Psalm 61, they were once again in the refuge of His strength.

So as we walk in disobedience, and as we find ourselves confronted with God's Word, our response should be grounded in a fear of God. Not necessarily an abject terror, but instead affection, worship, and trust, rooted in the person and character of God.

The Repentance of the People Led to the Restoration of the Temple

HAGGAI 1:13-15

The Messenger of the Lord Delivered the Message of the Lord (1:13)

Verse 13 is packed with helpful morsels that point us to the significance of the messenger of the Lord, the preacher of God's words. As we discussed in verse 12, the preacher of the word is a vital component to God's plan for the spread of His message. While this messenger is not infallible, the preacher is also not to be taken lightly or easily dismissed. The message of the preacher is a message of substantive weight and grave importance. While this verse says a number of things about the messenger of the Lord, I want us to consider two specific aspects concerning the words of the Lord and how we should understand the messenger of the Lord, the preacher of the word.

First, the word *messenger* is important. The root word for "messenger," unsurprisingly, is the same root as the word for "message" that we find a little later in the verse. While this is unsurprising, the meaning of the similarity has something important to say to us about the role of the preacher. The root of these words speaks to God's words being given to humanity. It is intended to convey the idea that the words we are hearing are directly from God. While this definition is helpful in understanding the weightiness of the words themselves, when we turn our attention to the messenger, the definition of the word becomes even more intriguing. The same root word that gives us "message"—or words from God Himself—gives us "messenger," only in the latter it is being applied to a human delivery system. It would appear that Haggai wants us to understand just how significant the role of the messenger and the content of his message are. They are explicitly linked together. While the messenger is not God Himself, the messenger represents God, he speaks for God, if you will. In fact, the word *messenger* is translated across Scripture in other contexts as "angel," "envoy," or "ambassador." It conveys the idea that the messengers have no inherent authority or truth in and of themselves, but they are to be listened to and honored because they carry the weight of the One who sent them. What's more, when they convey the message, they convey a message that is not their own, but a message that comes from God Himself.

In addition to the respect and trust that should be given the preacher, or messenger, of God's words, there is also a very important reality that must be embraced by preachers themselves. Namely, they do not represent themselves, nor do they have the freedom simply to say what they want to say. Messengers have a distinct responsibility to represent the one who sent them—in this case, God. Preachers represent and reflect God to their audience. This is why the Bible points out to us that the preacher will carry a greater responsibility before God than others will: "Not many should become teachers, my brothers, knowing that we will receive a stricter judgment" (Jas 3:1). I fear that too many preachers revel in the authority they believe they have without recognizing the great level of responsibility that comes with their position. Sadly, this has led to behavior that does little to represent well the character of God. Preachers, we must be careful of our position and responsibility as representatives—ambassadors—of God.

Further, not only does the messenger have a responsibility as a representative of God, the preacher also has a tremendous responsibility to ensure that the words they declare are, in fact, the words of God Himself. By virtue of the preacher's position, he is asserting himself as a sort of spokesman for the Lord. When the messenger, or preacher, is not careful to accurately reflect what God Himself has said, the preacher is responsible for a form of malpractice, and even worse than misrepresenting himself, there is the danger that he has guided his listeners away from God because of his sloppiness with regard to his message.

The second morsel from verse 13 that we should consider is the word *delivered*. The word speaks to the distribution of the Lord's message. It literally can be translated "to hand over." In other words, strengthening the point we have just tried to make about the messenger's responsibility, the messenger has no right or responsibility to deliver his own message. Instead, messengers are stewards, managers if you will, of God's message. To be a faithful messenger, or preacher, is to handle well the stewardship you have been given. This requires of the preacher an intimate understanding of the text he is declaring. It also requires a strict discipline to prioritize the content of the text and to refrain from changing the text into something else. It also expects a certain humility—that preachers would defer any praise received, as they acknowledge that it is not their wisdom, their brilliance, or their authority that is being delivered through the words of the Lord. Instead they are simply receiving the words from God and clearly passing these words along to those who are listening.

The Lord Promises His Presence to His People to Stir Them to Obedience (1:13)

The world is full of declarations. Maybe one of the most famous declarations in recent history was by Joe Namath, starting quarterback for the New York Jets, when they were preparing to play the Baltimore Colts in Super Bowl III. Namath was intoxicated and found himself facing down a loud Colts fan who was confident that the Jets could not survive the game against the Colts. So, in front of the crowd, Namath loudly declared that the Jets would win the Super Bowl. In fact, he even went so far as to say that he guaranteed the victory. This was significant because it was not just the loud Colts fan who was convinced that Baltimore would win. The Colts were favored by prognosticators to win by 18 points—a veritable landslide. Instead, the Jets would win 16-7, thus fulfilling Namath's promise from a few nights before.

Haggai 1:13 ends with a declaration. However, this declaration is more than someone simply making a statement. When Joe Namath made his statement, it was anything but a sure thing. While the outcome was what Namath promised, he was not able to know, for certain, that it would happen that way. This declaration from the Lord is different. Instead of just being a statement of confidence, this declaration actually carries the weight of a legal transaction. It is a certain promise from God to His now-repentant people. This promise is significant as it stands, but we see God make this promise again in Haggai 2:4. What is this promise that God felt so compelled to declare to His people? Simply put, He promises that He is with them. This is no small thing. This promise indicates a change in tone from the Lord. The people were disobedient, so He compelled them to obey. Then they turned from their sin and embraced righteousness, so God immediately began to affirm them and His presence among them. He is with them, and He will be with them. This is a promise of comfort, it is a promise of blessing, and most of all, it is the promise of grace.

First, **it is a promise of comfort**. In a time when the Israelites were still most likely aware of their recent Babylonian captivity and their return to Jerusalem, it would have been easy for the Jewish people to think that God had forgotten them. He had not. This is a theme that we see across the whole of Scripture. God's people find themselves in painful or lonely circumstances, and the desire is often to complain or be angry with God for the circumstances. Instead, God's promise to us is that He will never abandon us, and that commitment should compel us to be strong and faithful. "Be strong and courageous; don't be terrified or afraid of them. For it is the Lord your God who goes with you; He will not leave you or forsake you" (Deut 31:6). However, although we see this pattern communicated by God to His people over and over throughout Scripture, we continue to see the people of God forget it and attempt to abandon God.

As we walk through life today, we should not assume that we will be any different. Much like Peter in the courtyard when Jesus was on trial, we will be tempted to believe that God is not what we thought He was and that He is not able to do what He promised He could do. Then our natural response will be to reject the image of God that had, at one point, captivated our attention, and to turn to ourselves as our source of hope. In the face of that, God's promise to the Israelite people here rings true for you and me today. We see this same sort of redemptive promise on display through the prophet Jeremiah.

> *I am about to gather them from all the lands where I have banished them in My anger, rage and great wrath, and I will return them to this place and make them live in safety. They will be My people, and I will be their God. I will give them one heart and one way so that for their good and for the good of their descendants after them, they will fear Me always.* (Jer 32:37-39)

Furthermore, this is the lesson of Jesus' life. Quite possibly the most beautiful title for Jesus is that of Immanuel. "God with us," it means, and the truth that it communicates is stunning! This is the breathtaking lesson of the gospel, on display in these words of this often-overlooked minor prophet. God is our God and we are His people, and we should be comforted that He does not leave us and He is not changing. He is Immanuel, the God who is with us.

Second, **it is a promise of blessing**. These people, as the first 11 verses of Haggai 1 remind us, had been planting, drinking, dressing, and earning and yet were never satisfied; they never had enough. In the face of this, God promises His presence. It is a reminder that they will succeed and that they will persevere. They can be confident because of God's great affection for them and His advocacy on their behalf. John Calvin once said, "Nothing more inspirits men and rouses them from torpor, than, when relying on the promises of divine aid, they have a sure hope of a successful issue" (in Jamieson, Fausset, Brown, *Commentary*, 825). There have been times when Christians have, somewhat flippantly, stated that they had read the end of the book (the Bible) and they have seen that the Christian, in Christ, has won. While it is not helpful to approach that concept flippantly, it is absolutely true, nonetheless. God is with us, and He will conquer evil in the end. This confidence allows Christians to be like no other group throughout history and to thrive even when we are seemingly being defeated. The third-century lawyer, Tertullian, once said, "That's why you can't just exterminate us; the more you kill the more we are. The blood of the martyrs is the seed of the church" (*The Apology*, chapter 50).

Christians are able to persevere in a way that the rest of the world cannot for two primary reasons, both of which are intimately connected. First, we persevere because we have the promise, the hope, of resurrection. Paul said this well:

> *But now Christ has been raised from the dead, the firstfruits of those who have fallen asleep. For since death came through a man, the resurrection of the dead also comes through a man. For as in Adam all die, so also in Christ all will be made alive. But each in his own order: Christ, the firstfruits; afterward, at His coming, those who belong to Christ. Then comes the end, when He hands over the kingdom to God the Father, when He abolishes all rule and all authority and power. For He must reign until He puts all His enemies under His feet. The last enemy to be abolished is death. For God has put everything under His*

> *feet. But when it says "everything" is put under Him, it is obvious that He who puts everything under Him is the exception. And when everything is subject to Christ, then the Son Himself will also be subject to the One who subjected everything to Him, so that God may be all in all.* (1 Cor 15:20-28)

Not only are we reminded in this passage that the resurrection is our guarantee, but we are also encouraged to persevere because of the second, and equally important, truth: we will experience resurrection because Christ will conquer and He will reign eternally. We are adopted into Christ's family through our union with Him in His death and resurrection. Because of this great truth, we can have confidence. Therefore His declaration of His presence is more than just a statement of proximity, it is a statement of Jesus' victory and our share in that triumph!

Third, and finally, **they were recipients of God's grace**. The response of God to their repentance is a foreshadowing of God's response to our repentance today. They believed God's word, they turned from their sin, and God affirmed His presence among them. It is a reminder of God's consistent and unfailing love in the face of our own disobedience and unfaithfulness. There is no more precious truth in all of Scripture than "This saying is trustworthy and deserving of full acceptance: 'Christ Jesus came into the world to save sinners'—and I am the worst of them" (1 Tim 1:15). While we stand as perpetually unfaithful, unforgiving, unloving, and ungrateful, God stands, with affection and grace, ready to usher us into His family through the redemption that is offered in the life, death, and resurrection of Jesus, and all because of His radically sufficient grace. This statement from God that He is with them is not just a statement of presence or just a declaration of victory. It is, maybe most breathtakingly, a declaration of love. It is a message that points us forward to the message of Jesus, taught to us by the apostle Paul: "But God proves His own love for us in that while we were still sinners, Christ died for us!" (Rom 5:8).

The Lord Stirs the Spirits of the Leaders and the People to Encourage Them and Equip Them to Obey (1:14)

Leadership matters. It is not insignificant that the cascading order of obedience in verse 14 is first, the spiritual leadership is enabled; second, the political leadership responds; and finally, the people obey. God certainly does not need to use leaders to accomplish His purposes; for that matter, He does not need anyone to help Him accomplish His purposes.

However, in His wisdom and sovereignty, He has ordained humanity to accomplish His purposes, and He has specifically chosen to use leaders to move His people to accomplish His purposes. In this verse, not only does leadership respond, however, but we see leadership respond as God stirs up their hearts. This verse reminds us of a series of important principles that should guide all leaders and leadership processes. First, leadership leads as God enables them. Second, everything is theological. And finally, people generally only respond as their leaders call them.

First, **leadership leads as God enables them**. We are a fairly helpless lot. By "we" I'm referring to humanity. Our sinfulness and our finiteness limit our ability to do what God has called us to accomplish. Paul's words in Romans 3 speak to our depravity, but they paint a fairly hopeless picture:

> *There is no one righteous, not even one. There is no one who understands; there is no one who seeks God. All have turned away; all alike have become useless. There is no one who does what is good, not even one.* (vv. 10-12)

Thankfully, because of Jesus' redemption, the possibility of honoring God can be realized. Even then, however, it will only happen as God enables it. Paul also addressed that issue in his letter to the church at Colossae:

> *We proclaim Him, warning and teaching everyone with all wisdom, so that we may present everyone mature in Christ. I labor for this, striving with His strength that works powerfully in me.* (Col 1:28-29)

Leadership is unable to lead rightly unless God enables them by supplying His power. Acknowledgment of our weakness and need is a necessary component to faithful and successful spiritual leadership.

Not only is leadership dependent on God's supply, but this passage reminds us that everything is theological. Notice that the people had a problem. Their problem was their lack of progress on the building project. In spite of that, though, the answer is not viewed as primarily a physical problem but as a spiritual problem. Their lack of physical obedience was a direct result of their unwilling and disobedient hearts. All physical acts, both good and bad, initiate in the heart. Therefore, every behavior is ultimately a spiritual issue. Ultimately this means that every behavior is rooted in some sort of theological position. **Everything is theological**. Everything a person does reflects the relationship of that person's heart to God. Why does this matter, then, to leadership? It matters because, not only is leadership dependent upon God's supply to provide them with the strength to lead, but all leadership begins with the condition of the heart. Good leadership leads the heart first, recognizing that changed hearts lead to changed actions.

Finally we see one more leadership lesson, and that is the truth that every leader is in a position of authority for a purpose. **People generally only respond as their leaders call them.** God has designed the human heart to follow the leaders placed over them. Leaders lead and people follow. While there are certainly exceptions to that rule, generally speaking this pattern is the way life works, and this pattern honors God. Romans reminds us that all leaders exist in their positions because God placed them there: "Everyone must submit to the governing authorities, for there is no authority except from God, and those that exist are instituted by God" (Rom 13:1). Leaders are not a functional necessity, they are a God-ordained reality. When we understand this, we are enabled rightly to emphasize the importance of godly leadership, and leaders are able to comprehend the weightiness of their task. All leaders are stewards, or managers, of the responsibility that God has given them, and ultimately all leaders should lead like Paul, who told the Corinthian church, "For I didn't think it was a good idea to know anything among you except Jesus Christ and Him crucified" (1 Cor 2:2).

These three patterns, or lessons, are emphasized in this passage to highlight God and the way He works. As important as the leaders are in God's economy, this passage does nothing to highlight the leaders. They are recognized as part of God's plan—an important part, mind you—and as part of God's plan, like everything else in this passage, they reflect the goodness and glory of God. As is true of everything in life, good leadership is rooted in the goodness of God who enables us to lead. He allows us the privilege of leading so that others will follow us in such a way that God is honored and His purposes are advanced. This, in fact, is the crux of Paul's point when he calls us to "Imitate me, as I also imitate Christ" (1 Cor 11:1). This is the point of verse 14. Leadership matters, but only so far as it is empowered by God to lead others to honor God and advance His purposes. May it be so of each of us.

Reflect and Discuss

1. How do you give evidence in your daily life that you believe God's word to be powerful?
2. Does your church rightly recognize the authority of the preacher, without elevating him beyond where any person should be?
3. Are you a regular repenter? If not, is it possibly due to your lack of time in God's Word?
4. In what ways does your life and worship reflect "the fear of the LORD"?
5. Are you recognizing the importance of biblical preaching by placing yourself under it on a regular basis?
6. Do you examine the preaching you hear to make sure that it stands up to biblical scrutiny? Is it an accurate reflection of the preacher serving as a steward of God's Word?
7. How might the truth that God is with you encourage you to Christian faithfulness today?
8. Are you trusting in God and His grace as your only hope today?
9. Are you trying to lead today in your own strength? How might you be able to rest in the strength that only God can supply?
10. What situations in your life do you view as having little or nothing to do with God? What might change in your life if you understood that everything is theological?

Obedience Requires Strength but Results in Blessing

HAGGAI 2:1-9

Main Idea: The people of Israel heard the word of the Lord, repented together, and obeyed God. As they obeyed God, He affirmed His presence among them.

I. **The Presence of God's Spirit Motivates the People to Work for His Glory (2:1-5).**
II. **The Lord of Hosts Will Shake Everything to Fill His House with Glory (2:6-9).**

The Presence of God's Spirit Motivates the People to Work for His Glory

HAGGAI 2:1-5

I remember one of my earliest jobs. My uncle started a small business refurbishing riding lawn mowers. He would travel around to estate sales and yard sales, and he would purchase used lawn mowers that were in good structural condition. He would strip the mowers down, repaint them, put a new engine on them, and sell them at a much cheaper price than you could get at a retail store. He had a full time job, so he needed someone to help him out by stripping the paint off the mowers and painting them so they would look like new. This is where my younger brother and I came in. My uncle hired the two of us to strip and paint each mower. For each mower that we would finish, he would pay us $25, regardless of the time it required. I was pretty young at the time, so I was pretty excited about the opportunity to make some money. Recognizing that we could make more money if we worked faster, my brother and I developed a pretty nice little system to strip and paint these mowers. We were motivated by the possibility of making some money, so we worked hard because of that motivation. In a similar way, God makes a promise to the Israelite people at the beginning of Haggai chapter 2, only His promise is much more significant than a financial one. He promises His Spirit to them if they will repent and obey. In fact, we see four very clear and specific steps that occur in the first five verses of chapter 2 that culminate with the promise of God's Spirit.

God begins by helping them to **define the problem**. The problem is ultimately their sin, which is seen in the unfinished temple. In verse 3 He poignantly asks, "Who is left among you who saw this house in its former glory?" In other words, this house has been, and should again be, beautiful. Their disobedience, however, had left it unfinished. This conversation by God is the convicting work of God on display in their lives. He was bringing conviction of sin to them. Conviction always occurs through clarity. Their sin is laid bare for them to clearly see, and they can no longer deny it. The former glory of the temple and the lack of progress with the temple has clearly shown their failure to honor God with their actions. They were in sin.

He continues, however, by **calling them to hope**. "Even so, be strong, Zerubbabel!" This encouragement from God is a renewal of hope in their midst. It is a clarion call of potential in the midst of a growing awareness of sin. The reminder of sin is necessary to compel them to confession and repentance, but the reminder of grace is necessary to bring them hope. This statement is a reminder that God had not forgotten or given up on them. Yes, you have sinned, but there is hope yet—this is essentially the message of God at this point. God is doing what He has always done and will always do: He is encouraging them that even though they are sinful, His grace is greater than their sin. This is the glorious truth of the gospel, that "God proves His own love for us in that while we were still sinners, Christ died for us!" (Rom 5:8).

He goes on by **calling them to repent by working**. It was important that they understood their sin, and it was vital that they recognized God's grace, but all of that would be wasted potential if they did not respond in obedience, which demonstrated their repentance. Transformed hearts do not occur in isolation. Transformed hearts lead to transformed hands, and transformed hands do God's work. This was the point that God was making through Haggai. "Work! For I am with you" is the declaration of the Lord. In light of your sin and My grace, work!

Finally, God concludes with the point that motivates all of this. If they will understand their sin and if they will respond to His grace by repenting, then they will **experience His presence**. God's presence is directly connected to their ability to work. It is also directly connected to their ability to experience joy and satisfaction. Verse 5 points out that because God's presence is among them, they will not have to be afraid.

They can rest in God's presence. He is a strong tower that brings grace, yes. He brings hope, yes. Finally, though, He brings rest.

All things considered, the promise of God's presence is a powerful motivator. Much like the promise of $25 moved me to refinish lawn mowers, the promise of God's presence moves His people to confession, repentance, and action. As we see throughout the whole of Scripture, there are many reasons why one will be blessed by following God, but none is more significant than the promise of God's presence. "Better a day in Your courts than a thousand anywhere else. I would rather be at the door of the house of my God than to live in the tents of wicked people" (Ps 84:10).

The Lord of Hosts Will Shake Everything to Fill His House with Glory

HAGGAI 2:6-9

God will bring His glory. That purpose cannot be slowed or stopped. If there is one message that is constant throughout Scripture, it is that God's purposes cannot be halted. Verses 6-9 of Haggai chapter 2 are a consistent reminder of that fact. We are told here that God will assert His sovereignty, that He will provide for the completion of His purposes, and that He will ultimately deliver an even greater glory than the glory of the temple they would rebuild.

Verse 6 speaks of God shaking everything that is. This is a reference to the authority of God, **the sovereignty of God**. A. W. Pink, in his great work *The Sovereignty of God*, defined God's sovereignty this way: "What do we mean by this expression? We mean the supremacy of God, the kingship of God, the god-hood of God. To say that God is Sovereign is to declare that God is God" (*The Sovereignty of God*, 11). The shaking that is mentioned here is a rather colorful way of describing the fact that God is over every created thing. It was a reminder to the nation of Israel that His word was to be obeyed. It was also a reminder that He would be able to provide the strength necessary to accomplish the task. Finally, it was a reminder that He would provide the necessary resources to rebuild the temple.

In verses 7-8 Haggai continues on the sovereignty theme, specifically declaring God's ability to **provide the financial resources necessary** to accomplish the task. This is an important and needed lesson to an Israelite people who were surely frustrated over the lack of provision that they had experienced, which God previously told them was due to their disobedience. We see this promised provision fulfilled by King Darius, the ruler of the Persians, in Ezra 6:8:

> *I hereby issue a decree concerning what you must do, so that the elders of the Jews can rebuild the house of God: The cost is to be paid in full to these men out of the royal revenues from the taxes of the region west of the Euphrates River, so that the work will not stop.*

Not only would God provide the necessary resources, but He would do it without costing the Israelites anything at all. They were simply called to be obedient, and God would provide the means. This is an important lesson for us today, as we often struggle and resist God's call to obedience due to our lack of faith in His provision. God is always enough.

Finally, we see the capstone of these few verses, and ultimately the capstone of the entire book. Not only would God provide and would the Israelites rebuild the temple, but **God would eventually accomplish a greater work** by providing a greater temple. God promises that the "final glory" would be "greater than the first." He also goes on to promise that He will provide peace through the final temple. So what is this statement referring to? It is a Messianic promise. It is a promise of Jesus to come. In fact, in the gospel of Matthew Jesus Himself would declare that He was greater than the temple: "But I tell you that something greater than the temple is here!" (Matt 12:6). Jesus would also refer to Himself as a type of a temple in John's gospel: "Jesus answered, 'Destroy this sanctuary, and I will raise it up in three days'" (John 2:19). Jesus is the greater temple, and God was using the rebuilding of this temple, and the hope contained within it, to point to Jesus and the peace He would bring. In fact, He specifically describes this as *shalom* in the text, which means "peace." His promised presence would bring them peace, although only temporarily. No, it is not final, but there is One coming who can provide lasting and complete peace. This verse declares that Jesus is coming.

Reflect and Discuss

1. What motivates you most often? Is the thought or the truth of God's promised presence a comfort and motivator to you?
2. God promises hope, even when we know we are in sin. What sins do you have that you secretly fear God is unwilling to forgive?
3. How astonishing is God's promise of grace to you?

4. Are you aware that repentance is a heart issue? Do you understand that genuine repentance requires a heart change and that behavior will always follow the heart?
5. Have you spent time in the presence of God today? We can know God through His Word and prayer. Have you pursued Him through those avenues today?
6. How does the truth of God's sovereignty comfort and encourage you?
7. Are there times when you have struggled to obey God because you feared that you would not have the necessary resources?
8. How encouraging is it to know that there is a greater temple, Jesus, who is promised and is our hope?
9. Have you experienced the peace that comes from trust in Jesus, the greater temple?

Israel Would Flourish When They Obeyed

HAGGAI 2:10-23

Main Idea: God's people begin to flourish again as they obey His word.

I. The Sin of the People Had Turned Them Away from God and His Blessing (2:10-14).
II. The People Were to Consider Where They Had Come From and Be Encouraged by What God Had Called Them To (2:15-19).
III. God Will Shower His People with Blessing as His Chosen Ones (2:20-23).

The Sin of the People Had Turned Them Away from God and His Blessing

HAGGAI 2:10-14

Using the technique of conversation, God speaks through the prophet Haggai to the priests to define the extent of the nation's sin. He helps them to understand that holiness does not transfer, but unholiness does. Speaking to the priests about the law, God asks them about consecrated meat. He knows the answer to the question, but He asks it so that the impact would be felt by the religious leaders. Moving beyond the consecrated meat, God then compares their activity to a corpse. He wants them to feel the weight of their sin. As He uses the illustration of the corpse, the priests affirm that anyone who has touched a corpse is defiled and anything they touch is defiled. So the question must be asked: What does this have to do with the nation of Israel?

God is leading them down this path to help them understand the depth of their sin. This comparison to a corpse illustrates two central truths. First, their sin has caused them to become spiritually dead and defiled. Second, because they are dead and defiled, no amount of activity on their part would profit them until they had repented of their sin.

First, God illustrates for them a central truth that is found throughout Scripture: **our sin has separated us from God and has caused us to be spiritually dead**. In the book of Revelation we see another example of a church that thought of itself as alive but was dead. God once again uses the illustration of defilement to describe their condition:

> *Write to the angel of the church in Sardis:*
>
> *The One who has the seven spirits of God and the seven stars says: I know your works; you have a reputation for being alive, but you are dead. Be alert and strengthen what remains, which is about to die, for I have not found your works complete before My God. Remember, therefore, what you have received and heard; keep it, and repent. But if you are not alert, I will come like a thief, and you have no idea at what hour I will come against you. But you have a few people in Sardis who have not defiled their clothes, and they will walk with Me in white, because they are worthy. In the same way, the victor will be dressed in white clothes, and I will never erase his name from the book of life but will acknowledge his name before My Father and before His angels.*
>
> *Anyone who has an ear should listen to what the Spirit says to the churches.* (Rev 3:1-6)

This church at Sardis was also defiled. They were defiled and they were dead. As a result, their good works had earned them nothing and they were hopeless unless they repented. Because of the depth of their sin, they were in danger of experiencing God's wrath at any moment, and they were oblivious to the danger because of their belief in their own vitality. There are great similarities between the Israelites in the book of Haggai, the church at Sardis, and many churches today.

Being dead was not their only problem. Also, **no amount of effort on their part would improve their condition apart from repentance**. Verse 14 reminds us that not only were they defiled, but "every work of their hands" was also defiled. This would have been a crushing blow because of their confidence in themselves as children of God. Paul in his letter to Timothy describes a similar situation in the New Testament:

> *But know this: Difficult times will come in the last days. For people will be lovers of self, lovers of money, boastful, proud, blasphemers, disobedient to parents, ungrateful, unholy, unloving, irreconcilable, slanderers, without self-control, brutal, without love for what is good, traitors, reckless, conceited, lovers of pleasure rather than lovers of God, holding to the form of godliness but denying its power. Avoid these people!* (2 Tim 3:1-5)

Notice the description. It sounds like a group of depraved individuals. However, look again. At the end of the passage, it would appear that Paul was talking about people who claimed faith. The people guilty of all these disgusting sins were also guilty of "holding to the form of godliness but denying its power." In other words, these were people within the church—people who would have thought themselves to also be a part of God's family. They were claiming faith, but were in fact full of sin. In Jesus' strong condemnation of the Pharisees He offers a similar rebuke:

> *Woe to you, scribes and Pharisees, hypocrites! You are like whitewashed tombs, which appear beautiful on the outside, but inside are full of dead men's bones and every impurity.* (Matt 23:27)

All of their good works, as well as the appearance of godliness, would be for naught if it was not accompanied by repentance.

The People Were to Consider Where They Had Come From and Be Encouraged by What God Had Called Them To

HAGGAI 2:15-19

In order to walk in God's path, it is necessary to remember where we come from. Those who are deeply aware of their sin will also be deeply affected by grace. This was Jesus' message when the sinful woman anointed Him with oil in front of His disciples. In response to their objections, Jesus pointed out, "Therefore I tell you, her many sins have been forgiven; that's why she loved much. But the one who is forgiven little, loves little" (Luke 7:36). Verses 15-19 of Haggai 2 are God's means of calling the nation of Israel to repentance. It is a call to remember where they had come from so that they could celebrate what God, in His grace, would do.

Yes, they had been greatly disobedient; yes, they had long run from God, but that has now changed. They had confessed. They were repentant. They were ready to honor God with their actions, but most of all with their hearts. They had hope that God would bless them with His presence, and that ultimately He would build a greater temple—a temple that we would come to know as Jesus. In light of all of this, they were promised that God would bless them. He would restore to them the things they had lost, and then some. Because they had chosen to repent and obey, they would receive God's *berakah,* His blessing. Once again, as has been mentioned throughout the book, this is evidence of God's grace.

God Will Shower His People with Blessing as His Chosen Ones

HAGGAI 2:20-23

Finally, Haggai offers one last message to Israel, and particularly to Zerubbabel, Israel's king. They had sinned and they had repented, and in response, God promises three things: power will be restored to them, peace will reign, and they will have His presence.

First, He once again reminds them of His authority to do whatever He is about to promise. He uses the illustration that we saw in 2:6-9. He will exert His sovereignty through this process of shaking. This authoritative promise, then, is initiated with a promise to **restore them to political power**. This was important to the king because the kingdom had limited resources, political capital, and military strength. They were weak and vulnerable. Instead, God would overturn the kings and kingdoms of their enemies. He would transfer that power to the Israelites. Instead of a weak, resource-challenged kingdom, Zerubbabel would preside over a strong, resource-rich, and influential kingdom.

Second, God, through Haggai, promises **the return of peace**. Notice the language of the destruction of the weapons of warfare that were wielded against them. Verse 22 specifically points out that He will cause the chariots, the horses, and their riders to fall. This depiction of falling illustrates the death of the warriors and the machines of war that would come against the Israelite people. This is not a reference to their newfound political power, however. The warriors are not defeated by the Israelites, they are defeated by one another ("each by his brother's sword"). This is a reminder of the peace that God will provide to them, and it also points forward to the ultimate peace that God promises to provide in the Messiah. In John's gospel Jesus declared the peace that He brings: "Peace I leave with you. My peace I give to you. I do not give to you as the world gives. Your heart must not be troubled or fearful" (John 14:27).

Finally, God concludes the book with a powerful—and redemptive—promise that stands in stark contrast to the depravity that dominates the beginning of the book. He declares that He will take Zerubbabel (and by extension, all of Israel) and **make him His "chosen" one**. Even more descriptive, though, He promises to make them His "signet ring." This is a powerful reminder that God deeply loved Zerubbabel and Israel, and that God was also entrusting him with His authority, which is symbolized by the ring. This offer of authority is a step beyond forgiveness; it is a declaration of the restoration of the close relationship between God and His chosen people. God not only forgives, He not only redeems, He not only blesses, but He also restores.

What was initially a kingdom in shambles, slowly dying in its own disobedience, is now a robust and blessed kingdom, led well by a repentant and God-focused leader. The miserable has been made majestic, which is the power of God's redemptive activity.

Reflect and Discuss

1. Is there unconfessed, unrepentant sin in your life? What is keeping you from repenting of that right now?
2. How dead is the one who is enslaved to sin? Is it possible to be only partly dead?
3. Have you been guilty of deceiving yourself to believe you are fine, when in truth you are living in unrepentant sin?
4. Have you reflected on your sin? Do you find God's grace to be clearer as you meditate on where you have come from?
5. What examples of God's blessing have you seen on display in your own life after repentance?
6. How have you experienced God's promise of peace?
7. How encouraging is it to know that those who have repented and trusted in Christ are God's "chosen ones"? How can you reflect often today on God's compassionate love for you?

Zechariah

Go Home!

ZECHARIAH 1:1-6

Main Idea: God calls His people to return when we wander far from Him.

I. **God's Righteous Wrath Calls Us to Return to Him (1:1-3).**
II. **God's Repeated Warnings Call Us to Return to Him (1:4-6a).**
III. **God's Reassuring Words Call Us to Return to Him (1:6b).**

My sweet family likes to say that I am directionally challenged. Under my leadership, I have gotten us lost in some of the finest cities in the United States. By myself, I have been hopelessly lost over and over again in all kinds of places throughout the years. I have even been in communities within five miles of where I live without a clue how I got where I was or where I needed to turn next. That is why I was so happy several years ago to get a car with a satellite navigation system. For a directionally impaired person like me, that system, with its gentle but authoritative computerized voice instructing me where and when to turn next, has been a gift from heaven. I rarely get mixed up with my directions anymore. And even if I do, my navigation system has a fail-safe: the "Go Home" button. As long as I have that button, no matter where I am, I know I am never lost. I can push "Go Home," and instantly a voice begins to direct me back to my home address.

Until we come to know God, follow Him, and walk with Him, our hearts will not be at home. In his *Confessions* Augustine famously prayed, "You have made us for Yourself, and our hearts are restless until they rest in You" (*Confessions*, 45). There is a deep reality of lostness that we experience before we come to Jesus as Savior. Only hearing the gospel and placing saving faith in Christ can cure that restlessness of heart. Even as saved people, it is possible to wander from close fellowship with the Lord because of persistent sin without repentance. I have heard some older believers graphically describe this as "walking at a guilty distance." Pastor and author A. W. Tozer acknowledged, "One serious and often distressing problem for many Christians is their feeling that God is far from them, or that they are far from God, which is the same thing" (*Born*, 119).

The hope of the gospel is that lost people can be found and that distant and wandering believers can come back to the Lord. God has put something that says "Go Home!" inside every human heart. Jesus calls us to return when we wander far from Him. The need to return to the Lord is great. So many people who call themselves followers of Jesus simply are not following Jesus. In nearly every moral category professing Christians have become just like the lost world. Consider these measurements:

- Divorce rates among Christians are about the same as those for non-Christians.
- Christian men regularly view pornography as often as non-Christian men.
- Christians are more than twice as likely to have racist attitudes as non-Christians.
- One in four people living together outside marriage call themselves evangelical.
- Only about 6 percent of evangelicals regularly tithe.
- Domestic violence, drug and alcohol abuse, and most other problems are as prevalent among Christians as among non-Christians. (Putnam and Harrington, *DiscipleShift*, 20)

In so many regards there is no distinguishable difference between those who claim to be saved and those who do not know Christ at all. We have gotten far from the Lord, and we need to return.

God's call for His people to return to Him is the first prophetic message in the book of Zechariah. Before we delve into that message, however, let's set the table for our study by examining some important information. Notice the three names at the end of verse 1: "Zechariah son of Berechiah, son of Iddo." Here we have the name of the prophet, his father, and his grandfather. Each man's name has a significant meaning. Zechariah's name means "the LORD remembers." Each mention of his name reminded the prophet and others that God never forgets His people. As a side note, any time in the Old Testament a name ends with "-iah," that's the name of the Lord ("Yah," short for "Yahweh") at the end of that person's name, whether it's Isaiah, Jeremiah, Hezekiah, or Zechariah. So, Zechariah's name means "the Lord, Yahweh, remembers." The name of his father, *Berechiah*—again, you see the "-iah"—means "the LORD blesses." His grandfather's name, *Iddo,* means "in time."

Put those names together, and they provide us a clue as to the theme of this entire book: The Lord remembers and blesses at His set time.

At the beginning of the verse you will notice the time during which this book was written: "In the eighth month, in the second year of Darius." The eighth month, according to the Hebrew calendar, would have corresponded with our month of October or November. Additionally, God's message came to the prophet "in the second year of Darius." Darius was a Gentile king, a pagan ruler, governing the land of Persia. Based on what history tells us about the years of Darius's rule, Zechariah's prophecy would have been given to God's people about 520 years before the coming of Jesus Christ.

Zechariah was living in the land of Judah, in the vicinity of Jerusalem. He was there with many Jewish people who had returned from years of exile to the land of Judah. God's people had turned away from Him so greatly that He finally had given them over to their sin and sent in an invading army from Babylon. The Babylonian King Nebuchadnezzar had taken into captivity all the Jewish people from Jerusalem and throughout the region of Judah. They were separated from their homeland. Then God began to work to return His people back to the promised land.

By the time of Zechariah, God's people had been back in Jerusalem for nearly two decades. Sixteen years before, the people of Judah had begun rebuilding the temple in Jerusalem. They had laid the foundations with great fanfare and celebration, but they encountered opposition. They faced people living in the land who hated them. These people were constantly fighting against them and trying to get them to stop, criticizing them and doing everything they could to oppose them. So God's people got discouraged and stopped building. For 16 years they had taken no action. Now, God was speaking. He had spoken through His prophet Haggai, and now a word came through Zechariah, calling the people to continue the work that God had given them to do to return to Him.

In Zechariah 1:1-6 God sent a message to the Jews who had come back to Jerusalem. Now back in their homeland, they had grown cold in their spiritual lives. The initial enthusiasm they had for rebuilding the new temple had turned into complacency and discouragement. Their work had stopped, their faithfulness had wilted, and the Lord was not pleased. Haggai's primary purpose was to get the people to restart the work of building the Lord's house. Zechariah's purpose went even deeper. He called the people to a renewed closeness to the Lord. Our text shows how God works when we have strayed, calling us back to Himself. With compelling yet compassionate language, this text reveals three motivations for returning to the Lord.

God's Righteous Wrath Calls Us to Return to Him

ZECHARIAH 1:1-3

In the opening message of his prophecy, Zechariah reminded the Jewish people, "The LORD was extremely angry with your ancestors." The language of the Scripture conveys intense indignation on God's part.

The text literally says that the Lord was "angry with anger." In English we consider it redundant to use the same word twice. In Hebrew, however, repeating the same word amplifies the force of the expression. For God to say that He was "angry with anger" means that His displeasure with His people was severe and penetrating.

God further emphasized the seriousness of His anger by referring to Himself with the name *the* LORD or *Yahweh.* Using this personal, covenantal name was a reminder that God's anger came not from a distant, dispassionate Creator, but from *Yahweh,* who had lovingly pursued a relationship with the very people who had rejected Him.

Notice also that Zechariah was pointing back to Israel's history as he spoke of God's anger. The Lord's extreme displeasure had been directed toward the "ancestors" or the forefathers of the generation of Jews Zechariah was now addressing. Psalm 78 summarizes the rebellion and wickedness of pre-exilic Israel this way:

> *They did not keep God's covenant and refused to live by His law. They forgot what He had done, the wonderful works He had shown them.* (vv. 10-11)

The Lord—who had redeemed Israel out of Egyptian slavery, who had given them His law and made a lasting covenant with them, who had brought them into the promised land and established them there, who had shown them faithfulness and mercy even when they were rebellious and idolatrous, and who had sent numerous prophets to warn them—had now become intensely angry at the people of Israel and Judah because of their refusal to return to Him.

God instructed Zechariah to plead with the Jews who had come back to Jerusalem after the exile. Zechariah's words of warning were hedged on every side by reminders of God's sovereignty. Three times in verse 3 God instructs His prophet to invoke His authority: "This is what the LORD of Hosts says," "this is the declaration of the LORD of Hosts," and "says the LORD of Hosts."

The phrase LORD *of Hosts* describes *Yahweh* as King over His people and commander of the angelic armies of heaven. It is as though God were telling Zechariah, "Make sure everybody understands this is not just a man speaking; this is Almighty God speaking in power." In light of His righteous wrath with past generations, God called to His people, "Return to Me."

Recently, while I was driving down Interstate 4 in Florida, I saw a large billboard with these words: "God is *not* angry." There was no message on the sign. No phone number. No name of an organization that had sponsored the advertisement. Just the words: "God is *not* angry." Someone had invested a good deal of money to have the sign put up. The message must have been very important to that person. He or she wanted to assure the world—or at least everyone traveling on that highway—there is no need to fear the Lord's anger. In truth, to many people, God's anger seems incompatible with His overall character.

The problem is that when we hear "The LORD was extremely angry," our immediate assumption is to think that God's anger must somehow be like our anger. We cannot accept that God might be angry the way we become angry. Our anger causes us to lash out with words we later regret. Our anger causes us to hold on to grudges that eventually destroy relationships. Our anger can harden into long-term bitterness and an unforgiving spirit that destroys us. So when we read in God's Word that God is love, God is merciful, God is gracious, God is forgiving, and God is kind, it seems logical for us to say that this same God could not also be angry.

But God's anger is not like our anger. He does not pitch temper tantrums, nor is He an ogre in heaven, eagerly waiting to lash out at people.

God is slow to anger (Nah 1:3). Yet, the Bible is clear in our text that sin and rebellion make the Lord "extremely angry." Both the Old and New Testaments speak of God's wrath along with His love (Exod 34:6-7; John 3:16,36). There are circumstances where God does express His anger. Our attitudes and actions can evoke His anger. People can become the objects of His anger. When people deliberately take the path of sin and rebellion, when we determine to distance ourselves from Him, we experience God's anger, His righteous wrath, just as the Jewish people did in their history. God is angry at sin in my life and in your life. And when we rebel against Him, we place ourselves into His anger zone.

Several years ago our family spent a day at SeaWorld in Orlando and visited Shamu Stadium. As we came into the arena, we noticed that close to the tank where the huge black and white killer whales perform, the seats and concrete risers around them were all painted blue. These rows are known as the "Soak Zone." Before the show began, an announcement came over the PA system warning that everyone in the soak zone would definitely get wet, even drenched. Sure enough, when Shamu and the other killer whales circled into the tank and started jumping and splashing around, the soak zone lived up to its name. Most of the people in those seats took an impromptu bath. Now, Shamu did not soak those people because he picked them arbitrarily for splashing. They got drenched only because of where they were sitting, a place that had been duly marked and about which they had been warned.

God also has an anger zone. Just as the people sitting in the soak zone got soaked, those who place themselves in a posture of rebellion and sin against God will experience His righteous wrath. When we live a rebellious life, continue in sin, or refuse to trust and follow the Lord, we place ourselves in His anger zone, all because of where we have chosen to place ourselves spiritually.

The only way out of God's anger zone is to repent and return to Him. When we His people return to Him, He has promised He will return to us: "Return to Me . . . and I will return to you." God's promise to return to us if we return to Him is another way that His anger differs from human anger. Sadly, when we get angry with someone and they try to make amends, we often say, "I don't care what you do. I'm going to stay angry." That's not how God works. Even in His anger He is ready to forgive when we return. His anger is not temperamental or unpredictable, but righteous and just. Sinful choices on our part put us in God's anger zone, but returning to Him restores us.

God's Repeated Warnings Call Us to Return to Him

ZECHARIAH 1:4-6A

We should return to God because of His righteous wrath. But the text goes on to show that we should return because of God's repeated warnings. Again, the Lord points to the negative example of Israel's past in order to call His people to turn back to Him (v. 4). This marks the second of four times in this passage that God points to the "ancestors" of the present generation (see also vv. 2, 5, and 6). Here God reminds the Jews of the warnings the "earlier prophets" had proclaimed before the Babylonian captivity. In all likelihood these prophets were men like Isaiah, Habakkuk, and Jeremiah who warned God's people of the approaching exile that resulted from their sin.

Zechariah summarizes the proclamation of the earlier prophets with the command "Turn from your evil ways and your evil deeds." The major subject of these pre-exilic preachers had been repentance. The word translated "turn" in verse 4 is the same Hebrew word translated "return" twice in verse 3. Walter Kaiser draws a distinction between "evil ways" and "evil deeds." "Evil ways" refers to a mindset or an attitude that leans toward wicked choices. "Evil deeds" indicates going a step further, to the actual activity of evil and sin. While some people only lean toward evil and others actually commit evil acts, God condemned evil in all its forms, and called His people to turn away from it (Kaiser and Ogilvie, *Micah*, 305).

The theme of repentance had been especially prominent in Jeremiah's preaching. In Jeremiah 3 the prophet had declared to Judah that even the northern kingdom of Israel, with all of its idolatry and wickedness, could find hope by returning to the Lord:

> *Go, proclaim these words to the north, and say: Return, unfaithful Israel. This is the* Lord*'s declaration. I will not look on you with anger, for I am unfailing in My love. This is the* Lord*'s declaration. I will not be angry forever. Only acknowledge your guilt—you have rebelled against the* Lord *your God. You have scattered your favors to strangers under every green tree and have not obeyed My voice. This is the* Lord*'s declaration. "Return, you faithless children"—this is the* Lord*'s declaration—"for I am your master, and I will take you, one from a city and two from a family, and I will bring you to Zion."* (Jer 3:12-14)

In the final days of Judah, just before the people were taken into exile, Jeremiah had warned the people repeatedly, "Turn back to God. Return to God." But they would not listen. They refused to pay attention. Instead of repenting, they mocked Jeremiah. They tormented and tortured the prophet. Jeremiah had watched with tears in his eyes as his beloved city Jerusalem was destroyed and God's people were taken away. They did not heed. They did not pay attention. They continued in their rebellion against God.

Decades later, God asked these questions through Zechariah: "Where are your ancestors now? And do the prophets live forever?" Imagine the response of the Jewish people to those two questions the Lord asked. "Where are your ancestors now?" *Well, Lord, You know where they are. You took them from this land to a place far away, and they went there and died because they would not listen.* "And do the prophets live forever?" *No, Lord, they eventually stopped prophesying and our ancestors never paid attention.* We should return to the Lord because His warnings, though graciously repeated, do not last forever. Our time to respond to Him is limited.

The word *overtake* in verse 6 means "to catch up." The same word is used in Deuteronomy, when Moses promised the children of Israel that His blessings would overtake them if they obeyed God, but also warned that curses would overtake them if they disobeyed:

> *All these blessings will come and overtake you, because you obey the LORD your God.* (Deut 28:2)
>
> *But if you do not obey the LORD your God by carefully following all His commands and statutes I am giving you today, all these curses will come and overtake you.* (Deut 28:15)

Eventually, the word the Lord sent to Israel and Judah through the prophets caught up with them because they ignored His repeated warnings. It is a dangerous thing to decide to ignore the warnings that God gives us—warnings from His Word, warnings He gives through pastors and preachers, or warnings He brings through the godly people in our lives.

Pastor Bobby Welch tells a story, and for the setting he uses the longest bridge in the world over water, the 24-mile Lake Pontchartrain Causeway, which stretches from the north shore of New Orleans into the city. At times fog will roll in over the lake and you can barely see in front of you on that bridge. It was one of those foggy days, and a man was creeping along as bank after bank of fog came in. Suddenly, right in front of him, the man saw someone running straight toward his car, waving his arms and screaming. The driver changed lanes and kept creeping forward. The man running toward him got into the other lane and continued running toward him, still waving his arms and screaming. As the running man got closer, the driver began to make out the words he was screaming: "Stop! Stop! In the name of God, stop! The bridge is out! The bridge is out!"

Finally the man driving got the message and stopped. He got out of his car, and together, he and the other man crawled through the fog until they came to a place where a barge going across Lake Pontchartrain had hit the bridge and taken a whole section out. Half a dozen people had driven off into the water and had died instantly. The two men looked at the horrific scene of people who had plummeted into the lake, struggling for their lives. The man who had been driving that car was so thankful that someone had cared enough to warn him.

When a pastor preaches a message of judgment or a message that talks about God's anger, it is not usually popular. But it is an urgent message. And ultimately, it is a loving message motivated by concern for the souls of men and women. That's why we must share the message of repentance with others and heed it ourselves. Make no mistake: a time is coming when God's repeated warnings will stop. "Where are your ancestors now? And do the prophets live forever?" A time will come when our lives will be over. Or a time may come when the person who has warned us and called us to turn back to Jesus Christ will no longer be in our lives. People who sound the warnings in our lives may seem to be a thorn in our side and their message may seem negative or tiresome as they keep telling lost people to turn to Christ for salvation or urging wayward believers to return to the Lord. But the time will come when God's judgment will overtake those who reject God's warnings.

God's Reassuring Words Call Us to Return to Him

ZECHARIAH 1:6B

At the end of our text, the Lord provides a third motivation to His people to return to Him: reassurance of His kind and merciful intentions toward them. In all likelihood "they repented" refers to what the preexilic Israelites had done during and immediately after their captivity. They came to understand they had been taken away from their homeland because of their refusal to obey the warnings of God's prophets.

After they had been taken away into exile, the Jews realized how far they were from the Lord. Even in exile, some of God's people repented and turned back to the Lord. The word *repent* carries the idea of a radical change. Repentance is a change of understanding, creating a change of mind, leading to a change of heart, and culminating in a change of direction. The exiles came to the place where they understood what they were receiving from God was what God had promised. They said to themselves, "As the LORD of Hosts purposed to deal with us for our ways and deeds, so He has dealt with us." Then they trusted in the character of God enough to understand that, even after they were far from Him and though they had been carried away into captivity, He would return to them if they would repent and turn to Him. They recognized that the Lord had done with them exactly what He had planned and promised to do, and they could not question His purposes.

The Babylonian captives, who had experienced God's anger and who had, up to this point, rejected God's warnings, came to understand the truth of verse 3: "Return to Me . . . and I will return to you." Now, through Zechariah, God was reassuring those who had returned to Jerusalem, "I won't forget you. I won't reject you. I won't push you away. Return to Me." He tells us the same thing today. Our Lord has already given us the assurance that He will return to us when we turn to Him. Through the cross of Jesus Christ, God brings us to Himself and brings Himself to us.

When I'm driving and I'm depending on my GPS system, I've learned never to ignore one message it gives me: "Make a U-turn if possible." Has your GPS ever told you to do that? I like the fact that the voice always gives the caveat, "if possible." The GPS doesn't want me turning around in the middle of an interstate highway! But if I'm in a place where I can turn, the system warns me that I should turn.

When God tells His people, "Return to Me," He's not only saying that a U-turn is necessary in our lives, He's also saying the U-turn is possible. Through His grace and the power of Jesus Christ, we can repent and change direction. When our lives are directionally challenged, God commands us to return to Him. And He promises, when we return to Him, we will find that He is already turned toward us.

Reflect and Discuss

1. What are some of the factors or circumstances that can make believers feel far from God?
2. When we experience a sense that God is distant, what are some of the repercussions in our lives?
3. The people of Judah had stopped rebuilding the temple because of the opposition of the enemies. When you encounter spiritual opposition, how can you keep from quitting the work the Lord has called you to do?
4. Does God's righteous anger at our sin and rebellion draw His people back to Himself or repel us from Him? Why?
5. How is God's wrath against sin in your life compatible with His unfaltering love for you?
6. When you find yourself in God's "anger zone," what kinds of consequences do you experience? What can you do to get out of God's "anger zone"?
7. Explain how God's grace results in His strong warnings about judgment for sin.
8. How has God worked in your life to warn you when you were headed in the wrong direction?
9. What aspects of God's nature make repentance possible?
10. How does the gospel message speak to those who need to return to the Lord?

Extreme Jealousy

ZECHARIAH 1:7–2:13

Main Idea: The Lord is jealously committed to His people.

I. **We Can Depend on the Lord's Overcoming Comfort (1:7-13).**
II. **We Can Depend on the Lord's Overflowing Mercy (1:14-17).**
III. **We Can Depend on the Lord's Overriding Justice (1:18-21).**
IV. **We Can Depend on the Lord's Overwhelming Love (2:1-13).**

On a recent trip, my wife and I boarded a small helicopter in Juneau, Alaska, and landed on the surface of Mendenhall Glacier to visit a sled dog camp. As we landed on that snow-covered slab of ice, we saw dozens and dozens of white doghouses, each with a sled dog lying down in front, beside, or even on top of it. We got out of the helicopter to meet our musher, a young woman who would take us on our first ever dogsled ride.

"Welcome!" she said, "We're going to go out to the dogs that I'm training. We'll hook them up to the sled, and then we'll get going."

When we went out to where all the dogs were, nearly every dog seemed asleep. They looked lazy, lying down on the snow, with just a few dogs barely holding their heads up—until they saw their musher getting ready to hook them up to the harness. Then, the dogs went nuts. They were jumping all over on top of one another, trying to get to their spot in front of the sled.

Michele and I were tempted to reach out and touch one of those beautiful animals, but before we could, the musher stopped us, warning, "Don't pet one of them. If you do, you'll have to pet all of them."

Then she told us, "They are just incredibly jealous of each other. If one gets food, all the others want food. If one gets attention, the others want it, too. They are jealous over everything. And, especially when it's time to pull the sled, all of them just turn into green-eyed monsters."

People often talk about jealousy the way that musher did, as a "green-eyed monster," a phrase coined by William Shakespeare in *Othello*. Mark Twain, in an essay disparaging God, called jealousy "the trademark of small minds" (*Letters from the Earth*) Science fiction writer

Robert Heinlein, who also was no respecter of God, identified jealousy as "a symptom of neurotic insecurity" (*Time Enough for Love*, 250). In its human expressions, jealousy can truly be spiteful and destructive. Our jealousy is rooted in insecurity, fear, and anxiety that come when we anticipate losing something, such as a relationship, status, or possession. Jealousy creates friction and problems for us in our interactions with others.

As a result, we rarely consider it a virtue to be jealous. Instead, jealousy is ugly, petty, and hurtful. We think of jealousy as a negative emotion that leads to negative actions. Moreover, Scripture cautions us strongly against human jealousy as a work of the flesh (Gal 5:20), calling it inconsistent with love (1 Cor 13:4), and demonic in its source (Jas 3:14-15).

That's why, for many people, it is surprising—and even offensive—to hear that God is jealous. We tend to think, "Surely God, in His perfection and goodness, could never display anything as base and ugly as jealousy." Yet, the Old and New Testaments bear witness that jealousy is an essential part of God's character. Consider just a few portions of Scripture (all emphases mine):

> *Do not make an idol for yourself, whether in the shape of anything in the heavens above or on the earth below or in the waters under the earth. You must not bow down to them or worship them;* ***for I, the Lord your God, am a jealous God,*** *punishing the children for the fathers' sin, to the third and fourth generations of those who hate Me.* (Exod 20:4-5)

> *You are never to bow down to another god because* ***Yahweh, being jealous by nature, is a jealous God.*** (Exod 34:14)

> *But Joshua told the people, "You will not be able to worship Yahweh, because He is a holy God.* ***He is a jealous God;*** *He will not remove your transgressions and sins."* (Josh 24:19)

> *Judah did what was evil in the Lord's eyes.* ***They provoked Him to jealous anger*** *more than all that their ancestors had done with the sins they committed. They also built for themselves high places, sacred pillars, and Asherah poles on every high hill and under every green tree.* (1 Kgs 14:22-23)

> *They enraged Him with their high places and* ***provoked His jealousy*** *with their carved images.* (Ps 78:58)

> *You cannot drink the cup of the Lord and the cup of demons. You cannot share in the Lord's table and the table of demons. Or* ***are we provoking the Lord to jealousy****? Are we stronger than He?* (1 Cor 10:21-22)

> *Adulteresses! Don't you know that friendship with the world is hostility toward God? So whoever wants to be the world's friend becomes God's enemy. Or do you think it's without reason the Scripture says that* ***the Spirit who lives in us yearns jealously****?* (Jas 4:4-5)

In each of these cases God expresses His jealousy in response to unfaithfulness on the part of His people. He conveyed His jealousy when Israel turned to idols or when the church became like the unregenerate world. As such, God's jealousy flows out of His great love toward His redeemed ones. His jealousy is akin to the type of human jealousy described by poet and essayist Joseph Addison: "Jealousy is that pain which a man feels from the apprehension that he is not equally beloved by the person whom he entirely loves" (*The Spectator, Volume 1*, No. 170; Friday, September 14, 1711). God's jealousy is His passionate commitment to that which rightfully belongs to Him—whether it is His glory that cannot be shared with another, His right to be worshiped as the one true God, or the affections and devotion of His people.

Zechariah 1:7-17 presents the first vision in a series of eight that the prophet experienced approximately three and a half months after his initial prophecy. The remaining visions continue through Zechariah 6:8. These visions were not dreams that came to Zechariah in his sleep, but waking revelations from God. Throughout the visions, Zechariah indicates that his eyes are wide open, using phrases such as "I looked" (1:8), "I looked up and saw" (1:18; 2:1; 5:1,9; 6:1), and "he showed me" (3:1) as he introduces the visions. In each vision an angelic messenger brought a message from the Lord to the prophet. The first three visions are of horsemen (1:7-17), four horns and four craftsmen (1:18-21), and a man with a measuring line (2:1-13).

In some way these first three visions point to the central truth that God is jealously committed to His people. Through His angel, God proclaims His jealousy in Zechariah 1:14: "So the angel who was speaking with me said, 'Proclaim: The LORD of Hosts says: I am extremely jealous for Jerusalem and Zion.'" The language the Bible uses in these verses is absolutely clear and unambiguous. In Hebrew the words translated "extremely jealous" are literally "jealous with a great jealousy." God's holy jealousy springs from His great love and unfaltering desire to have an exclusive relationship with those He has delivered and redeemed as His own. In this passage we see that God's jealousy also moves Him to act against those who would harm or oppress His people. Zechariah's initial visions demonstrate four assurances that God's extreme jealousy brings to His people.

We Can Depend on the Lord's Overcoming Comfort

ZECHARIAH 1:7-13

In his first vision Zechariah saw a man riding a red horse. According to verse 8, this rider was among some myrtle trees in a deep valley. Accompanying the first rider were other horsemen, riding horses of three different colors: red, sorrel (from a Hebrew word only found here in the OT that might mean "brown" or "speckled"), and white. While it may have been that there were only three riders on these horses, the language leaves open the possibility that there were many riders on multiple horses, the horses being of three different colors.

The language here is symbolic. Some biblical symbolism that seems mysterious to modern audiences would have been readily understood by the ancient recipients of Scripture. Certain colors and objects have an implied meaning within a culture. For example, if someone were to tell you about a vision of three eagles flying—one red, one white, and one blue—you would probably assume that the vision pertained in some way to the United States. The image of the eagle and meaning of the colors of the U.S. flag are common and understood. While the significance of every part of Zechariah's vision can appear complicated, much of the symbolic language would have been quite clear to the Jewish people of the day.

Zechariah saw a grove of myrtle trees. The myrtle was a shrub that grew throughout Israel. Consequently, "myrtle" actually became a popular name for Israel. The myrtle tree, then, represents Israel. Zechariah saw a rider in a valley. The valley, being a low place, likely symbolized that Israel was in a time of deep humiliation. The people had been taken into exile. Their temple had been destroyed. They were now coming back to rebuild but faced great opposition. The different colors of the horses Zechariah saw also may have symbolic significance. He saw horses of red, white, and sorrel. Red is a color that often symbolizes war in Scripture. White may have represented peace. While the meaning of the color translated "sorrel" is harder to discern, the mixed color may suggest a time of tension—not all-out war, but not peace, either.

The Bible also identifies the first rider in the valley of myrtle trees as "the Angel of the LORD." When the term *Angel of the* LORD is used in Scripture, this messenger of God is sometimes described as the Lord Himself (Gen 16:10-13; Exod 3:2-6; 23:20; Judg 6:11-18). The Angel of the Lord accomplishes actions closely associated with God, such as revelation, deliverance, and destruction, even though the Angel is also portrayed as distinct from God (2 Sam 24:16; Zech 1:12). The unique relationship this Angel has with God has led many students of the Bible to understand that the Angel of the Lord in the OT is, in fact, the Second Person of the Trinity. Though this book was written more than 500 years before Jesus was born, the Son of God has always existed, from eternity past. Prior to His incarnation, God's Son manifests Himself from time to time in the OT Scriptures, where He is often called "the Angel of the LORD." This appears to be the case in this text. The riders on the other horses can be seen as other angelic messengers sent out at the Lord's command.

With all of these things in mind, the symbolic picture that emerges in Zechariah 1:8-10 is this: Christ is standing in a valley of myrtle trees that represents Israel in her humiliation. He is sending out angelic patrols to discover what is going on in the other nations surrounding them. He is asking for the conditions: Is there war? Is there peace? Is there tension?

The report comes back in Zechariah 1:11. The surrounding nations of the earth are enjoying "calm" and "quiet." The word *quiet* translates the Hebrew word *shaqat*, describing a state of undisturbed tranquility. The term is used elsewhere in the OT to signify the condition during the absence of war (Judg 3:30) or a sense of safety and security (Ezek 38:11). In most contexts "calm" and "quiet" would describe a positive and comforting environment.

However, from the perspective of Zechariah and the people of Judah living in Israel, this is not a good report. Though Israel has been torn to pieces and left wounded and low, other nations—even the ones that have harmed God's people the deepest—are enjoying peace and tranquility.

The report of the horsemen prompted the Angel of the Lord to bring this question to Yahweh at the end of verse 12: "How long, LORD of Hosts, will You withhold mercy from Jerusalem and the cities of Judah that You have been angry with these 70 years?" Usually in the OT the

Angel of the Lord's function is to communicate messages from God to His people. Here, remarkably, the Angel intercedes to God Almighty on behalf of the people, and asks "how long" Yahweh will continue to "withhold mercy." "How long?" is a lament formula often found in Scripture. (See Exod 16:28; Ps 94:3; and Hab 1:2, along with numerous other passages.) It conveys a profound need for the Lord to deliver His people. The primary idea behind the Hebrew word translated "mercy" (*racham*) is "cherishing" or "soothing." The word carries the thought of tender affection and compassion. Even after 70 years of captivity, Jerusalem was still in ruins. In the wake of the defeat and discouragement that God's people were experiencing, the peace and tranquility of the surrounding wicked nations caused even the Angel of the Lord to question whether God would ever stop being angry with Israel.

Yahweh answers: "The Lord replied with kind and comforting words to the angel who was speaking with me." Here the heavenly messenger who receives the message is probably not the Angel of the Lord but another angel who was interpreting the vision for Zechariah. "The Lord," in turn, may refer to "the Lord of Hosts" (v. 12) or to the Angel of the Lord. Regardless of the details of the chain of communication, the nature of the message from heaven is clear. The words from God were "kind" (*tov*, meaning "pleasant" or "agreeable") and "comforting" (*nichum*, from a root word meaning "breathing deeply," reflecting a physical display of compassion and sympathy).

Because God loves His people with a jealous, unfailing love, we can depend on His comfort, even when our enemies appear to be prospering and the consequences for our past failures linger. Through the Angel of the Lord, God extended overcoming comfort to Israel in four significant ways in this part of Zechariah's vision:

(1) He showed concern for their situation. The horsemen, whom the Angel of the Lord sent in every direction to survey the situation of the earth, demonstrate God's care for the state of His people. Then, as now, God is "very compassionate and merciful" (Jas 5:11) toward those who are hurting.

(2) He interceded on their behalf. The Angel of the Lord Himself articulated the heart-cry of Zechariah and all of God's people: "How long?" The Bible promises that Jesus Christ "is at the right hand of God and intercedes for us" (Rom 8:34).

(3) He spoke words of encouragement. The kind and comforting words of the Lord brought encouragement to Zechariah, which he could then share with God's people. All of these expressions of comfort are consistent with God's character as

> *the God of all comfort, who comforts us in all our affliction, so that we may be able to comfort those who are in any kind of affliction, through the comfort we ourselves receive from God.* (2 Cor 1:3-4)

(4) He was intimately present in their lives. Perhaps most powerfully, Zechariah's vision revealed that the Angel of the Lord "stood among the myrtle trees in the valley" (1:8). During Israel's time of physical weakness, emotional anguish, and spiritual discouragement, the Son of God was in the midst of God's people, as He is now: "The LORD is near the brokenhearted; He saves those crushed in spirit" (Ps 34:18).

During a recent conflict in the Middle East, a friend of a missionary couple serving in Israel watched as a shepherd cared for his flock near an area where the fighting was intense. Each time shots fired, the frightened flock would scatter. The shepherd would walk over to each of them, speak words of comfort, and touch each sheep with his staff. When another shot sounded, the shepherd did the same thing again. With each attack of the enemy, the sheep needed the shepherd to reassure them with his presence (Larson, *1001 Illustrations*, 114).

Like those sheep, God's people need to hear the soothing voice and feel the calming touch of our Shepherd. His jealous love for believers moves the Lord to reassure us with His overcoming comfort.

We Can Depend on the Lord's Overflowing Mercy

ZECHARIAH 1:14-17

Beginning in verse 14, the angel sent to interpret Zechariah's vision begins to deliver the message that Yahweh had spoken. In answer to the question "How long?" Yahweh professes His intense jealousy for Jerusalem and Zion. Then, in verse 15, He reveals that, while it may appear the oppressive nations surrounding Israel are enjoying peace and tranquility, the truth is that He is "fiercely angry" with them. In both His descriptions of His jealousy over Jerusalem and Zion and His anger toward the nations, God used double emphases in the Hebrew language, literally declaring that He is "jealous with great jealousy" (v. 14) and "angry with great anger" (v. 15). Indeed, He had only been "a little angry" toward Israel (v. 15), intending for His people to be punished for a season by the surrounding nations but not to be oppressed to the extent and intensity that Israel had been.

Motivated by His jealous love and offended at Israel's mistreatment by the nations that were now at ease, God declared in verse 16, "In mercy, I have returned to Jerusalem." God's tender mercy (*rachamim*) toward His people reached out to them in spite of the judgment they deserved. In Deuteronomy, long before the time of Zechariah, God had prophesied Israel's apostasy and eventual exile but had also promised that Israel's return to the Lord would be met with God's mercy:

> *When all these things happen to you—the blessings and curses I have set before you—and you come to your senses while you are in all the nations where the LORD your God has driven you, and you and your children return to the LORD your God and obey Him with all your heart and all your soul by doing everything I am giving you today, then He will restore your fortunes, have compassion on you, and gather you again from all the peoples where the LORD your God has scattered you.* (Deut 30:1-3)

God's mercy—which had spared Israel from utter destruction even when they had been unrepentant—would now work to restore His repentant people. Because of His mercy, God made four promises to Zechariah and Israel.

(1) He promised His returned presence. "I have returned to Jerusalem; My house will be rebuilt within it." Prior to the exile, Ezekiel had seen a vision of God's glory departing from the temple (Ezek 10:18-19; 11:22-23). Now God declared that He had returned and that His dwelling place, the temple, would be rebuilt in Jerusalem.

(2) He promised restored stability. "A measuring line will be stretched out over Jerusalem." This measuring line, prophesied earlier (Jer 31:38-40), is a symbol of restoration. The holy city, which had been desecrated in the past and which now was fragile and vulnerable to attack, would become established and stable.

(3) He promised rich blessing. "My cities will again overflow with prosperity." Though the towns of Judah were currently impoverished, God foretold a coming day when they would, in the most literal sense of the words, "spread out with prosperity." The language paints a picture of towns that were so blessed with God's abundance that the city walls would not be able to hold all the wealth.

(4) He promised renewed favor. "The LORD will once more comfort Zion and again choose Jerusalem." The Lord promised to make Jerusalem His chosen place. The renewed city would become a model for the world, reflecting God's favor and affection.

From a dispensational eschatological perspective, the ultimate fulfillment of these promises to Israel will only be realized with the second coming, the millennial temple, and the thousand-year reign of Christ on earth (Lindsey, "Zechariah," 1551). Even so, the anticipation of God's fullest expression of His mercy to Jerusalem would have invigorated the people of Israel to continue rebuilding the temple in Zechariah's day. Understanding the hope and encouragement of God's mercy also spurs us on when our situation seems bleak and hopeless.

God shows His people mercy. His words to Jerusalem centuries ago have never changed: "In mercy, I have returned." He loves us so much that He overflows with mercy for us. His mercy moves Him to love us deeply. Because of His mercy, God is compassionate toward us with a kindness that we could never deserve. Whoever you are, wherever you have been, and whatever you have done, God longs to be merciful to you.

Luis Palau tells a beautiful story about a mother who approached the French emperor Napoleon Bonaparte seeking a pardon for her son. The emperor listened to her request, but then he replied that this young soldier had committed a certain offense twice and that justice demanded death.

The mother said, "I'm not asking you for justice; I'm asking you, I'm pleading, for mercy."

Napoleon answered, "Your son does not deserve mercy."

And the mother cried, "Sir, if he deserved it, it wouldn't be mercy, and mercy is all I ask for."

The emperor said, "Well, then, I shall have mercy," and he spared the woman's son (Palau, "Hope for Healing").

Mercy is God withholding from us the judgment we deserve because of our sin. Had Judah been guilty of rebelling and sinning against God? Yes. Had they deserved to be trampled by the nations around them? Yes. But in God's mercy, He promised to restore them and give them prosperity again. Here's why: His love will not let His people go. You can come to the God of the universe, throw yourself at His feet, and He will show you mercy. God extends His mercy to us because of the cross of Jesus Christ. God's people can count on His overflowing mercy.

We Can Depend on the Lord's Overriding Justice

ZECHARIAH 1:18-21

Beginning in verse 18, Zechariah receives a second vision from the Lord, this one consisting of four horns and four craftsmen. Among the Jews, the horns of an animal were a measure of that animal's power. We have the same idea today. The avid hunter goes after the twelve-point buck. The rancher prizes the longhorn bull. Because horns represent strength in the animal world, the horn was also used figuratively in the OT to symbolize political or military strength. For instance, in Micah 4:13 God said, "Rise and thresh, Daughter Zion, for I will make your horns iron and your hooves bronze, so you can crush many peoples." Horns were also used to symbolize kingdoms, as in Daniel 7:24. The four horns that Zechariah saw represented the power of the nations that had scattered Jerusalem, an interpretation made clearer by the words of the angel in verses 19 and 21.

A more difficult interpretive question is the significance of *four* horns. Why that specific number? What nations or kingdoms are being symbolized? Some interpreters have suggested that the four kingdoms are the world empires of Babylonia, Medo-Persia, Greece, and Rome. Some have countered that earlier kingdoms—Assyria, Egypt, Babylonia, and Medo-Persia—are in view (Barker, *Zechariah*, 615). Others have proposed the four horns represent attacks against Israel from all sides: north, south, east, and west (Kaiser and Ogilvie, *Micah*, 318). No matter what the exact significance of the number, the four horns clearly portray total domination of the people of Israel by the powers that attacked and conquered them.

Because of His jealous love, God assured Zechariah that He would act with justice to override the great power of these conquering kingdoms. The four craftsmen in Zechariah 1:20 represent God's instruments to bring justice to the nations that had abused God's people. The image of the craftsmen is somewhat unusual. The Hebrew term *charash* refers to someone who is skilled at working in some type of medium, including metalwork (1 Chr 29:5), woodwork (Isa 40:20), or stonework (Exod 28:11). Zechariah himself does not ask about the identity of the craftsmen, however. Instead, he asks about their function: "What are they coming to do?" (Zech 1:20). The answer, which presumably comes from the angel, is that they have come to "terrify" the four horns that have abused Judah and "to cut off the horns" of these nations, indicating a dismantling of their power.

Perhaps the vision of the four craftsmen is meant to evoke the idea that just as a craftsman does his work slowly, carefully, and skillfully, so God skillfully works His justice in His own time. Also, sometimes we can only understand the work of a craftsman once it is finished. In the same way, God's ultimate justice will only be fully understood when time has drawn to a close and God's purposes are complete.

Ravi Zacharias tells the story of visiting the city of Varanasi in northern India. There he walked into the small side room of a building where a father and son were working together to make a wedding sari, a spectacular traditional garment that every bride in India wants to wear on her wedding day. He writes,

> The father sits on a raised platform with huge spools of brilliantly colored threads within his reach. The son sits on the floor in the lotus position. . . . Before my eyes, though it did not appear so at first, a grand design appears. The father gathers some threads in his hand, then nods, and the son moves the shuttle from one side to the other. A few more threads, another nod, and again the son responds by moving the shuttle. The process seems almost Sisyphus-like in its repetition, the silence broken only occasionally with a comment or by some visitor who interrupts to ask a question about the end design. The father smiles and tries in broken English to explain the picture he has in mind, but compared to the magnificence of the final product, it is a mere lisp. Throughout the process, the son has had a much easier task. Most likely he has often felt bored. Perhaps his back has ached or his legs have gone to sleep. Perhaps he has wished for some other calling in life—something he might find more stimulating or fulfilling. He has but one task, namely to move the shuttle as directed by the father's nod, hoping to learn to think like the father so that he can carry on the business at the appropriate time. Yet, the whole time, the design has remained in the mind of the father as he held the threads. (Zacharias, *Grand Weaver*, 15–16)

In the same way, sometimes we look at our lives and, from our limited earthly human perspective, we cannot see the pattern or the plan. We cannot see God's justice at work, and life looks incredibly messy and unfair. Life is *not* fair, but God is fair, God is just, and God is greater than this life.

We may not experience the fullness of His plan for us in this lifetime. We may find ourselves wondering, Why am I suffering this way? Why am I going through this? But, like a craftsman, God is working everything together (Rom 8:28). As a result, we can say, "God, I know that You are just. I know that You are righteous. And I am counting on Your ultimate justice, that You're going to take care of things, even if I don't quite understand how." God promised overriding justice to His people Judah. He promises that to us, as well.

We Can Depend on the Lord's Overwhelming Love

ZECHARIAH 2:1-13

Zechariah 2 records a single vision that continues the theme of God's jealous commitment to His people. In this vision Zechariah sees a man with a measuring line in his hand. The prophet asks the man where he is going, and the man indicates that he is on his way to take the measurements of Jerusalem (vv. 1-2). Then, as now, surveying property in this way was done in preparation for building. The man in the vision represents God's desire to restore and rebuild the city. In verses 3-4 another angel instructs Zechariah's interpreting angel to tell Zechariah, to whom he refers as "this young man," that Jerusalem would have to expand its walls because so many people and livestock will be in it. This would have been a surprising message. At the time of Nehemiah, the city was in such ruin and so unstable that very few wanted to live in it, preferring the surrounding area in Judah (Neh 11:1-2). Verse 5 shows the reason the city would once again become safe for inhabitants. The Lord Himself would be the city's defense, with His protection circling the city like "a wall of fire" and His glorious presence providing stability within it.

Based on this vision, in verses 6-13 Zechariah proclaims a message to the people of God. The message includes the following elements:

(1) The exiles remaining in Babylon should return to Jerusalem as quickly as possible (vv. 6-7). In verse 6 the "land of the north" is Babylon, identified explicitly in verse 7. The people of Zion, whom God has scattered out "like the four winds of heaven" in every direction, are urged to return immediately to Jerusalem.

(2) The nations that had been harming Israel will be judged (vv. 8-9). God promises to judge Babylon and other nations that have harmed Israel, which is another reason that the people of Judah needed to leave Babylon so quickly. Ironically, those who have plundered God's people will now be plundered by the Lord Himself. The word for "plunder," *shalal*, means to take by force.

(3) God will bless Israel and many nations through Israel (vv. 10-12). The expressions of God's blessing on Israel include the Lord "coming to dwell" among them, other nations that "will join themselves to the LORD on that day and become My people," and the Lord taking possession of Judah "as His portion in the Holy Land."

(4) All people should be silent in the presence of the Lord (v. 13). In light of what God had revealed to His people, the only fitting response was awe-filled and silent submission to the Lord's might.

Verse 8 contains a key phrase that reveals the overwhelming love of God for His people: "Anyone who touches you touches the pupil of His eye." The figure of speech originates in Deuteronomy 32:10, where Moses says that the Lord found Jacob in a desolate wilderness, surrounded him, cared for him, and "protected him as the pupil of His eye." More famously translated "the apple of His eye," the word literally means the gate or opening of the eye, which is the part of the eye most easily injured and most in need of protection. Because of His love for His people, God placed Israel under His own protective and powerful care.

John Hyde, a missionary to India who died in 1912, became known as "Praying Hyde." He told of the greatest lesson God ever taught him about prayer. Hyde was praying for a national pastor in India, a man who was causing problems.

Hyde began his prayer, "O God, Thou knowest this brother, how . . ." He was going to say "cold," when suddenly a voice seemed to tell him, "He that touches him touches the apple of My eye." Horror swept over Hyde. Falling to his knees, Hyde confessed his own sin and then prayed, "Father, show me what things are lovely and of good report in my brother's life."

Hyde instantly remembered the many sacrifices this pastor had made for the Lord, how he had given up all for Christ, how he had suffered deeply for Christ. He thought of the many years of difficult labor this man had invested in the kingdom, and the wisdom with which he had resolved congregational conflict. Hyde remembered the man's devotion to his wife and family, and how he had provided a model to the church of godly husbanding. John Hyde wound up spending his prayer time that day praising the Lord for this brother's faithfulness.

Shortly afterward, Hyde traveled to see this pastor, and he learned that the man had just experienced a personal revival and spiritual renewal (Carre, *Praying Hyde*, 136–37).

God's overwhelming love for us that protects us, draws us back to Himself, and renews us is the ultimate root of God's extreme jealousy for us. He will not let us go, because we are precious to Him!

Reflect and Discuss

1. What gives God the right to be jealous over His people?
2. How is human jealousy like God's jealousy? How is it different? If a friend asserted that jealousy makes God seem petty or insecure, how would you respond?
3. Assuming that the "Angel of the Lord" is a preincarnate appearance of Jesus, in what ways does the Angel reflect the character and activity of Christ?
4. Zechariah's vision revealed that the enemy nations surrounding Judah were enjoying peace while Jerusalem remained in ruins. How do you reconcile the prosperity of wicked people with the suffering of faithful believers?
5. God spared Israel even when the nation was unrepentant. What are ways that God has gone to extravagant measures to extend His mercy for you?
6. What are some of the circumstances both the church at large and individual believers face that can rob us of hope? How can we continue to live for God's glory when our situation seems hopeless?
7. How does God's jealousy for His people result in Him acting with justice on our behalf?
8. When does it become difficult to trust in the Lord's justice?
9. Who are some people in Scripture, history, and your own life who experienced God's goodness after a time of trial and testing? What areas of commonality can you see in their stories?
10. How does knowing that God's people are like "the pupil of His eye" affect our thoughts, emotions, and responses to life's challenges?

Guilt Stripped

ZECHARIAH 3:1-10

Main Idea: Satan deceives regarding our guilt, while God tells the truth.

I. Satan Wants Us to Feel Hopeless When We Are Guilty (3:1).
II. God Wants Us to Feel Sorrowful When We Are Guilty (3:2).
III. Satan Wants Us to Feel Innocent When We Are Guilty (3:3).
IV. God Wants Us to Feel Guilty When We Are Guilty (3:4-5).
V. Satan Wants Us to Feel Guilty When We Are Forgiven (3:6-7).
VI. God Wants Us to Feel Forgiven When We Are Forgiven (3:8-10).

It's a ridiculous story: A man goes into a restaurant and orders a soft drink. As soon as he receives it, he throws it in the waiter's face. The waiter is ready to fight, but the man says, "Oh, I am so sorry. I have a horrible compulsion. I can't help it. Every time someone hands me a drink, I throw it in their face. I feel so guilty. Please forgive me." Then the guy says, "Look, I'm working hard to overcome this compulsion. Would you bring me another soda?"

The waiter says, "You promise not to throw it in my face?"

The man says, "I promise. I'm trying really hard to resist. I'll do better."

The waiter says, "Okay, I'll get you another one." The waiter comes back with another Coke, serves it to the man, who immediately throws it in his face. The waiter's beside himself: "I thought you weren't going to do that!"

The guy is so embarrassed. "I'm sorry. I feel so guilty. I'll get help. I won't come back until I'm cured." Then, he runs out of the restaurant.

Ninety days later, the same guy comes back to the same place. He sits at the same table, where the same waiter comes to wait on him: "May I take your order?"

The man says, "Yes, I'll have a soda, please."

The waiter says, "Hold on. I recognize you. Three months ago you threw two drinks all over me."

The man says, "I know, and I felt so guilty. But I've been in intensive therapy for the last 12 weeks. I'm completely cured."

The waiter hesitates, but says, "Okay, if you're cured, I'll bring you a soda." The waiter brings out the drink, the man takes it—and throws it in the waiter's face. The soaked waiter sputters, "I thought you said you were cured."

The man says, "I *am* cured."

The waiter says, "But you threw the drink right in my face."

The man answers, "Yes, but I don't feel guilty about it anymore!"

That's a silly story, but it illustrates a serious truth: There's a big difference between *being guilty* and *feeling guilty*. Being guilty is objective. It means we are responsible for doing something wrong, harmful, or sinful. Feeling guilty is subjective. It means we feel ashamed or embarrassed for something we've done. Guilt is a squishy thing.

We can feel "not guilty" when we are guilty. It's possible for our consciences to become so calloused that sin and evil in our own lives no longer bother us. We can also feel guilty when we are not guilty. A lot of people spend their lives on guilt trips. They carry misplaced guilt that is not based in reality.

Zechariah 3:1-10 talks about having our guilt *stripped*. By the grace of God, our guilt can be taken from us. Through Jesus Christ, the Lord can deliver us both from *being guilty* and from *feeling guilty*.

Our text records Zechariah's fourth vision in a series of eight visions from the Lord. The people of Judah have come back to Jerusalem after spending years in Babylonia in exile. They have been back in the land of Israel now for about 20 years. God's people have started rebuilding the temple in Jerusalem. But because they faced great opposition from the others who live in the area of Jerusalem, the people have stopped rebuilding the temple. Zechariah, who prophesied 520 years before the time of Christ, has been sent as God's messenger, calling them to return to the Lord. With the guidance of an interpreting angel, God has shown Zechariah eight visions, of which this is the fourth.

In this vision there are three major actors in addition to Zechariah the prophet:

(1) Joshua the high priest. It is important to note that this is not the Joshua who fought the battle of Jericho. That Joshua lived centuries and centuries before this time. Instead, this Joshua, a high priest, is one of the 49,697 exiles who have returned to Jerusalem. As a priest, his job is to represent all of God's people. In this vision Joshua embodies the humanity that God loves and that God has called to serve Him. Joshua is wearing soiled garments (v. 3), representing the guilt of his sin.

(2) The Angel of the Lord. This is not the first time the Angel of the Lord has appeared in Zechariah (see 1:7-17). The Angel of the Lord should be understood to be the second member of the Trinity, the pre-incarnate Christ. A simple way to say it is that the Angel of the Lord in the OT is Jesus before He was born. Because Jesus has always existed, He occasionally shows up in the OT before His birth, appearing as the Angel of the Lord.

(3) Satan, the sworn enemy of God and His people. Satan's work in this vision is to accuse and slander God's people—represented by Joshua—and to deceive them regarding their guilt.

When it comes to your guilt, Satan will always deceive you and God will always tell you the truth. Everyone needs to hear the message of Zechariah 3. Some people feel guilty who do not need to feel guilty. Their guilt has been taken away by Jesus Christ, but Satan has deceived them into self-condemnation and guilt over their past failures and sins. Others, who are indeed guilty, have been deceived by the Devil so that they feel no guilt at all. Satan has blinded their eyes to their own sinfulness in order to keep them from bringing their guilt and sin to Jesus for forgiveness.

Our text presents six principles regarding what Satan does and what God does concerning our guilt. These six principles are actually three pairs of principles. The first half of each pair shows how Satan deceives us in our guilt, while the second half shows how God tells us the truth.

Satan Wants Us to Feel Hopeless When We Are Guilty

ZECHARIAH 3:1

When we are legitimately guilty before God, Satan uses our guilt to make us feel hopeless so that we will stay far from God. Zechariah saw Joshua the high priest "standing before the Angel of the LORD, with Satan standing at his right hand to accuse him." The word *standing* was used in the OT as a technical term to talk about a priest in the presence of the Lord, prepared to perform his ministry (see Deut 10:8; 2 Chr 29:11). As a member of the tribe of Levi and a descendant of the family of Aaron, Joshua, the high priest, is standing ready to serve the Lord and to serve as a mediator for God's people. But as he does so, Satan is standing there as well. In fact, Satan is at Joshua's right hand, which signifies where Joshua is supposed to draw his strength for service.

Satan's purpose is "to accuse him." In Hebrew the name *Satan* and the verb *accuse* are forms of the same root word. Satan's very name means that he is an adversary and an opponent. His nature is always to malign and attack God by slandering and accusing God's people. Here Satan is pointing to Joshua's guilt, represented by his filthy clothes (v. 3), and saying, in effect, "There's no hope for him. He's guilty of evil and sin. He can't serve God."

I once heard about a young lady who was dating a man whom she hoped to marry. However, they had some differences in belief. So she went to her mother and said, "I'd like to marry John. I think I'm in love with him. But I'm concerned, because John doesn't believe there's really a Devil."

Her mother said, "Honey, don't worry about a thing. Go ahead with the wedding, and once you get married, I'll show John there's a Devil!"

The truth is, according to God's Word, Satan is indeed real. He's not merely a representation of evil or a fantasy character invented to frighten people. The Bible talks about Satan as a real spiritual personality. And just as he accused Joshua the high priest, Satan is our accuser. He opposes and attacks all of God's people. Revelation 12:10, which describes Satan's ultimate defeat, also gives insight about his constant activity:

> *Then I heard a loud voice in heaven say: The salvation and the power and the kingdom of our God and the authority of His Messiah have now come, because the accuser of our brothers has been thrown out: the one who accuses them before our God day and night.*

According to Scripture, Satan accuses and opposes believers day and night in the presence of God.

Since Satan is a consummate liar (John 8:44), we might imagine that he lies to God about our sinfulness, accusing us of things we have never done. Often, however, our enemy does something far worse. He comes into the presence of God and tells the truth about us. We *are* sinners. We *are* sinful. We *have* done, said, and thought things that offend and displease our holy God. But Satan's accusations against us are always accompanied by hopelessness. He not only accuses us of having sinned, which is true, but he also tells us that we are beyond God's reach, which is a lie. Satan uses our guilt as his weapon to make us feel hopeless and to keep us from God.

God Wants Us to Feel Sorrowful When We Are Guilty

ZECHARIAH 3:2

When believers sin against God, He desires for us to feel sorrowful for our guilt so that we will turn from our sin. In Zechariah 3:2 the Lord strongly rebukes Satan for opposing Joshua. The Hebrew term *ga'ar*, "rebuke," is also used to describe Jacob chastising Joseph for telling his dream (Gen 37:10) and God rejecting the offerings of priests and spreading excrement on their faces and their offerings (Mal 2:3). The term means "to scold" or "to offer a sharp criticism." God's sovereign ability to reprimand Satan in this manner is a reminder that the Lord and Satan are by no means equal forces in the universe. As powerful as Satan's tactics against God and God's people can be, he is no match for the Lord. Accordingly, when Yahweh rebukes Satan, the enemy becomes silent.

The end of verse 2 reveals the foundation for the Lord's rebuke. First, the Lord had "chosen Jerusalem." By His grace and love, God had shown favor to Jerusalem and the Jewish people. Second, the Lord specifically identified Joshua as "a burning stick snatched from the fire." The "fire" suggests the judgment of the Babylonian captivity. While Joshua's people had sinned and had suffered because of that sin, God was offering hope through repentance. This truth corresponds to one of the major themes of this book: "Return to Me . . . and I will return to you, says the LORD of Hosts" (1:3). God had been faithful to bring His people out of exile, and He was not going to abandon them now, not even when they were covered with the filth of their sin.

Will God allow believers to feel bad about our sin? Absolutely. In fact, one of the signs that you have been saved is that you will not be able to continue in a life of sin and feel good about it. The writer of Hebrews says, "The Lord disciplines the one He loves and punishes every son He receives." Based on that fact, God's Word commands us, "Endure suffering as discipline: God is dealing with you as sons. For what son is there that a father does not discipline?" (Heb 12:6-7). God wants His children to feel grief and sorrow over our sin because grief and sorrow over sin are the ways that God brings us back to Him. Second Corinthians 7:10 says, "For godly grief produces a repentance not to be regretted and leading to salvation, but worldly grief produces death." Repentance has been called a change of mind that leads to a change of heart that creates a change of direction that culminates in a change of life.

God loves us too much to allow us to sin and feel good about it. But God's kind of guilt will never lead us to hopelessness or despair. He allows His people to feel the weight of their sin so they can return to Him. So while Satan comes to us when we are guilty saying, "There's no hope for you. You might as well be dead," God comes to us when we have sinned and says, "Repent. Turn from your sin and I'll save you. I'll make things right again."

When I was a kid, after our family enjoyed a meal at my grandmother's house I would sometimes get drafted to help wash dishes. Standing next to my grandmother at her kitchen sink, I would usually wash the dishes while she did the drying. I would scrub a plate or a pot and hand it over to her to dry and put away. Every now and then I would hand a dish to her only to have her hand it back to me. She would say softly, "Honey, I'm sorry, but this one is not clean."

Any time my grandmother did that, I had a few choices in how to respond. I could have countered angrily, "This plate is clean to *my* satisfaction. Get over it." But I never would have said that, even if the plate looked completely clean to my eyes. I loved my grandmother too much—and I feared her punishment too much—to do that. I could have become crushed and humiliated when she handed a plate back, thinking that I was a hopeless failure at washing dishes. But I knew my grandmother loved me too much to make me feel that way. Instead, I would take the dish back, ask her to show me the unclean spot, and rewash it. And sometimes I would realize that I didn't have the ability to find the spot or scrub the plate like my grandmother could. That was typically when she would say, "Honey, you dry. I'll wash." And she would get it clean.

Genuine guilt is a gift from God. When we sin, the Lord wants us to feel the sense that something is not right, that something in our lives is not clean. His purpose is that our sorrow and guilt will lead us to get things right with Him. When we feel guilt over sin, God wants us to realize that we cannot make ourselves clean and righteous on our own. Just as a child would hand over a dirty dish for his grandmother to scrub, God wants us to hand our lives to Him and say, "Lord, take this sin, take this guilt, and cleanse me of it."

God loves believers so much that He won't allow us to sin and feel good about it. However, unlike the way Satan attacks us with guilt, God's kind of guilt will never lead us to hopelessness and despair. Instead, He will allow His people to experience godly sorrow over their sin so that they will return to Him. He's always ready for us to return to Him so that we can be forgiven.

Satan Wants Us to Feel Innocent When We Are Guilty
ZECHARIAH 3:3

The enemy of our souls has two major strategies when we are guilty of sin, both of which are designed to keep us from coming to God for forgiveness. One strategy, we have seen, is to make us feel hopeless, so we conclude that we can never be forgiven or loved by God and there is nothing we can do about our guilt. There is an equally dangerous way the enemy deceives. This other strategy, illustrated here, is to make us feel innocent, so we will continue in the sin that is destroying us.

Zechariah saw Joshua the high priest standing before the Angel of the Lord, the preincarnate Christ, wearing "filthy clothes." It is almost impossible to describe how strongly the Hebrew language talks about the filth of Joshua's garments. These were not simply clothes stained with just a few spots of sweat and dirt. Nor were they garments that have gone too long unlaundered, with a whiff of body odor on them. "Filthy" translates perhaps the strongest expression that the Hebrew language had to talk about something loathsome and vile. The word used here is directly related to the Hebrew term for human excrement. Joshua is standing there, trying to serve the Lord, yet he is absolutely contaminated.

The irony, though, is that Joshua seems to think he is acceptable. After all, he is "dressed," showing that he considers himself to be prepared to serve and minister in the temple. He is standing before the Angel of the Lord, apparently believing that he is ready to do God's work and to be in the Lord's presence. He thinks he is fine. This is a portrait of how Satan will work when we are contaminated with sin. He will try to convince us that we are innocent, even when there is great guilt in our lives.

On a recent visit to New York City I challenged myself to learn how to use the subway system. I had a good time figuring out how to read the subway maps to get from place to place, planning my route, and then pushing my way into the crowded subway cars with all of the other riders. I learned an important lesson, though, on the first day of my trip there. I was waiting for my train to come, standing on a subway platform that was absolutely crammed with people. The next train rolled in and every car was packed full of people, except for one car. One car, right in front of me, was nearly empty. I thought, "This is great. I'll get on this car." As soon as I stepped in, I instantly learned a lesson that I will never forget. If you see an empty subway car, and the cars in front of it and behind it are full, *do not* get on that empty car. Here's why: something unpleasant has happened in there, and the horrendous effects will still be lingering in the air when you get on board. You may not be able to see the problem, but you will be able to smell it. Everything looks okay, but something is not right.

In the same way, Satan tries to convince us that things are okay with us spiritually when things are not right. He makes us feel innocent when we are guilty, clean when we are dirty, virtuous when we are wicked, and godly when we are unholy. Satan hates us and will do anything he can so that we will continue in the sin that is destroying us. That's why God's Word is so careful to warn against this type of self-deception. In 1 John 1:8 and 10 God says, "If we say, 'We have no sin,' we are deceiving ourselves, and the truth is not in us. . . . If we say, 'We don't have any sin,' we make Him a liar, and His word is not in us."

When the truth of God's Word is not in us, we are easy prey for Satan's deceptive work regarding our sin. Before we encounter the objective standard of God's Word, we can do all kinds of things and yet be deceived about our guilt. We can be deceived into thinking that times have changed and we have no need to be concerned about sexual sin. We can be fooled into supposing that we had a good reason to lie and we should feel no guilt over being dishonest. We can be tricked into believing that everybody around us is cheating and it is only fair for us to cheat as well. We can be deceived to reason that since we are in a committed relationship with the person with whom we are living and having sex, we do not have to have a wedding ceremony or a piece of paper to make things right.

Then, when we come to the Scriptures, God's Word speaks to us and says that God is truth, and therefore He wants us to be truthful; that God is pure, and therefore He wants us to be pure. When we, as believers, fail to hold our lives up to God's Word and do not allow Scripture to determine whether our lives are pure or defiled, we open ourselves us to Satan's deception. He wants us to feel innocent when we are guilty so that we deceive ourselves and continue in our sin.

God Wants Us to Feel Guilty When We Are Guilty

ZECHARIAH 3:4-5

God wants us to feel guilty when we actually *are* guilty, because only then will we bring our guilt to Him and be forgiven. Apart from the convicting work of God, we are likely to keep deceiving ourselves and continuing in our sin, even as our sin destroys us. Zechariah 3:4-5 describes the cleansing of Joshua the priest, symbolizing the forgiveness and restoration of the people of Israel.

Verse 4 says that the "Angel of the Lord spoke," commanding those standing by the High Priest—evidently other attending angels—to remove Joshua's filthy garments. The word *spoke* is instructive, in that the Hebrew term used here most often means "to answer" or "to respond." The word indicates a response to a request or a question, even though that request may not be explicitly spoken. In this case the reader may assume that Joshua made a request of the Lord, namely, "God, take this filth off of me. Take away my guilt." Then God does what Joshua could never do for himself: He answers, ordering that the contaminated clothes be removed.

After removing the garments of Joshua's guilt, the Lord does something even more beautiful. He tells Joshua, "See, I have I have removed your guilt from you" (v. 4). The Lord's words are a reminder that, when we bring our guilt to God, He is not only gracious enough to cleanse us, but also to show us ("See") and tell us that that we have been cleansed ("I have removed your guilt from you"). There is no lingering doubt in our minds about where we stand with God. Even more, the Lord promises Joshua, "I will clothe you with splendid robes" (v. 4). The Hebrew word translated "splendid" is only used here and in Isaiah 3:22. Joshua's new garments represent purity and holiness. They also signify his restoration and readiness to resume his ministry as a priest. In verse 5 Zechariah himself interjects, desiring to see Joshua's restoration made complete: "Then I said, 'Let them put a clean turban on his head.'" The turban, adorned with a golden medallion, was worn by the priest. Exodus 28:36-38 indicates that the medallion was engraved with the words "HOLY TO THE LORD."

The end result is a picture of complete cleansing. Joshua—representing all of God's people—had been filthy and contaminated. Now he is robed in festal attire, crowned with God's holiness, ready to meet with the Lord and to serve in His name. Joshua's cleansing portrays vividly the salvation and restoration that God brings to sinners when we confess our sin and receive His forgiveness. When sinners recognize the state of our guilt, when we acknowledge that we have departed from Him and then repent, God uses our real guilt as a tool to bring His grace to us. God wants His people to feel guilty when we are guilty so that we can turn from our guilt and be cleansed.

Our need to feel guilt over our sin brings to mind the story of a Sunday school teacher who had just concluded her lesson on forgiveness and wanted to make sure that she had made her point. She said, "Children, tell me, what do you have to do to be forgiven for your sin?"

For a few moments, nobody answered. Finally, one boy in the back of the class said, "First, you have to sin!"

That may not have been the answer the teacher was looking for, but she could not deny the kid was right. Until we know that we have sinned and we come before God and say, "God, I have sinned and I need You to cleanse me," we will never receive the forgiveness that we need. The Bible promises, "If we confess our sins, He is faithful and righteous to forgive us our sins and to cleanse us from all unrighteousness" (1 John 1:9). God's forgiveness and grace come when we agree with God that we have sinned and that we are guilty, and when we then seek His cleansing.

We live in a generation of people who never want to feel guilty about anything, even great sin. Sometimes seemingly well-intentioned people will come to a pastor and say, "Don't load guilt on people. Just always be positive." But it is a false positive to make guilty people feel innocent. We need to feel guilty when we are guilty, so that we can bring our guilt to God and He can take away our guilt.

Guilt should move us to confess our sins to God. I often tell my congregation that we must confess our sins the same way we commit our sins. Sometimes people will mistakenly pray, "Lord, forgive me of all my many sins." That type of prayer is really not confession, because the person did not commit his sins as a lump sum. Instead, just as we commit one sin at a time, we should confess one sin at a time. Specific repentance involves praying this way: "Lord, I lied. Forgive me. I mistreated this person. Forgive me. I had an attitude that was hateful and unkind. Forgive me. Through the blood of Jesus, I ask you to forgive me." As we confess individual sins, the Bible promises that God is faithful and righteous to cleanse us from our guilt.

So far in this text, Zechariah has shown us how God counters the work of Satan *before* we are cleansed of our guilt. The last two principles show how Satan deceives us and God tells us the truth *after* we have been forgiven.

Satan Wants Us to Feel Guilty When We Are Forgiven
ZECHARIAH 3:6-7

After God has forgiven believers, Satan's desire is to make us continue to feel guilty in order to debilitate us spiritually and to keep us from serving the Lord. Once Joshua had been cleansed of his iniquity, the Lord spoke a strong word of assurance to him. The Hebrew word translated "charged" is extremely instructive regarding the Lord's intentions. It means "to bear witness" or "to give testimony." In this instance the Lord is countering any lingering accusations of Satan regarding Joshua's guilt by providing a solemn declaration that the high priest was not only cleansed but ready for renewed ministry. Warren Wiersbe notes, "Joshua and his fellow priests weren't put on probation; they were cleansed and restored to service" (*Be Heroic*, 100).

In Zechariah 3:7 the Lord describes the nature of Joshua's service by presenting an "if/then" type of conditional promise, with two conditions and three results. The first condition involves obedience: "If you walk in My ways." God was calling Joshua to pursue a life of personal righteousness now that he was forgiven. The second condition involves faithfulness: "If you . . . keep My instructions." The Lord's "instructions" speak of Joshua's duty as a priest to fulfill the requirements of his office. In response to Joshua meeting these two conditions, the Lord promised the following results:

Leadership among God's people. God promised that Joshua would "rule My house." God's "house" refers here to His people. This same image is used in Numbers 12:7, where God describes Moses as being "faithful in all My household." Joshua's obedience would result in him being a leader and judge over the people of God.

Authority over the temple. The Lord assured Joshua that he would "take care of My courts." The Lord was not only promising that the temple, which was presently in ruins, would surely be rebuilt, but also that Joshua would have the honor of serving the Lord there. The phrase *take care of* carries the idea of both watching over something to protect it and also taking charge of something.

Access to God. The Lord's final promise is that Joshua would be granted "access among those who are standing here." The word translated "access" means a passageway or a stretch of road. Joshua was promised the right of passage into the very presence of God, even among the angelic beings. Walter Kaiser observes that the Jewish Targums make this comment on the promise: "In the resurrection of the dead, I will revive you and give you feet walking among the seraphim" (*Micah*, 334).

Reflecting on the "if/then" pattern of these promises, it is important to note that Joshua's cleansing had been given unconditionally when he repented. All Joshua had to do to be cleansed was turn to the Lord and receive the gift of forgiveness. However, Joshua's usefulness to the Lord was conditional. The Lord said, in effect, "Joshua, now that you are cleansed, obey Me and be faithful to Me, and I will use you for My glory and bless your life."

Amputees often experience some sensation of a phantom limb. Somewhere, locked in their brains, a memory lingers of the nonexistent hand or leg. Invisible toes curl, imaginary hands grasp things, a "leg" feels so sturdy a patient may try to stand on it.

For a few, the experience also includes pain. Doctors watch helplessly, for the part of the body screaming for attention does not exist. Phantom limb pain provides a powerful insight into the phenomenon of false guilt. Christians can be obsessed by the memory of some sin committed years ago. It never leaves them, crippling their ministry, their devotional life, and their relationships with others (Galaxie, *10,000 Sermon Illustrations*).

God has great plans for us once we have been cleansed. But Satan wants to make us feel like we are still what we once were. He will bring up our past. He will bring up our failures. He will bring up our weaknesses. He will bring people into our path to discourage us. Or he will stir up our own self-doubts so that we negate ourselves. Once we are forgiven, Satan will often use misplaced guilt—the phantom pain over sin that God has already forgiven—in order to keep us from being used by God. That is why forgiven people need to be reminded of who they have become through Jesus Christ. We are no longer guilty. We are forgiven.

Even the most shameful things from our past have been cleansed by Him and redeemed as a testimony to His glory in our lives. This brings us to the final principle illustrated by this text.

God Wants Us to Feel Forgiven When We Are Forgiven

ZECHARIAH 3:8-10

At the conclusion of this vision, the Lord tells Joshua that he and those with him are a sign of things to come, pointing to what God is going to do in the future. The word translated "sign" indicates a symbol with prophetic significance. The name *Joshua* (Hb *Yeshua*) is itself a sign since it is the Hebrew form of the name *Jesus*. Joshua, the high priest, points forward to the coming Messiah, the great high priest. He and his companions receive a message concerning the coming of the Lord Jesus. This passage uses two titles to describe the coming Messiah: "My servant" and "the Branch." "Servant" is the most common name in the Old Testament for the Messiah, used even more frequently than the word *Messiah* itself. The title *Servant* emphasizes the work of the Messiah in obeying the will of the Lord and doing His work.

The other messianic title used here, *Branch*, is more unusual. Notably, the Messiah is called "the Branch" four significant times in the Old Testament, and each mention connects to an aspect of Jesus revealed in the four Gospels. The Branch is called the royal "king" in Jeremiah 23:5. In Matthew, Jesus is revealed as Israel's King. The Branch is called God's "servant" here in Zechariah 3:8. In Mark, Jesus is revealed as God's servant. The Branch is called "a man" in Zechariah 6:12. In Luke, Jesus is revealed as the Son of Man. The Branch is described as belonging to God in Isaiah 4:2. In John, Jesus is revealed as the Son of God. In talking about the Messiah as the Branch then, God is unveiling the fullness of who the Messiah will be as revealed in the Gospels.

In verse 9 the Lord sets before Joshua a stone, a further image of the coming Messiah. In other prophetic passages, the Messiah is identified as the cornerstone (Ps 118:22-23; Zech 10:4), the rock that causes stumbling (Isa 8:14), the stone the builders rejected (Ps 118:22-23), and the stone that strikes and crushes evil (Dan 2:34-35). The idea of the Messiah as a stone depicts His dependability and sureness, His ability to overcome God's enemies, and His distinctiveness as the foundation for the church. Notably, the stone presented to Joshua has "seven eyes." In Scripture the number seven often speaks of fullness, completion, and perfection. A number of different explanations have been given for the seven eyes on this stone: (1) Some English Bibles, including the NIV and ESV marginal translations, render the Hebrew "seven facets" or "seven sides." If the "eyes" are facets, like those of a gemstone, then the gem in the high priest's turban or gold plate worn over his breast bearing the seven-letter Hebrew inscription *qds yhwh*, "Holy to the LORD," may be in view here, as described in Exodus 28:36-38. (2) Another alternate, but acceptable, translation renders this "seven springs" of water, referring to the springs flowing from the altar of sacrifice, as in Ezekiel 47:1-2 and Zechariah 14:8. This idea is consistent with the rock that yielded water for Moses in the wilderness (Exod 17:6; Num 20:8) (Stuhlmueller, *Rebuilding*, 79–80). (3) The most commonly accepted explanation, however, is that the seven eyes symbolize the full wisdom of the Messiah, who sees and knows all, and who judges with perfection and fullness. This interpretation is in concert with Zechariah 4:10, which describes the seven eyes of the Lord, "which scan throughout the whole earth."

The Lord promises to "engrave an inscription" on this stone. The early church fathers understood this cutting into the stone to symbolize the scars borne by Jesus during His crucifixion (Barker, "Zechariah," 7). While this interpretation may see somewhat fanciful, the message of the inscription is clearly redemptive: "I will take away the guilt of this land in a single day." The complete spiritual cleansing of the nation was indeed accomplished in "one day" by Jesus on Calvary. This "one day" also points forward to the time when Israel will look to Jesus in repentance and be forgiven (12:10).

The results of the Messiah's redemption and forgiveness are described at the end of our passage: "On that day, each of you will invite his neighbor to sit under his vine and fig tree." The image of each Israelite sitting under his own vine and fig tree is a common Hebrew figure of speech expressing absolute peace (see 1 Kgs 4:25; Isa 36:16; Mic 4:4). The text moves from Joshua in the filth of his sin to every Israelite enjoying the blessings of peace and harmony with the Lord. Through the Messiah—the Servant, the Branch, the Stone—God has made the way for His people to overcome the accusations of Satan and the condemnation of sin.

In a cemetery not far from New York City a grave is said to have been marked with an unusual headstone. The headstone does not indicate a date of birth, the date of death, or even the name of the person whose grave the stone marks. Instead there is just one word: *Forgiven*. For the person whose body lies beneath that stone, the most important thing that could be said at the end of life was that one word. Far better than having a cold word chiseled in stone at the end of our lives, God desires to engrave "Forgiven" in our hearts and our minds each day. Though our sin is great, Jesus has cleansed us from our sin. Through Jesus, God has made the way for people to experience the joy and freedom of *being* forgiven and *feeling* forgiven.

Reflect and Discuss

1. How can you distinguish between objective and subjective guilt from a Scriptural standpoint?
2. Does objective guilt always result in feelings of guilt? Why or why not?
3. What are some specific ways that Satan deceives God's people about our guilt?
4. Why does Satan accuse God's people about our sinfulness? What are his intentions in doing do?
5. How do feelings of guilt over real sin in our lives confirm that we belong to God?
6. What is the difference between sorrow over sin and repentance? Is it possible to have one without the other? How?
7. What are some expressions in our world today of people being objectively guilty of sin, but feeling innocent?
8. In what ways is genuine guilt a gift from God?
9. How does Satan cause forgiven believers to continue to feel guilty? What does he accomplish by doing this?
10. When a forgiven believer experiences the knowledge and assurance that he is indeed right with God, how does that affect his emotions, his devotion to the Lord, and his service in God's kingdom?

Our Strength, or God's Spirit?

ZECHARIAH 4:1-14

Main Idea: Our greatest need is God's Spirit, not our own strength.

I. God's Spirit Conquers the Greatest Obstacles (4:1-7).
II. God's Spirit Overcomes the Smallest Beginnings (4:8-10).
III. God's Spirit Uses the Unlikeliest People (4:11-14).

Hundreds of thousands of spectators lined San Francisco Bay on September 25, 2013, to watch two boats battle one another for the oldest trophy in international sport, the America's Cup. That year, Oracle Team USA overcame a 1–8 deficit to defeat Emirates Team New Zealand 9–8 in the largest comeback in the race's 162-year history.

Larry Ellison, the billionaire who sponsored Oracle Team, reportedly spent more than $100 million to win the race. He commissioned a 72-foot catamaran yacht that weighed seven tons, sported carbon fiber sails 131 feet tall, and reached incredible speeds of over 50 miles per hour. He hired an experienced 11-member crew to man the ship and put veteran captain Sir Ben Ainslie in charge.

But none of those things were the most essential part of the ship's victory—not the expert crew, not the high-tech sails and engineering, not the big money, not even the tactics of the captain. None of those things were the most essential part. As with any sailing race, victory ultimately depends on the wind.

Perhaps the best-known phrase from the book of Zechariah is, "'Not by strength or by might, but by My Spirit,' says the LORD of Hosts." The Hebrew term for "Spirit" is *ruach,* a word that also means "wind" in some contexts. The Greek word for "Spirit" used in the New Testament, *pneuma,* also can mean "wind."

It is important to understand that God's Spirit is a person, a part of the triune God along with the Father and the Son. God's Spirit is not merely a force, a presence, or a power. Still, there is something instructive and insightful in the fact that the word for "Spirit" can also mean "wind."

Consider just a few of the implications:

(1) Like God's Spirit, wind is unseen but creates visible results. Jesus told Nicodemus, "The wind blows where it pleases, and you hear its sound, but you don't know where it comes from or where it is going. So it is with everyone born of the Spirit" (John 3:8).

(2) The wind's strength can only be accessed when the conditions are right. A sail must be turned toward the wind in order to be moved by it. In the same way, God commands believers to be "filled by the Spirit" (Eph 5:18). The Spirit only operates fully in believers when our hearts are in a posture of surrender.

(3) Like the Spirit, wind has greater power than human effort. While the wind-powered yachts in the America's Cup reached speeds of 55 miles per hour, an 8-man Olympic rowing crew cannot even reach half that speed. The wind makes the difference. To an even greater degree, we need God's Spirit—God's divine wind in our sails—in order to live for Him and serve Him with power.

If you have been saved, the Holy Spirit of God is in you. To belong to Jesus is to have the Holy Spirit. In Romans 8:9 Paul writes, "if anyone does not have the Spirit of Christ, he does not belong to Him." So failure to have God's Spirit is failure to belong to Jesus. However, if you do indeed belong to Jesus Christ, then God's Holy Spirit has come to live inside of you. The Bible says in 1 Corinthians 6:19, "your body is a sanctuary of the Holy Spirit who is in you, whom you have from God." On the basis of His presence in our bodies, God's Spirit is available to "fill" believers (Eph 5:18), which speaks of His control, dominance, and power in our lives.

Our greatest need is for God's Spirit, not our own strength. That's the message of Zechariah 4. This is true in every area of life, including marriage and family, business and career, and ministry and church. Absolutely, undeniably, and essentially, we must have God's Spirit, because God's Spirit can do what God alone can do. Chapter 4 describes the fifth vision that the Lord gave to Zechariah to proclaim. The vision can be understood by viewing it through the lens of Zechariah 4:6:

> *So he answered me, "This is the word of the LORD to Zerubbabel: 'Not by strength or by might, but by My Spirit,' says the LORD of Hosts."*

God wanted Zechariah to take the message of this vision to a specific person, Zerubbabel, the governor of the land of Judah. Along with the rest of the remnant who had returned to the land, Zerubbabel was given the task of rebuilding the temple of God in Jerusalem. Under

Zerubbabel's leadership, the work had started over a decade before. He had led the people to lay the temple's foundations, but nothing had happened since then. For the temple—which represented God's presence, His blessings, and His power—to be left incomplete was a burden to the heart of the Zerubbabel and the people. Seeing it still in ruins so long after they had returned to rebuild it must have been discouraging and defeating for them. More than that, they probably doubted whether they would ever be able to build the temple, since they had been powerless to do so for such a long time.

In the midst of their hopelessness and discouragement, the Lord sent a message of hope to Zerubbabel. Take a moment to consider each part of the text of Zechariah 4:6. **Not by strength.** Strength refers to the military power of Zerubbabel and his people. God was saying, in effect, "Zerubbabel, the answer is not in the power of your armies or your weapons or your horses or your chariots. That's not how you're going to accomplish this task." **Or by might.** Might refers to human manpower. God was telling Zerubbabel, "Getting people motivated so that they put their all into this effort will not get this work done." Instead, God promised to achieve what needed to be accomplished **by My Spirit.** Only God's Spirit could accomplish the task that was in front of God's people. As the vision unfolds, this passage reveals three things that only God's Spirit can do.

God's Spirit Conquers the Greatest Obstacles

ZECHARIAH 4:1-7

The angel who has been interpreting the visions wakes Zechariah up as though the prophet had been sleeping, and the angel begins to show him objects related to worship in the temple. Zechariah sees a golden lampstand, a furnishing for the temple that would look much like a candelabra. The Hebrew for "lampstand" is *menorah.* This lampstand seems to be similar to the one in the tabernacle described in Exodus 25:31-40 or to the 10 lampstands that were in Solomon's temple as described in 1 Kings 7:49. This lampstand has a significantly different source of oil from either of those lampstands. In both the tabernacle and the temple, the duty of the high priest was to trim the wicks of the lampstands each morning and evening and to fill the lamps with oil so that they would keep burning (Lev 24:2-3). In Zechariah's vision, however, the prophet sees a bowl, or a reservoir of oil, suspended above the lampstand. The bowl has seven channels coming out of it for each bowl, making a total of 49 conduits. Oil pours down from these channels into the lamps in an abundant supply. Zechariah also sees olive trees standing on either side of the lampstand, one to the right and other to the left. Later in the passage, Zechariah will note that these trees are tapped with "two gold conduits, from which golden oil pours out" (v. 12). Instead of requiring human effort to keep the lamps burning, the Lord has provided a perpetual supply of oil.

The imagery thus far is straightforward. The golden lampstand symbolizes God's people, Israel. The oil—produced by the olive trees, supplied by the suspended bowl, and delivered by the 49 channels—represents the work of Holy Spirit, empowering Israel to be a light to the nations, directing them to God.

When Zechariah asks the angel the meaning of what he is seeing, instead of giving an immediate explanation of the symbolism of the lampstand, bowl, and olive trees, the angel explains the spiritual truth behind the symbols: "Not by strength or by might, but by My Spirit." The vision portrays an endless supply of God's Spirit, an endless supply of God's power for His people to accomplish God's purpose, supplied by God Himself. In the vision the bowl is above the lamp. This indicates that God's power is not something that human beings work up. God's power is something that He sends down. When the channels are open in our lives to receive His Spirit's power, He is ready to send down everything we need to do His work.

Then in verse 7 the Lord gives this message to Zerubbabel: "What are you, great mountain? Before Zerubbabel you will become a plain." The "mountain" refers to the opposition that stood in front of Zerubbabel as he tried to do God's work in rebuilding the temple. God's enemies living in the area came against Zerubbabel and the Jews with words of discouragement and hostility. Imagine their taunts: "You cannot rebuild this temple. You have barely gotten started, and you will never finish. You might as well quit. We are going to fight you at every turn." In the face of that mountain of opposition, God was saying, "What are you? Zerubbabel will flatten you by the power of My Spirit."

God's Spirit can overcome mountainous obstacles in our way and reduce them to level ground so that we can do what God is calling us to do. God promised that, by His Spirit, Zerubbabel would one day "bring out the capstone accompanied by shouts of: Grace, grace to it!" In other words, the leader of God's people would complete the temple and place the final touch on its highest point, and the beauty of the rebuilt house of the Lord would be evident to everyone who saw it. All this would come about through the work of God's Spirit, not because of Zerubbabel's strength or the might of the people.

God's Spirit can conquer our greatest obstacles. Too many times, though, we allow our obstacles to conquer us. In his book *Fuzzy Memories*, humorist Jack Handey wrote, "There used to be this bully who would demand my lunch money every day. Since I was smaller, I would give it to him. Then I decided to fight back. I started taking karate lessons. But then the karate lesson guy said I had to start paying him five dollars a lesson. So I just went back to paying the bully" (*Fuzzy Memories*, n.p.). Too often, that is what too many of us do. Instead of finding the strength and courage to defeat the obstacles that oppose us, we decide that it is easier just to keep paying the bully.

By the power of God's Spirit, when there is a bully, a mountain, or some other opposition or obstacle standing in front of you, daring you to even try to trust God, you can say, "Who are you, great mountain?" Whether you face the mountain of discouragement, the mountain of financial crisis, the mountain of past failures, the mountain of addiction, the mountain of criticism, the mountain of the misplaced guilt from your past, or the mountain of doubt about your future, you can stand in front of that mountain and say, "What are you, great mountain?"

And if you listen carefully, you may hear the mountain reply, "I am a great mountain. What are you?" Standing on our own, we would never have an answer for the mountains we face. But standing in the power of God's Holy Spirit, when the mountain says, "I'm a mountain. What are you?" we can say, "I am a child of God, living in the power of God's Spirit. The blood of Jesus Christ has redeemed me. His Spirit lives inside of me. Mountain, you will become level ground in front of me." Praise the Lord!

There may be a mountain you have faced for years, just as Zerubbabel faced the mountain of the incomplete temple. Each day of continued opposition and the increasing sense of defeat makes the mountain seem larger and more overwhelming. By now, you may think that you simply will never overcome it. And, in the deepest sense, you are right. You cannot overcome your obstacle. You cannot flatten the mountain on your own. But the Holy Spirit of God can overcome it. He lives inside of you, and He will empower you. The greatest obstacles can be conquered. As you trust in Him, God's Spirit conquers even the greatest of obstacles.

God's Spirit Overcomes the Smallest Beginnings

ZECHARIAH 4:8-10

In verses 8-10 Zechariah's fifth vision continues with a word of encouragement for Zerubbabel. In verse 9 the Lord acknowledges that Zerubbabel had laid the foundation for the temple. He had started on the rebuilding project a number of years before, in 537–536 BC (Ezra 3:8-11; 5:16). When the rebuilding began, the priests had dressed in their robes and held trumpets while the Levites stood with cymbals in hand to lead the people of Israel in praise. Together, the people shouted and gave thanks to the Lord for His goodness and His eternal love. There had been tremendous celebration when the foundation of the Lord's house had been laid. Now the year was 519 BC. Over 17 years had passed, and the foundations had become a bitter visual testimony to an unfulfilled hope.

How encouraged Zerubbabel must have been to hear this promise from God: "Zerubbabel's hands have laid the foundation of this house, and his hands will complete it." The language here uses synecdoche, in which the parts, "Zerubabbel's hands," represent the whole, the man himself. Repeating the figure of speech—"Zerubbabel's hands have laid the foundation" and "his hands will complete it"—emphasizes the fact that Zerubbabel, who had personally begun building the temple, would also personally fulfill his God-given task by completing it. When Zerubbabel finished the temple, the angel promised, "Then you will know that the Lord of Hosts has sent me to you." With those words, which repeat identical pledges made in 2:9 and 2:11, the angel offered not only a confirmation of Zechariah's prophetic ministry, but also an assurance of the validity of all the visions the angel had shown the prophet.

As a result, the angel asks this rhetorical question: "Who scorns the day of small things?" The word translated "scorn," *buz* in Hebrew, means to despise or hold in contempt. It indicates showing disrespect for someone or something. The word is used in Proverbs to caution fools against despising God's wisdom (Prov 1:7; 23:9), to warn about the danger of disrespecting a mother or father (Prov 23:22; 30:17), or to judge those who hold God's Word in contempt (Prov 13:13). The angel's question in 4:10 also carries a cautionary tone. The NET Bible captures this warning especially well: "Who dares make light of small beginnings?"

"The day of small things" refers to the day when Zerubabbel and other returning Jews had started work on the temple. The longer Zerubbabel and company went without completing the building, the more insignificant that foundation seemed to be. You may have watched what happens in your community when someone starts to build a house but never finishes it. You drive down the road and see the building has been started. Workers dig the footings and pour the concrete for the foundation. They start to put up the walls or go even further. Then one day you drive by and you notice that construction has stopped. Maybe the builder ran out of money, or perhaps something tragic happened in the life of the family that was building the home. But for whatever reason, the building just sits there unfinished. Eventually, weeds begin to overtake the foundation. Rain starts to rot the wood of the uncompleted walls. A building that had looked promising at the beginning becomes more and more insignificant as the days pass with no progress.

A similar thing had happened with the temple in Jerusalem. More than a decade and a half before, Zerubbabel had laid the foundation. He had marked out all the footings to show where the temple was going to be. He and his workers, along with the rest of the returning Jews, must have been brimming with excitement to think that they were going to rebuild the house of God. Then, because of opposition and challenge, the work stopped. For days, then weeks, and eventually years, nothing happened. Now there were among God's people those who despised the day of small things, who held the construction of the temple in contempt. They said, "Nothing is going to happen. Nothing has happened in 10 years. Nothing has happened in 15 years. Nothing is going to happen, ever." As time passed, the project began to look less and less significant and more and more ill advised.

The Lord's message for Zerubbabel was that when His Spirit touches something that looks small and inconsequential, God will do something significant. Perhaps those who scorned the day of small things were the older Jews who believed the new temple would be lackluster compared with the former temple before the exile (Ezra 3:12-13). Or those who scorned that day may have been the surrounding enemy nations who were at ease as the returning remnant of Israel sought to rebuild Jerusalem (Zech 1:15). Whether the scorn came from enemies on the outside or critics from within Israel, God Himself promised to rejoice as His mission for Zerubbabel was achieved: "These seven eyes of the LORD, which scan throughout the whole earth, will rejoice when they see the plumb line in Zerubbabel's hand."

The language at the end of verse 10 holds some difficulties. The phrase "the seven eyes of the LORD," reminiscent of the stone with seven eyes in 3:9, suggests the Lord's omniscience. The Hebrew translated "plumb line" can also be interpreted to mean "separated stone," which might be a reference to the capstone in verse 7. If the meaning is "plumb line," Yahweh, who sees and knows all, promises to rejoice as the construction of the temple begins again under Zerubbabel's supervision. If the meaning is "capstone," then Yahweh's rejoicing comes at the temple's completion. In either case, the idea is very similar: though Zerubbabel's detractors scoff at his attempts to rebuild the temple, the Lord will overcome meager beginnings through His Spirit.

Just as Zerubbabel had an assignment from the Lord to rebuild the temple, every follower of Jesus has a specially designed life assignment from God. For each of us, there is a project God has for our lives. While all believers have the same ultimate purpose of living for God's glory (1 Cor 10:31), the way that purpose fleshes out in the details of our lives every day differs for each Christian. But many of us have been in the same place that Zerubbabel was. God has given us an assignment, and maybe we have started it but we have unfulfilled dreams, uncompleted goals, dead visions, or half-built projects. We have laid the foundation but now we feel stuck. God's Word assures us that, through the power of God's Spirit, we can finish what we have started. God's Spirit can overcome small and even frustrated beginnings and, in the end, the small things that some people despised will become finished projects over which people rejoice.

A friend of mine says that every church has a "Cold Water Committee." These are people who have appointed themselves to discourage the dreams of other people and throw a bucket of cold water on them. Sometimes they even throw the cold water "in Jesus' name"! As a pastor, people come to me often with ideas and dreams they believe the Lord has given them. At times, some of their ideas seem outlandish and impossible, and I am tempted to join the "Cold Water Committee" myself and tell them all the reasons their idea will never work. But then I remember that I serve a God for whom nothing is impossible (Matt 17:20). I am thankful for people who have encouraged me to pursue God's calling on my life, rather than dousing every dream I have had. We need people like that in our lives. And, even when no one else sees the vision God has given us, the Holy Spirit of God who lives in us will encourage us and overcome the smallest beginnings. In Philippians Paul assures believers, "I am sure of this, that He who started a good work in you will carry it on to completion until the day of Christ Jesus" (Phil 1:6).

God's Spirit Uses the Unlikeliest People

ZECHARIAH 4:11-14

At the conclusion of the fifth vision, Zechariah asks the angel who has been revealing the vision to him two questions that both reiterate and clarify the initial questions asked in verse 4. The first question, found in verse 11, concerns the olive trees on either side of the menorah. The second question, found in verse 12, is more specific, asking for the identity of the two olive branches beside the gold conduits out from which "the golden oil" (literally "the gold") flows.

After further conversation in verse 13, the angel gives the answer to the first question: "These are the two anointed ones . . . who stand by the Lord of the whole earth." According to the angel, these branches are people, the "two anointed ones," which means "two sons of oil." The phrase indicates that two men had been set apart and anointed by God as His special representatives. While the identity of these two men is not explicitly mentioned in this text, the context strongly indicates they must be Zerubbabel the governor and Joshua the High Priest (Barker, "Zechariah," 631). Zerubbabel, a member of the line of David, embodies the political leadership of Judah. Joshua the High Priest, whom we met chapter 3 and will meet again in chapter 6, personifies the spiritual leadership of God's people.

Joshua and Zerubbabel were unlikely people for God to use. These two branches, through whom God's Spirit flowed and by whom God promised to complete His work in Jerusalem, were not Moses, not Aaron, not David, not Solomon, but Joshua and Zerubbabel.

Consider Zerubbabel. He was, by all accounts, a godly man, yet he had an ungodly name. His name means "descendant of Babylon." Zerubabbel's very name brought to mind a wicked kingdom. Although Zerubbabel descended from the kingly line and was the grandson of King Jehoiachin of Judah (see Ezra 3:2 and 1 Chr 3:17-19), he was not a king himself. Instead, he was a governor, a vassal ruler under the authority of a pagan king.

Now consider Joshua. He is a high priest with no temple. We last found him in chapter 3 being cleansed from the horrendous filth with which he had been clothed. He has a famous and beautiful name, which means "Yahweh delivered." Yet, any time we teach or talk about him, we have to distinguish this Joshua from the storied leader of Israel who first took control of the promised land of Canaan. Imagine meeting a man in heaven one day who introduces himself as "Joshua from the Old Testament." Your elation at meeting him would no doubt diminish a little when he told you, "Now, before you get too excited, I need to tell you: I'm Joshua the high priest, not Joshua the son of Nun who fought the battle of Jericho." This is Joshua with a lowercase "j," Joshua the minor character in a book written by a minor prophet! He served alongside a mere governor. Still, God promises that He will use these unlikely men to do great and mighty things.

Conventional wisdom says that you have to have great resources to accomplish great things. It says you have to be a great person to accomplish great things. We tend to believe we can only do great things if we have large financial resources and talented people and innovative ideas. The truth is that our abundance of resources and abilities do not really help God accomplish His work, and our lack of resources and abilities cannot hinder God from doing His work. God works not by our might or strength but by His Spirit.

Consider a few examples. In Judges 3:31 a man you have probably barely even heard of, Shamgar, delivered Israel from the Philistines singlehandedly. He won a great victory by killing 600 Philistines with nothing more than an oxgoad, a stick sharpened at one end to drive along slow-moving oxen. Shamgar was an unlikely hero—as was Moses. When God asked Moses to lead the Israelites out of Egypt, he was afraid no one would listen to him or follow him. God asked him, "What is that thing you have in your hand?" Moses answered, "It's a rod, just a stick." And God used that rod to convince the people to follow Moses, to turn the Nile River into blood, to bring great plagues on Egypt, to part the Red Sea, and to perform miracles in the wilderness (Lee, "Two Sticks").

God uses ordinary instruments and unlikely people to do great things. We might be tempted to say, "I'm not much. I don't have much. I don't know much. I can't do much." Those things don't matter to God. Here's what matters: Are you willing to take who you are and what you have and place all of yourself into His hands? Zerubbabel, the unlikely governor descended from the line of David, points forward to the coming Messiah who would sit on David's throne and rule the nations (Isa 9:7). Lower-case "j" Joshua reminds us of the coming *Yeshua*, whose name belongs in all caps, underscored, and bold print, whom the Bible calls our Great High Priest "who has passed through the heavens—Jesus the Son of God" (Heb 4:14). Through Him, we can turn a discouraging deficit into a stimulating success. Are you willing to turn the sails of your life toward His Spirit so that His Spirit can be the wind in your sails and take you where He wants you to go? God's Spirit can conquer incredible obstacles and turn mountains into plains. His Spirit can make great things out of small beginnings. His Spirit can use the least likely people for His glory. His Spirit can do what our might and strength could never do as we give ourselves to Him.

Reflect and Discuss

1. The people of Judah had allowed the temple in Jerusalem to remain incomplete. What aspects of our spiritual lives do believers sometimes leave unfinished?
2. The Lord reminded Judah that they would accomplish their work by His Spirit rather than through military power or human effort. What substitutes for the work of God's Spirit may we be tempted to rely upon?
3. What are some of the mountainous obstacles we face in our lives and ministries?
4. Why do those difficulties often seem to become bigger as more time passes?
5. How does God's Spirit work in our lives to overcome our biggest challenges?
6. When you have a God-given vision, how do you respond to those who "scorn the days of small things"?
7. In what ways does the Holy Spirit encourage us when others "throw cold water" on God's calling for our lives?
8. Why do you believe God often chooses to use unlikely people in His kingdom?
9. This chapter listed a few unlikely people mentioned in Scripture whom God used. Who are some others? How did God's Spirit use them?
10. What adjustments do you need to make in your life in order for the Holy Spirit of God to use you to the fullest extent?

The Power of God's Spirit

ZECHARIAH 5:1–6:15

Main Idea: The Spirit's power works in our lives to accomplish what we never can.

I. The Power of the Spirit to Reveal Sin (5:1-4)
II. The Power of the Spirit to Remove Sin (5:5-11)
III. The Power of the Spirit to Renew Hope (6:1-15)

Preacher and author Steve Brown tells the story of an airline flight he took. During the flight, the plane began to have extraordinary problems. Though he flies often, Steve Brown does not enjoy flying. He was nervous about the flight from the start because, before boarding this particular flight into Pittsburg, he learned that another plane had recently taken the same itinerary and had crashed.

"As we were flying into Pittsburgh," he said, "that airplane began to experience such turbulence, that it was as though God was just shaking that airplane like a gigantic piggy bank, and just shaking it and shaking it and shaking it." So Steve Brown was sitting white-knuckled in his seat and scared to death when he noticed the woman seated next to him was not moved or shaken by the turbulence at all. Instead, she was sound asleep! This was irritating to Steve. Even worse, the woman was snoring throughout the whole flight!

When the plane landed, the lady woke up, yawned, and stretched. Steve looked over at her and said, "Lady, you don't know it, but we almost died up there. And you really don't want to sleep through your own death. One should be fully awake for that experience." Exasperated, he continued, "And not only were you sleeping, but you were actually snoring!"

That was when the woman said something that Steve Brown says he'll never forget. The lady smiled and said, "Mister, I don't know how to fly this plane." That's all she said: "Mister, I don't know how to fly this plane." Her words are a wonderful illustration of a spiritual truth.

When it comes to life, none of us really has the ability to "fly the plane" successfully. We sin. We fall short. We miss the best that God has for us. We lack the power and wisdom to navigate through life. The good news is this: Our God is in control. His Spirit's power works in the lives of believers to accomplish what we never can. Zechariah 5 and 6 record the last visions given to Zechariah. Understood in light of the message of Zechariah 4:6—"Not by strength or by might, but by My Spirit"—these visions expand on the theme of the power of God's Spirit to work in the lives of His people.

The Power of the Spirit to Reveal Sin

ZECHARIAH 5:1-4

God's Spirit has the power to reveal and remove the darkest sin. In chapter 5 of Zechariah we see the sixth and seventh visions that the Lord showed His prophet. These visions go together. Some interpreters see them as one vision because they work together to provide one message. In the sixth vision, recorded in Zechariah 5:1-4, the prophet sees a flying scroll, which represents the power of the Spirit to reveal sin.

Unfurled, this giant scroll looks like a flag flying over the land. The Hebrew text describes the scroll as 20 cubits long and 10 cubits wide. Understanding that a cubit is roughly the distance from an adult's elbow to the tip of the fingers, typically about 18 inches, the dimensions of the scroll are, as translated in the HCSB, "30 feet long and 15 feet wide." The enormous scroll is flying over the entire land of Israel. A good way to imagine the flying scroll is to think about an advertising banner that you might see when you are at the beach. An airplane flies by, towing a huge banner behind it advertising something. In much the same way, this scroll is flying over the land, huge and impossible to ignore.

Additionally, words are written all over the scroll declaring the charges of God against His people because of their sin. On one side, the scroll describes their theft, and it promises to remove the thieves from the land. The other side of the scroll lists their acts of deception, and it promises God's curse for all the people's lies. Warren Wiersbe addresses the question of why the Lord selected only two of the Ten Commandments in this vision, stealing and swearing falsely: "The third commandment is the central commandment on the first tablet of the Law, and the eighth commandment is the central commandment on the second tablet of the law, so these two commandments represent the whole law" (*Be Heroic*, 109).

The flying scroll filled with charges and judgments is a reminder that evil offends God. He looks, He knows, He cares, and He judges when God's people cheat one another or steal or fail to tell the truth. When students who are believers cheat on a test, God knows and cares. When a Christian businessperson takes unfair advantage of a client, God knows and cares. When Christian husbands and wives deceive each other or break the covenant of their marriage, God knows and cares. The large flying scroll in the sixth vision represents God's knowledge of the people's guilt and the promise of God's judgment because of their sin. The Lord promises swift and severe judgment for the sin of the people, banishing thieves from the land and bringing complete destruction to the house of those who swear falsely by His name.

We can thank God, though, that His Spirit does not simply reveal our sin and leave us to deal with the guilt and the consequences. If the Holy Spirit only convicted us of sin, He would leave us miserable all the time. Zechariah's next vision shows what God's Spirit does after He reveals our sin.

The Power of the Spirit to Remove Sin

ZECHARIAH 5:5-11

This seventh vision is filled with strange imagery, though its symbolism is fairly straightforward and simple to understand. The interpreting angel shows Zechariah a basket that represents the iniquity of the people. The container is an *ephah*, a large barrel or basket that was used for measurement. The measuring basket, a tool for commerce, symbolizes the iniquity of the people in using false measurements. They were cheating one another and being dishonest in business. Prior to the exile, Amos decried the same type of dishonesty:

> *Hear this, you who trample on the needy and do away with the poor of the land, asking, "When will the New Moon be over so we may sell grain, and the Sabbath, so we may market wheat? We can reduce the measure* [literally, *ephah*] *while increasing the price* [literally, *shekel*] *and cheat with dishonest scales. We can buy the poor with silver and the needy for a pair of sandals and even sell the chaff!" The Lord has sworn by the Pride of Jacob: I will never forget all their deeds.* (Amos 8:4-7)

Now, even after the return from Babylon, dishonest scales and false measurements were still a problem among the Jews.

The capacity of a normal *ephah* used by the Jews was somewhere between 5 and 10 gallons. However, just as the scroll in the previous vision was much larger than a normal scroll, the basket in this vision must have been considerably bigger than an ordinary *ephah,* as evidenced by what happens next. When the leaden cover of the basket is removed, Zechariah discovers a woman inside the basket. The woman is called "Wickedness." The woman in the *ephah* is forced back down into the basket and sealed into the container with the lead weight (v. 8).

Then, something significant happens in verse 9. Two unidentified women with wings like those of a stork pick up the basket containing the woman. Whether these winged women are instruments of evil or of good is debatable. The stork is an unclean animal (Lev 11:19; Deut 14:18). Their actions toward the woman in the *ephah* could be interpreted as protecting her. Yet, these creatures are doing the work of God in removing wickedness from the land. Two verbal clues indicate the winged women are God's servants. First, the women are said to have the "wind in their wings." The idea is that the women were carried by the wind, which helped them in their flight. As noted in our explanation of Zechariah 4:6 in the previous section, the word *wind* is closely associated with God's Spirit, using the same Hebrew word. The wind is also used also an instrument in God's hand. Psalm 104:4 speaks of the Lord "making the winds His messengers." Further, their wings are said to be "like those of a stork." The Hebrew word for "stork" sounds similar to another word that can mean "loyalty," which may suggest loyalty to God on the part of these creatures that remove evil from God's people (Clark and Hatton, *Zechariah,* 158).

The winged women carry the woman in the basket through the air to Shinar, that is, Babylon, where the basket is placed on a pedestal in a shrine. The idea is that wickedness, which is so offensive in the promised land, has a home and a place of honor in Babylon. In Scripture Babylon is not just the place of Israel's exile. It also represents sin, idolatry, rebellion, and wickedness. The Bible mentions Babylon in the Genesis account of the tower of Babel (Gen 11:1-9), when the people of Shinar tried to build a tower to take them all the way up to God. From its earliest appearances in Scripture, Babylon represents a system proudly opposed to God. The book of Revelation contains a prophecy equating Babylon in the last days with a religious and political world system based on rebellion against God (Rev 17–18). So, from the beginning to the end of Bible, Babylon signifies sin.

This vision communicates a clear message from God. He was promising to take the guilt, iniquity, and wickedness of His people and carry it away from His presence in Jerusalem. He was promising, by His own initiative, to remove the people's sin from His presence and confine it to its natural habitat, Babylon. From a premillennial eschatological perspective, removing wickedness and idolatry from Jerusalem and returning it to Babylon can be seen as part of God's final judgment on Babylon described in Revelation 17–18. The removal of idolatry prepares Israel for the second coming of Christ, the final conflict between God and all the nations of the earth with Babylon at the center, and Christ's millennial reign, as portrayed in Revelation 19–20 (Lindsey, "Zechariah," 1557).

From the perspective of personal application, the sixth and seventh visions of Zechariah are a reminder that God's Spirit has the power to remove the darkest sin. Putting these visions together creates a picture of the convicting and cleansing work of the Spirit. In the flying scroll we can see how the Holy Spirit reveals the sinfulness of His people. In the woman of wickedness in the basket, flown back to Babylon, we can see how the Holy Spirit removes the sin from God's presence.

God's Spirit convicts us of sin, and then He cleanses us from sin. According to Jesus, the Holy Spirit works even in the lives of unbelievers, as the Spirit convicts the world about "sin, righteousness, and judgment" (John 16:8). For Christians, the Holy Spirit not only cleanses and removes sin at the time of salvation (1 Cor 6:11), but He continues to produce the fruit of God's holiness in our lives (Gal 5:22-23) and transforms us into the image of Jesus (2 Cor 3:18). By the Spirit, believers are able to "put to death the deeds of the body" and live holy lives (Rom 8:13).

A man purchased a white mouse to use as food for his pet snake. He dropped the mouse into the snake's glass cage. The tiny mouse saw that he had a serious problem on his hands. The snake was sleeping in a bed of sawdust and though the snake was asleep, the mouse knew at any moment the snake could wake up and eat him. So the mouse did the only thing he could think to do: He started covering up the snake with sawdust chips. He dug down and pushed the sawdust chips onto the snake until the snake was completely buried under the sawdust. When he had finished burying the snake, the mouse sat down and rested. He thought the problem was solved.

But the man watching knew the problem was not solved, but only hidden. The solution to the mouse's problem could not come from the mouse, the solution had to come from the outside. The man took pity on that little mouse and reached in, picked him up, and removed the mouse from the cage.

No matter how hard we may try, we cannot cover our sin or deny our sinful nature. Our own sin will eventually awake from its sleep and shake off its cover, and sin's consequences will devour us. Were it not for the saving grace of the Master's hand, sin would eat us alive. But, praise God, His Spirit can convict us of our sin and guilt, and then He can take the guilt and shame of sin away from us! His Spirit can deliver us from the power of sin and temptation. He removes the darkest sin. There's no sin that Jesus Christ didn't die for. There's no sin that His resurrection did not conquer. There's no sin from which the power of the Holy Spirit cannot deliver us. Sometimes God delivers us from sin instantly: we ask God to deliver us from a particular sin, He takes away the inclination of our heart toward that sin, and we never struggle with that sin again. Sometimes God takes sin away from us that way. But many times, I have found, God takes sin away from us on a day-by-day basis as we walk with Him. He teaches us to trust in the power of His Spirit for daily deliverance from sin's power in our lives.

The Power of the Spirit to Renew Hope

ZECHARIAH 6:1-15

Chapter 6 brings us to Zechariah's eighth vision. The vision indicates that God's justice was brought to the wicked nations that have oppressed Israel. Following this last vision, God acts to give hope to His people.

At the beginning of Zechariah 6, the prophet sees four chariots coming out from two mountains. The location of these mountains in Judah is uncertain, though some have speculated that the use of the definite article (i.e., *the* two mountains) points to specific mountains, perhaps Mount Zion and the Mount of Olives. In this case, though, it is hard to understand why the mountains would be described as being made of bronze, since the mountains in Jerusalem are made of limestone. The material of the mountains, however, does seem significant. Bronze is often used in Scripture to depict the sureness and resoluteness of God's judgment. For instance, the bronze altar in Exodus 27:2 and the bronze snake in Numbers 21:9 both speak of God's judgment on sin. Likewise, Jesus is described as having feet of bronze in Revelation 1:15 and 2:18 as He stands in judgment over His churches.

Powerful horses draw the chariots that come from between the two bronze mountains. The horses are reminiscent of the ones described in the first vision (Zech 1:8-9), though the colors of the horses are not the same in the two visions. These horses are red, black, white, and dappled (6:2-3). Walter Kaiser notes that the horses bear a strong resemblance to the four horsemen of Revelation 6:1-8 and suggests that the red horse indicates martyrdom, white stands for victory, black stands for famine, and dappled symbolizes death (*Micah*, 355). When Zechariah asks what the horses and chariots are, the interpreting angel explains that they are "the four spirits of heaven going out." While the Hebrew word can mean either "spirits" or "wind" as in 5:9, the context seems to indicate these are angelic spirits sent from the Lord to go throughout the earth.

The chariots are going north and south, each direction representing enemies faced by God's people. The chariots pulled by the black and white horses go to the north, referring to Babylon, while the dappled horses traveled to the south, which represents Egypt (v. 6). Though no specific mention is made of the direction of the red horses, all of the horses and their chariots go out to exert God's control and sovereignty over the nations. Following these patrols, the Lord Himself speaks in response to the chariots that have gone out to Babylon: "See, those going to the land of the north have pacified My Spirit in the northern land." The report from Babylon pacifies God's Spirit and puts His Spirit to rest. Though God had been angry at the oppressive nations (1:15), His work of judgment has been completed and His Spirit is satisfied.

The remainder of Zechariah 6 is a denouement based on the reports from the chariots. Because the Lord's wrath against the nations was satisfied, in verses 9-11 God instructs Zechariah to crown Joshua the high priest. The crown was of silver and gold, precious metals that were to come from a small delegation of exiles from Babylon, namely Heldai, Tobijah, and Jedaiah. The crown was to be an elaborate one, as indicated by the plural of majesty (HCSB reads "crowns"). Joshua's coronation united the priesthood with the monarchy. While there was no precedent in Scripture for a priest to be crowned as a king, the message the Lord gave to Joshua in verses 12-15 explains the reason behind this coronation.

In these verses the Lord offers Joshua, Zechariah, and all the people of Judah a renewed hope through His promises. Just as the Lord had promised to use Zerubabbel to rebuild the temple by His Spirit in Zechariah 4, He now specifies how His Spirit will work through Joshua.

The oracle given to Joshua contains both promises that are contemporaneous to Zechariah's time and those that await future fulfillment. While God indeed used Joshua to rebuild the temple in the days of Zechariah, the final realization of these promises from God will come when Jesus Christ establishes the millennial temple described in Ezekiel 40–46. God's message to Joshua includes several noteworthy and emphatic promises concerning the Messiah, or "the Branch."

- He will build the temple of the Lord (v. 12).
- He will be clothed with majesty and glory (v. 13).
- He will sit and rule on his throne as a priest (v. 13).
- He will unite the role of priest and king, creating "peaceful counsel between the two of them" (v. 13).

In Zechariah's day Joshua's crown would be placed in the completed temple as a remembrance of the men who donated the silver and gold (v. 14). Morever, people from far away—presumably other Jews who were presently in Babylon—would come to complete the construction of the temple as a validation of the Lord's message to Zechariah (v. 15). God concluded this vision with a warning: "This will happen when you fully obey the LORD your God." These words, evocative of Deuteronomy 28:1, remind God's people that the blessings that come from His Spirit and the hope that flows from those blessings are reserved for those who diligently obey Him.

Some time back I was with a group of friends at a retreat near a small lake. On the banks of the lake there was an old sailboat that looked like it had been abandoned and unused for a long time. On the first evening of the retreat I was talking to my friend, Paul.

"What did you do this afternoon?" I asked.

Paul answered, "I took that little sailboat out on the lake."

"I figured nobody ever took that thing out," I said. "Did you have any trouble?"

Paul replied, "Oh, no, I had no trouble at all."

"But the wind was barely blowing," I said.

Paul smiled and answered, "Stephen, I've got some experience with sailboats. And I know how to trim the sails to catch the breeze." And then he said, "If you know how to catch the wind, there's almost always enough wind to sail."

So it is with the power of the Spirit. There is always enough of Him to keep the wind in the sails of our spiritual lives. God wants us to learn how to keep His wind in our sails. The Spirit's power will work in our lives when we (1) obey the book of the Spirit, the Bible, (2) surrender each day to the filling and control of the Spirit (Eph 5:18), and (3) stay connected to the family of the Spirit, the body of Christ.

Reflect and Discuss

1. Would we be aware of our sins without the work of the Holy Spirit? Why or why not? What verses or passages of Scripture support your answer?
2. What aspects of our fallen nature require that God reveal our individual sins to us?
3. How has God worked in your life to uncover otherwise hidden sin?
4. In Zechariah's vision, sin was carried away from Jerusalem, where it did not belong, to Babylon, where it was given a place of honor. In what ways is sin honored in our culture today?
5. Is the church accommodating culturally accepted sins or dealing biblically and redemptively with them? How?
6. How does the Holy Spirit work to remove our sin from us and cleanse us?
7. From an eschatological perspective, what is God doing to deal with the cosmic problem of sin?
8. How is God's Spirit working in time and history to reveal and remove sin and to renew hope?
9. How does the promise of Christ's return and reign on earth affect our struggle with sin and evil today?
10. What practical steps can followers of Christ take to experience the power and hope of the Holy Spirit in their lives each day?

From Fasting to Feasting

ZECHARIAH 7:1–8:23

Main Idea: Experiencing God's living presence requires deep transformation in our lives.

I. **Transformed from Fasting to Feasting (7:1-3; 8:18-23)**
II. **Transformed from Serving Ourselves to Serving Him (7:4-7)**
III. **Transformed from Pursuing Religion to Pursuing Righteousness (7:8-10)**
IV. **Transformed from Listening to Our Desires to Hearing His Voice (7:11-14)**
V. **Transformed from Trusting Our Capabilities to Trusting His Faithfulness (8:1-17)**

A few years ago, Michele and I were invited to a picnic for our church's preschoolers and their families. The picnic was on a Saturday morning in a grassy park area on the church campus. It was a fun event, with baskets filled with sandwiches, chips, and cookies, dads and moms sitting on blankets on the ground, and children running around everywhere playing games and laughing.

After we had been picnicking for about an hour I noticed a group of people walking past us on the sidewalk. They were headed toward our church's worship center wearing dark suits and dresses. In contrast to the laughter of our picnic, they looked somber and subdued. It was then I realized that they were going into the worship center for a funeral.

What do you do when you're having a picnic and someone else is going to a funeral?

We did our best to quiet things down for a few moments as the funeral-goers passed by. But the preschoolers pretty much kept laughing and playing. After all, it *was* a picnic.

I have kept that Saturday in mind ever since. It's a reminder of a reality in life: When you're having a picnic, somebody else, somewhere, is having a funeral. And when you're having a funeral, somebody, somewhere, is having a picnic. At the moment when you're celebrating the greatest joy of your life, someone else is experiencing their greatest sorrow.

Here's the good news about our God: He can take a funeral and transform it into a picnic. He can take our mourning and turn it into dancing. He can take our sorrows and transform them into joys. He can take our times of fasting, and turn them into seasons of feasting. That's the truth we discover in Zechariah 7 and 8.

Transformed from Fasting to Feasting

ZECHARIAH 7:1-3; 8:18-23

It is important to understand that about two years have passed between Zechariah 6 and Zechariah 7. In the first six chapters of the book the Lord gives Zechariah a series of visions. The eight visions told God's people that the Lord would be faithful to rebuild the temple in Jerusalem and that God was going to do something great in the middle of the city of Jerusalem 70 years after His people were carried away into captivity.

As chapter 7 begins, it is now two years later and the temple is about halfway through construction. A delegation of men comes to Jerusalem from the outlying town of Bethel to ask Zechariah and the other priests and prophets who were there, "Do we keep on fasting? Do we keep on mourning? Do we keep on remembering that our city, Jerusalem, was torn down, and that the temple was torn down? Do we keep on fasting now that the temple is being rebuilt?"

When Jerusalem and the temple were destroyed, it became traditional for the Jewish people to fast four times during the year. There was only one fast God commanded His people to observe, the fast on *Yom Kippur,* the Day of Atonement (Lev 23:16-32). No other fast was mandated or commanded by the Lord. But when Jerusalem was destroyed, the people began to fast at four other times of the year:

- They fasted in the tenth month to commemorate when the Babylonians had begun to lay siege to the city of Jerusalem.
- They fasted in the fourth month to commemorate when the city walls of Jerusalem had been broken through.
- They fasted in the fifth month to commemorate when the temple in Jerusalem had been burned.
- Finally, they fasted in the seventh month, the month when Governor Gedaliah had been assassinated.

The delegation of men from Bethel came to Jerusalem saying, "Listen, the fifth month is coming, and we've always fasted in the fifth month to commemorate the burning down of the temple. Now that the temple is being built back up, do we continue that fast?" The answer that God eventually gave is found at the end of chapter 8. The prophet answered the men's question by telling them the day was coming when all of Israel's fasts would become "times of joy, gladness, and cheerful festivals for the house of Judah." All of Israel's fasts would be transformed into feasts. And God promised that people would come from all over the world one day just to experience the presence of the Lord in Jerusalem. The culmination of Zechariah's message comes in verse 23, as the prophet envisions a time when "10 men," a Hebrew expression that implies "many, many men," would come to Jerusalem from the nations of every tongue, from every direction, and of every nationality. God graphically promised these multitudes would grab the robe of a Jew and beg him to take him to the temple because "we have heard that God is with you." In short, God was going to transform their fasting into feasting, and everyone would know that God was with them.

For the nation of Israel, this day that is prophesied in Zechariah 8 has still not yet fully come. It will come one day when, for a thousand years, Jesus Christ reigns on the throne of David in Jerusalem, and all nations will come to worship and serve Him. But even now, when Jesus Christ is ruling and reigning on the throne of our lives, He can transform our fasting into feasting. He can take the most difficult circumstances, the most broken times of your life, and turn them into times of feasting and fruitfulness through His power.

The opening verses of Zechariah 7 and the closing verses of chapter 8 serve as a frame for understanding all the verses in between. Between being asked the question "Do we have to keep fasting?" and giving the answer "You can start feasting," Zechariah addresses the heart attitudes of the people that had to change in order to experience the living presence of God. The intervening verses unfold with the central idea, **experiencing God's living presence requires deep transformation in our lives.** By the power of the gospel, God transforms us. Some believers make the mistake of thinking that God's transforming work begins and ends at the moment of salvation. But throughout Scripture, God reveals His desire to work in His people, day by day, to transform our lives into what He desires us to be. In order to move from fasting to feasting, there is a deep transformation that we have to allow God to work in our lives. Zechariah 7 and 8 reveal four ways that God wants to transform His people.

Transformed from Serving Ourselves to Serving Him

ZECHARIAH 7:4-7

God wants to transform us from serving ourselves to serving Him. The men from Bethel came to Zechariah and the priests asking, "Should we mourn and fast in the fifth month as we have done these many years?" (v. 3). Upon asking, the men discovered the Lord had some questions of His own. He asked, "When you fasted and lamented in the fifth and in the seventh months for these 70 years, did you really fast for Me?" The tone of the question seems to imply its own answer: No, the people were not truly fasting for the Lord. The next question makes the Lord's meaning even clearer: "When you eat and drink, don't you eat and drink simply for yourselves?" God took the occasion of their question to reveal what was truly in the hearts of the people. Yes, they were fasting faithfully in the fifth month and during the other times that they had set aside, but their religious activity was designed primarily to please themselves. The Lord reminded the people that the earlier prophets, who had ministered prior to the exile, taught the Jews to perform their acts of worship and devotion to God from something deeper than a sense of duty, obligation, or tradition (v. 7). Even back in the days of Samuel, God had sought to impress upon the people that He desired obedient hearts more than acts of sacrifice (1 Sam 15:22).

When God's people observe a fast or any other religious tradition to please ourselves or to win the admiration and approval of others, God is not pleased and the activity is wasted. If we are serving ourselves instead of serving Him, our activity becomes empty, no matter how outwardly commendable our actions may be. For many of the Jews in Zechariah's day, fasting four times each year had become a meaningless tradition or, worse yet, a type of idolatry. Our attachment to traditions usually shows up most powerfully when we are asked to break the tradition. For example, at my church a long-lasting tradition has been for the congregation to stand in worship for the reading of Scripture. There are beautiful reasons for this tradition, including a biblical precedent in Nehemiah 8:5. I believe standing to read Scripture can also help us to focus on what we're reading. Standing can also be a way of showing reverence for God's Word. But, most agree, standing to read Scripture is just a tradition. It may be nice and meaningful, but it's nonessential . . . until the pastor doesn't have everyone stand when he reads the text for his sermon! One Sunday I preached the very text we're discussing in this chapter and I left my congregation in their seats as I read the Scripture at the beginning of my message. There was an almost tangible tension in the room. I could see the questions and objections on the people's faces: "I was expecting to stand! I had put down all my stuff so I could stand, and then we didn't. What's going on? Did he forget? Could he be doing this to make a point later on the sermon?" The tension came because I was stepping on their tradition.

The danger of any religious tradition—whether it is keeping a fast or singing a certain song or praying with certain words at a certain time in a certain way—is that tradition easily degenerates into traditionalism. In an interview with *U.S. News & World Report,* theologian Jaroslav Pelikan once said, "Tradition is the living faith of the dead. Traditionalism is the dead faith of the living" (*Vindication of Tradition,* 65). Here is what he meant: Tradition is what those who have gone before us have done to express their living faith in the living God. They established those traditions because it meant something in their own hearts. But traditionalism is when we take the form of what has been done before and we just go through the motions without considering the meaning.

Experiencing God's living presence requires deep transformation and we begin to say, "Lord, I want to serve You and not myself. I don't want to just go through the motions. When I pray, I want to communicate with You. When I fast, I want to prepare my heart to meet with You. When I worship, I don't want just to come to church and stand up and sing and sit down and listen to a message. I want to see Your face. I want to hear Your voice. I want to know Your heart."

In essence, God asked the people of Judah, who had been fasting dutifully for 70 years, four times a year, "Were you fasting to honor Me, or were you fasting for yourselves so that you would feel and appear godly? When you feast and eat, are you feasting to give praise and glory to Me, or are you just having a good time for yourself?" God wants to transform us from serving ourselves to serving Him.

Transformed from Pursuing Religion to Pursuing Righteousness

ZECHARIAH 7:8-10

Zechariah reminded the people that their ancestors had been very faithful in their appearance when practicing their religious rituals in the temple, but they had failed to pursue God's righteousness. He gave the people a series of tests to show where they really were spiritually. The first test is, "Make fair decisions." This instruction involves treating others fairly and legally in business and commerce.

For the second test He said, "Show faithful love and compassion to one another." The term for "faithful love," often translated "kindness," is the Hebrew word *chesed.* The word speaks about the faithful and compassionate love that God has for His people and that God wants His people to have for one another. This type of faithful love and compassion should govern all of our relationships as God's people.

The third test is, "Do not oppress." That's the general command. Then the Lord listed some of the weakest and neediest, most defenseless and most disadvantaged people who had to be protected. He said, "Don't oppress the widow. Don't oppress the fatherless. Don't oppress the stranger, the person not of your nationality, who's living there with you. Don't oppress the poor." God was warning His people not to mistreat or take advantage of those who have no power.

The last test cautions against taking advantage of other people or seeking revenge. God said, "Do not plot evil in your hearts against one another." Righteous living requires letting go of grudges and refusing to devise ways of hurting others, even those who had inflicted hurt on God's people.

God gave these tests so that His people could hold up their hearts to His pure and holy standard, to make sure they were not just being religious, but instead, pursuing righteousness. Zechariah 8:16-17 contains a similar call to practical righteousness in the way God's people live. It lists actions God approves and those He hates. We can pursue religious activity all day long and yet be far, far from God. A transforming relationship with God will cause hearts to act rightly toward others.

Early on in our marriage, when we were trying to decorate our apartment, Michele bought pieces of Chinese pottery to put on display. She bought plates, bowls, pitchers, teapots, cups, and all kinds of things. The pieces were white with pale blue designs all over them. While they were pretty, the pieces were also very inexpensive. Michele put them up on the shelves in our house, and they were beautiful and ornamental. One day I noticed that every one of these pieces had either a sticker or even words painted on the piece in the blue paint with a warning message: "For decorative purposes only. Do not use for cooking, drinking, or eating. Could result in poisoning." The blue and white Chinese cups, saucers, plates, and bowls looked like something you could eat on or drink from, but something inside of them was poisonous and very dangerous.

Pursuing religion without righteousness is much like that. Too many times, our faith is for decorative purposes only. It may be attractive and impressive on the outside, but on the inside the poison of sinfulness and selfishness remains—just like the Pharisees Jesus described who cleaned the outside of the cup and plate but left the inside filled with greed and self-indulgence (Matt 23:25-26). For the Lord, the issue is not what I show everybody on the outside but what is going on in my heart, on the inside.

Only the power of the gospel can cleanse us from the inside. We can give ourselves a spiritual makeover or a religious face-lift and attempt to make ourselves look better but we cannot change who we are on the inside. But God can. He makes us right with Himself through the blood of Jesus Christ, so we can live transformed lives that move beyond our greed, self-indulgence, and selfishness. Through the transforming work of the gospel, we can begin living with selflessness, kindness, and compassion toward others.

Transformed from Listening to Our Desires to Hearing His Voice

ZECHARIAH 7:11-14

A third way that God moves us from fasting to feasting is by teaching us to hear and obey His voice rather than following the voice of our own desires. This passage talks about the people of Judah before the exile, describing their unwillingness to listen to God's voice. After stating that they "refused to pay attention," the Lord portrays His people's deliberate inattention with several powerful and picturesque phrases: (1) They "turned a stubborn shoulder." This phrase, also used in Nehemiah 9:29, describes the rejection communicated by unmistakable body language when a person turns his back to someone who is speaking. The people had turned their backs on the Lord with a defiant attitude that said, "God, You can talk all You want, but we're not listening." (2) They "closed up their ears." The Hebrew here is literally, "They made their ears heavy." Similar language is used in Isaiah 6:10:

> *Dull the minds of these people; deafen their ears and blind their eyes;*
> *otherwise they might see with their eyes and hear with their ears,*
> *understand with their minds, turn back, and be healed.*

Like a disobedient child plunging her fingers into her ears to keep from hearing her mother's instruction, the people of Israel had worked hard not to listen to what God was saying. (3) They "made their hearts like a rock." The Hebrew word for "rock" is also translated "diamond" in Jeremiah 17:1. The word denotes an extremely hard, impenetrable, and unbreakable stone. The people had made their hearts as hard as the hardest stone.

Though by His Spirit God had sent multiple prophets as His messengers bearing His Word to the pre-exilic Jews, the people were determined not to hear the Lord (v. 12). In effect, they were telling God: "We won't hear You. We're not interested in what You have to say. We'll keep our rituals and we'll do the religious things that make us feel spiritual, but we're not going to change the way we live our lives. We will do whatever it takes not to listen to You."

The subsequent verses reveal God's response: (1) God became angry with the people (v. 12). (2) God stopped listening to Israel when they called on Him (v. 13). (3) Ultimately, God scattered them "with a windstorm," a reference to the attacks of nations such as Assyria and Babylon, and "pleasant land" became a "desolation." Now, decades later, God reminded the current generation of Jews that the reason they were having to rebuild the destroyed temple and the ruined city of Jerusalem was simply because their forefathers had not listened to Him. God's judgment in Israel's history stands as a warning to people who are more intent on obeying their own desires rather than obeying God's voice.

The anechoic chamber at Orfield Labs, in Minneapolis, is the quietest place on Earth. You enter the room by passing through two soundproof vaults. Once inside, there is absolutely no sound. The chamber has a sound level of negative nine decibels. The human ear can only detect sounds above zero decibels. While a quiet place like that may seem appealing when compared to the busyness and noise of our world, the truth is, you would probably hate it. Though you cannot hear any sound in the room, you will hear things. You will hear your heart beating. You will hear your lungs functioning. You will hear every single noise your stomach makes. You will hear your own ears working. The silent room can actually cause hallucinations. What might seem like a peaceful place actually becomes a torture chamber. No one has ever been able to stay in that room, by themselves, for more than 45 minutes. Human beings cannot take that kind of silence.

Imagine what it would be like if God were to become absolutely silent. What if we stopped hearing from Him at all? What if the only things we could hear were our own thoughts, our own flawed ideas, the echoes of our own past and guilt, and the clamoring opinions and empty words of other people? What if God were simply to become silent? We would drown in hopelessness, despair, and lostness. We can praise God today that He is not silent. Our God is speaking. By His Spirit, He speaks through His Word. The question is, are we, His people, listening? Are we obeying our own desires, or are we listening to His voice? Are we able to tell the difference between what we want and what God wants? Are we able to tell the difference between our own voice and His voice? As we walk with Him, and as He transforms us, He wants to teach us how to follow Him rather than our own desires. He wants to transform us so that we learn to obey His voice.

Transformed from Trusting Our Capabilities to Trusting His Faithfulness

ZECHARIAH 8:1-17

The fourth way that God transforms His people is by teaching us to trust His faithfulness rather than our own capabilities. In Zechariah 8 the prophet begins to tell the people exactly what God will do as He transforms their fasting into feasting. In the opening verse God reminds His people of His jealous love for Zion, that is, Jerusalem. These words point back to God's declaration of holy jealousy for His people and His city in 1:14. This jealousy is what moves God to righteous anger and judgment (8:2). In the verses that follow, God makes promises to His people, revealing His faithfulness to accomplish what they are incapable of doing on their own.

(1) He will return to Jerusalem (v. 3). The Lord's return to Jerusalem is a recurring theme in Zechariah (see 1:16; 2:10). This promise especially anticipates the personal reign of Christ on the throne of David during the millennial kingdom. Indeed, all of the promises made in the verses that follow will have their fullest completion in the future.

(2) He will bless the residents of the city with both long life and new life (vv. 4-5). When a community is filled with only senior adults, it is a sign that youth and vitality have left. However, I have been in countries with a very low average age and was surprised to be told it is actually a bad sign, showing that few people lived to old age. God told the people of

Jerusalem, "You will have both. You're going to have people who live long, but your city will be filled with children as well." God acknowledges that His intentions toward His people may seem "incredible to the remnant this people in those days." Yet, in the same verse He inquires, "Should it also seem incredible to Me?" The implied answer is clear. Nothing, including all of the blessings promised to His people here, is too hard for the Lord.

(3) He will bring the nations to Jerusalem and make them His own (vv. 7-8). God's plan has always been to bring nations far beyond Israel to Himself. By shining the light of His goodness and mercy through the Jewish nation, God desired the Gentiles to come to Him (Gen 12:3; Isa 49:6). Through the Messiah, Jesus Christ, everyone can come to the living God.

(4) He will bring peace, productivity, and power to His people (vv. 9-13). In verses 9-11 the Lord encouraged the people to "let their hands be strong" so that they could complete the building of the temple, fulfilling the "words that the prophets spoke when the foundations were laid," a reference to the prophetic ministries of Zechariah and Haggai. The work of rebuilding had been unproductive and dangerous in the early stages, but now God promises a different outcome for His people: this remnant of Israel will be blessed and will be a blessing to the nations.

(5) He will drive away the fear they have experienced (vv. 14-17). Because of the sin and rebellion of their ancestors, God had judged them and given the people reason to fear. But now, just as He had once resolved to treat them badly, He resolves to do good to the people of Judah. The verb *resolved,* used in both verses, derives its meaning from the idea of talking to oneself in a low voice in order to arrive at a conclusion. By the using this word, God was indicating that His decision to do good to Judah was deliberate, fixed, and settled. For that reason, He assures them, "Don't be afraid." Then in verses 16 and 17 the Lord warns the people against repeating the kind of evil and dishonesty that had gotten their forefathers into such trouble to begin with.

The prophetic words that fall between the question from the people of Bethel in 7:3 and God's promise to replace His people's fasting with feasting in 8:19 are a strong reminder that, in the midst of our brokenness, discouragement, and heartbreak, God can do a renewed work of transformation. He meets us in our broken places to transform us from serving ourselves to serving Him, from pursuing empty religion to pursuing His righteousness, from listening to our own desires to hearing

His voice, and from depending on our own capabilities to trusting His faithfulness.

Several years ago our family discovered a lemon tree in our backyard. One summer I was walking near the tree and I saw that its biggest limb had broken. In fact, the limb was broken at least three-quarters of the way through. When I saw that cracked limb, my immediate reaction was to go get my saw and cut the limb off. But then I noticed something: there were lemons all over that broken limb, and the leaves were still green. So I picked all the lemons off of the limb and filled a large basket with the fruit. A few weeks later, I went out again to the tree. The break had gotten even bigger, but there were more and more lemons on that one branch that was broken. So again, I harvested another basket full of lemons. All summer long, I kept getting fruit off that broken limb. It was, by far, the most productive limb on the tree. In fact, because the broken limb bowed itself to the ground, I was able to get even more fruit off of it than I could have if it was standing up straight.

That limb was a reminder from the Lord that just because we're broken doesn't mean we can't still bear fruit. Just because you've experienced times of devastation in your life and have gone through seasons of fasting, those times when life became lean and when you were sorrowful, it doesn't mean that God still can't use you for incredible things. The Lord can take those times of brokenness in our lives, those times of fasting, and transform them into seasons of feasting, as we trust in Him.

Reflect and Discuss

1. Why is it so easy for God's people to turn spiritual disciplines like fasting, prayer, or giving into self-serving activities?
2. Can you think of other places in Scripture where people did spiritual-looking things for their self-interest? What areas of commonality can you identify in those passages?
3. From your perspective, what is the difference between spiritual tradition and religious traditionalism? What values do you see in tradition? What dangers in traditionalism?
4. What are the tests that God gave the people of Judah in Zechariah 7:8-10? How well would you or the believers who are closest to you do on those tests?
5. What areas of practical righteousness do you need to strengthen and emphasize—personally and as a leader?

6. Can you identify some ways churches make it easy for people to pursue religion rather than righteousness? How can pastors and leaders create a church climate that is focused on gospel-centered living?
7. God wants His people to hear His voice. If it were possible for God to stop speaking, and He became absolutely silent at seven this morning, how long would it have taken you to find out? Why?
8. What other voices can we allow to substitute for God's voice in our lives? How can we tune our ears and heart to hear Him speak daily?
9. This passage culminates with the Lord returning to reign in Zion, to accomplish what He alone can do. What in your life can you attribute only to the faithfulness and power of God? What would it take for His work in your life to increase?
10. Understanding that both seasons can be spiritually profitable, is right now a season of fasting or feasting for you? What type of season does it need to be? How does God use times of brokenness in our lives to produce fruitfulness?

Your King is Coming

ZECHARIAH 9:1-17

Main Idea: King Jesus desires to reveal Himself to us.

I. **King Jesus Expresses God's Righteousness (9:1-8).**
II. **King Jesus Extends God's Deliverance (9:9-13).**
III. **King Jesus Exhibits God's Glory (9:14-17).**

Years ago, a Cheyenne hunter found an eagle egg. He was interested to see if the egg would hatch because it was all by itself. He placed that egg in the nest of a prairie chicken and waited. The eagle egg did, indeed, hatch. The mother prairie chicken noticed that this young bird in her nest looked different from all the other birds. He acted different. He sounded different. But, as far as she knew, the chick that hatched from this egg was hers.

Consequently, she raised it as a prairie chicken. The eagle learned to act like a prairie chicken. Like all of his adopted brothers and sisters, this eagle pecked around on the ground for his food. He thought prairie chicken thoughts. He did prairie chicken things. His mother told him, "You're a prairie chicken." So did his father. Everything about his environment validated his identity as a prairie chicken.

Then one day this eagle, who thought he was a prairie chicken, heard the call of a mighty eagle flying overhead. He looked up, mesmerized, as he watched this bird flying higher and higher, until it finally disappeared above the clouds.

He cried out, "What was that?"

One of his adopted brothers said, "Oh, that's an eagle."

The prairie chicken, who really was an eagle, then said to himself, "Man, I wish I could fly like that." And then, with a sigh, he shook his head and went back to pecking at the ground and scratching for his food.

Too many people mistakenly believe that they are really something significantly less than what they are. So many people sell themselves short and fail to soar the way God intends them to soar.

For instance, a 2006 survey by the Pew Research Center asked 18 to 25 year olds their generation's most important goals in life.

- 81 percent said their goal was to be rich.
- 51 percent aspired to be famous.
- 30 percent wanted to help people who need help.
- 22 percent wanted to be leaders in their community.
- 10 percent desired to become more spiritual. (Pew Research, "How Young People," 12)

But a life of money and fame, and even a life of service or a so-called "spiritual" life, is settling for something less than God's best if our lives are not fixed on Jesus Christ.

Zechariah 9 begins a new section. Chapters 9–14 differ from the first eight chapters in that no reference is made to the rebuilding of the temple, no visions are given to the prophet, and individuals such as Zerubbabel and Joshua, who were so prominent in the earlier chapters, are not mentioned at all. Instead, the last portion of Zechariah's prophecy focuses on the coming of the Messiah.

Zechariah's prophecies about King Jesus and both His first and second comings reveal wonderful aspects of who Jesus is and what He can accomplish through His people. Whether we are young or old, the Lord Jesus desires to work in us to reveal Himself. Perhaps you have asked the question, what does Jesus want to do through me? You will find answers in our text, which reveals three aspects of the character of Christ.

King Jesus Expresses God's Righteousness

ZECHARIAH 9:1-8

Zechariah 9:1 begins by identifying the forthcoming message as "An Oracle." The Hebrew term *massa'*, repeated in Zechariah 12:1, comes from a word with two meanings: "to bear" and "to lift up" (Lindsey, "Zechariah, 1562). Accordingly, some translations take *massa'* to mean a burden or weighty judgment borne by the prophet. Others—following the meaning "to lift up"—use the term *oracle* to indicate a message that was lifted up by the prophet. Zechariah concludes with two oracles, the first found in chapters 9–11 and the second in chapters 12–14.

In the beginning of his first oracle Zechariah prophesies against Israel's enemies who have acted unrighteously in God's sight. Many conservative interpreters view Zechariah 9:1-8 as predictive prophecy of Alexander the Great's conquests in the areas to the north and east of Judah. After defeating the Persians at the Battle of Issus in 333 BC, Alexander was used as a tool in God's hand to bring defeat to the enemies of Judah. Though he did so unintentionally, Alexander was an instrument of God's righteous judgment in preparation for the coming of Zion's messianic King.

First, Zechariah's oracle addresses "the land of Hadrach," a land not mentioned anywhere else in the OT. The location of Hadrach, known only by its mention in an Assyrian text, appears to have been situated to the north of all of the other places Zechariah names (Klein, *Zechariah*, 260). In the rest of the verse Zechariah explains why the word of the Lord is against Hadrach, along with Damascus, the capital city of Syria: "For the eyes of men and all the tribes of Israel are on the LORD." By judging these places, God would show His glory and righteousness to His people. He also mentions "Hamath," bordering Syria in the northern part of the promised land, along with "Tyre" and "Sidon" on the Phoenician coasts of the Mediterranean, as recipients of the Lord's judgment.

In Zechariah 9:3-4 the prophet turns his attention to Tyre specifically. Personifying the city as a woman, he speaks of her military defenses. Tyre's fortifications included a breakwater that was 2,460 feet long and 27 feet thick (Kaiser, *Micah*, 381). With its elaborate fortifications, the city of Tyre seemed indomitable. He also uses similes to describe Tyre's wealth. From a human standpoint, Tyre had good reason to boast about her invulnerability. Failed attacks from Tyre's enemies in the past had proven the city's strength. Tyre had withstood a five-year siege by the Assyrians under Shalmaneser V in 722 BC and a 13-year siege by the Babylonians under Nebuchadnezzar in 527 BC.

In spite of Tyre's strength and prosperity, God promised to "impoverish her and cast her wealth into the sea." Moreover, the city itself would be burned. History shows that Alexander captured Tyre and conquered it in 332 BC. He won his victory by taking the ruins from the old city on the mainland and piling them up in the Mediterranean to build a causeway out to the island city. Alexander then blockaded Tyre for seven months until he was victorious. Diodorus Siculus records that he massacred between 6,000 and 8,000 of Tyre's men, as well as crucifying 2,000 and selling between 13,000 and 30,000 people into slavery. The city's weapons were thrown into the sea, and the remainder of the city was set on fire (Hindson and Kroll, *KJV Bible Commentary*, 1823–24).

Zechariah 9:5-8 describes the repercussions that the fall of Tyre brought to the neighboring Philistine cities farther south along the Mediterranean coast. Four of five major Philistine cities are mentioned here: Ashkelon, Gaza, Ekron, and Ashdod. Only Gath is left unnamed, presumably because the city had already deteriorated by this time. As they were attacked and conquered, God promised that the Philistine cities would lose hope and become uninhabited. In the end, the Lord would "destroy the pride of the Philistines," as Alexander moved southward.

Even this devastating prophecy of judgment, however, contains promises of grace for God's enemies and protection for God's people. The "blood" in verse 7 is a reference to the Philistine practice of eating meat that had not been drained of its blood, while the "detestable things" suggest not only polluted and ceremonially unclean foods they would have eaten, but also other idolatrous practices. The Lord prohibited both drinking blood and eating unclean animals (see Gen 9:4; Lev 11:2-47; Deut 14:3-21). With this promise, then, God was graciously pledging to change the lifestyles of pagan people to reflect His righteousness. Even more astonishing than changing the lifestyle of the Philistines, the Lord actually promises to transform their identity, so that He would treat these traditional enemies in the promised land as he would the people of Judah, and the inhabitants of Ekron like the Jebusites (v. 7), the original people of Jerusalem itself (2 Sam 5:6-10).

Verse 8 contains good news for Jerusalem. God would encamp around His "house," a use of metonymy indicating not only the temple itself, but the entire region surrounding Jerusalem. According to the ancient Jewish historian Josephus, after Alexander's siege of Gaza he started for Jerusalem. Frightened, the high priest ordered the Jews to offer sacrifices to God and ask for deliverance. That night, God spoke to the high priest in his sleep and told him to decorate the city with wreaths and to have the people of Jerusalem wear white garments, while the priests dressed in their holy robes to welcome Alexander. When Alexander approached the city, he was so impressed by the sight that he prostrated himself and offered sacrifices to the Lord, sparing the city (Josephus, *Antiquities*, XI, viii.3–5).

In addition to protecting Jerusalem, verse 8 concludes with God's promise to guard the city completely from attack. With this verse the prophet seems to take a great leap forward in time. While the immediate meaning of this verse can be seen as a promise that Judah would not be carried away into captivity as before, this prophecy finds its ultimate fulfillment in the future, when, during the millennial reign of Christ, by His own presence in the city He will safeguard Jerusalem from any kind of threat.

While the return of Christ will bring about God's perfect righteousness on the earth, right now we live in an unrighteous, unjust world. As we get closer to the time that Jesus Christ returns, the world is not going to become better and better. Instead, our world will become increasingly more sinful. God has called His people to stand for His righteousness. Romans 12:21 tells us, "Do not be conquered by evil, but conquer evil with good." Expressing God's righteousness requires looking at ourselves and asking, Am I right with God? Am I who He has called me to be? What can I do where I am to work for His justice and righteousness?

Walking home from class, a college student saw a little girl standing on a street corner, begging. The little girl's clothes were paper thin and dirty. Her hair was matted and unclean, her cheeks red from the cold. The student dropped a few coins into the little girl's cup and smiled slightly at her. As this college student walked on, she began to feel guilty, thinking, "How can I go back to my warm room, where I've got plenty of money, plenty of food, and plenty of clothes to keep me warm, while this little girl is out on the street, begging, cold, and shivering?" The young woman began to feel angry at God. She prayed a sort of protest prayer, asking, "Lord, how can You let things like this happen? Why don't You do something, God, to help this little girl?" And then, deep in her heart, she heard God answer: "I did do something. I created you, and I sent you to that girl."

Expressing God's righteousness requires a deep commitment to see that God's justice is done. It means being willing to risk and to work in order to make things right. We all know that there are big, world-scale problems when it comes to righteousness and justice. We could list things like world hunger, the mistreatment of the poor, and worldwide human trafficking. God is calling out a generation of people, in Jesus' name, to say, "We will stand for righteousness and justice world-wide." But smaller scale opportunities to stand for righteousness are no less significant, whether that involves ministering God's grace during a friend's addiction, praying faithfully for a marriage going through crisis, or sharing the gospel with someone who needs Christ. Jesus calls us to step into those situations and express His justice and righteousness.

King Jesus Extends God's Deliverance

ZECHARIAH 9:9-13

Verses 1-8 of this chapter prepare for the arrival of Israel's coming King. In verses 9-13 the King enters the city of Jerusalem and delivers His people. Verse 9 begins with God addressing the people of the city, personified as "Daughter Zion" and "Daughter Jerusalem." God gives the people of Jerusalem three commands: "Rejoice greatly," "Shout in triumph," and "Look." At the coming of King Jesus, God is telling His people, "I want you to rejoice, I want you to shout out loud, and I want you to pay careful attention to the One who is coming."

The first thing God calls our attention to about Jesus is His righteousness (v. 9). The Hebrew word *tsaddiq* speaks of the Lord's personal righteousness, indicating that He holds within Himself moral uprightness, spiritual perfection, and legal righteousness. He alone fulfills the righteous standard of God's law, something no one else on earth ever has done. The word *righteous* also refers to the justice of Christ. He upholds what is right.

Next, God calls attention to the Messiah's deliverance. Verse 9 continues by saying that King Jesus is "victorious." Walter Kaiser notes that the word here is the Hebrew term for "to save" in the passive form, literally meaning that the Messiah is "endowed with salvation" (*Micah*, 386). By saying that the Messiah is entrusted with salvation, the meaning can either be that the Messiah has experienced victory or that He brings deliverance to others.

The Messiah is further described as "humble," an idea that is emphasized by His entrance into the city "riding on a donkey, on a colt, the foal of a donkey." In the ancient Near East a king coming in peace would ride a donkey rather than a warhorse. In contrast to the pride and destruction of Alexander the Great, Israel's King comes in humility and gentleness, bringing salvation and peace. Zechariah 9:9 is one of the most significant messianic passages in Scripture. The gospel writers quote this verse, applying it to Jesus's triumphal entry into Jerusalem on the Sunday before His crucifixion and resurrection (Matt 21:5; John 12:15).

While verse 9 concerns the first advent of the Messiah, the verses that follow concern His second coming. When Jesus Christ comes again, He will abolish warfare during His reign on earth, removing weapons of war (v. 10). Zechariah's prophecy of peace also mentions both Jerusalem and Ephraim, both in verses 10 and 13, signifying a restoration and reunion of the southern and northern kingdoms of Israel during Messiah's reign. But even beyond the borders of Israel, Christ will "proclaim peace to the nations" through His work of deliverance .

In verses 11-13 God promises that the Messiah, King Jesus, will save and deliver the people of Jerusalem from those that would harm them.

Verse 11 contains one of the most powerful word pictures of His deliverance. The blood covenant not only pointed back to the Abrahamic and Mosaic covenants, both confirmed with sacrifices (Gen 15:8-21; Exod 24:8), but also pointed forward to the new covenant mediated by the blood of Jesus (Heb 12:24). Because of the price paid by His blood, Jesus releases prisoners from the "waterless cistern," an empty pit used as a dungeon.

Years ago I heard something called the "Parable of the Pit." The parable talks about a man who suddenly falls into a deep pit. It's too deep for him to jump out of. The walls of the pit are impossible to climb, and so he's stuck there. The question is, How will he get out of the pit?

People begin to pass by.

A self-righteous person passes by, looks down at the man, and says, "Only bad people fall in pits. You must be a really bad person to fall into a pit like that." And the man's still in his pit.

A philosopher passes by and says, "You're not really in that pit; you just think you are." The man's still in the pit.

A politician passes by and says, "I've got a new program that I'm proposing in Congress, and it's going to eliminate pitfalls just like yours." And the man's still in the pit.

A county inspector passes by and says, "Do you have a permit for that pit?" And the man's still in the pit.

A pessimist passes by and says, "You're never going to get out of that pit. And it looks like it's going to start raining." And the man's still in the pit.

An optimist passes by and says, "So you fell in a pit. Make the most out of it. Maybe you could decorate it." And the man's still in the pit.

An engineer passes by and says, "The pit you are in is 20 feet deep, 15 feet wide, and 25 feet long." And the man's still in the pit.

A preacher passes by and says, "I want you to notice three things about that pit. It's a deep pit. It's a dark pit. It's a dirty pit." And the man's still in the pit.

A psychologist passes by and says, "Maybe your mother pushed you into that pit. And how does being in that pit make you feel?" And the man's still in the pit.

A self-pitying person passes by and says, "You think you're in a pit? You ought to see my pit!" And the man's still in the pit.

But then Jesus sees the man in the pit, and He takes him by the hand and lifts him out. He extends God's deliverance.

Jesus gives the gifts of peace and salvation. When we need rescuing, salvation, and deliverance, we look up from the pit of our sin and we wonder: "Does someone love me? Does someone see me? Is someone strong enough to get me out of here?" The gospel of Jesus Christ answers each of those questions with a loud and audacious, Yes! Jesus loves you. Jesus sees you. Jesus is strong enough. We don't have the ability, on our own, to rescue ourselves or anybody else from a spiritual pit. But through His blood shed on the cross, Jesus has already done everything that needs to be done to lift us out of that pit. Simply sharing the gospel of Jesus with those around us extends His deliverance to others.

King Jesus Exhibits God's Glory

ZECHARIAH 9:14-17

The final section of this chapter describes the Messiah's triumph on behalf of His people, as well as His shepherdly care for them. In these verses Zechariah uses four images to describe the glory of God revealed in the Messiah. The first image is that of a thunderstorm (vv. 14-15). The Lord appears above His people, fighting on their behalf from heaven. Lightning is portrayed as the Lord's arrows. The blasting thunder is His trumpet. He marches in a furious storm to defend Israel. The Hebrew word for "defend" in verse 15 is related to the word for a shield. As a result of the victory the Lord will win for them, the armies of God's people will "consume and conquer" their enemies and become drunk on their blood—a gruesome image, but one that nonetheless graphically describes total victory for the people of Israel. The second image is of a flock of sheep (v. 16). God will "save them" or deliver them. The underlying idea is bringing them to a place of safety, with wide pasturelands to protect the flock. The third image is of a crown (v. 16). His people will be like jewels in the crown, shining on His land. The final image is agricultural, with the young men nourished by grain and the young women by new wine (v. 17). This is a picture of the physical health and wellbeing of the Lord's people that the Messiah will bring.

In each image an aspect of God's glory is revealed in the coming Christ. He is glorified in His conquering power, in His care for His flock, in the delight and treasure He finds in His people, and in the strength and beauty He bestows to those who follow Him. To make a difference for Christ, God calls His people to reflect His glory. He tells us, "You were bought at a price. Therefore glorify God in your body" (1 Cor 6:20).

Antonio Stradivari set up his workshop in a small Italian town, in Cremona, in the 1600s. You've probably heard of the Stradivarius violin, and you know they're very expensive, very rare instruments. But if you're like me, you don't know why they're so expensive, why they're so rare. Here's why: During the time that Stradivari began making his violins, the best violins made in the world were made by the Amati family. The Amati violins were made for performances in small places, performances in drawing rooms and in courts. But music was changing. It was moving from the small room to the concert hall. The violin had to be loud enough and clear enough to be heard clearly to the back reaches of the room.

Stradivari adjusted to those changes, and that's why he became so great. He chose bigger and better pieces of maple. He experimented with stronger varnishes. He arched the belly of the violin differently to give it a distinctive and loud and brilliant sound, unlike any before their time.

When Stradivari died in 1737, they found a particular violin in his studio. This violin had never been played. And they gave the violin the name *the Messiah.* It has an incredible tiger-striped pattern on its back, and it's said to be the perfect violin. In form and finish and everything about it, it's flawless. It's on display in a museum in Oxford, England, and it's the only instrument in that museum to have its own showcase.

But the Messiah Violin has never, ever, in nearly 300 years, been played. Wait a minute. The perfect violin? Never played? Is that a perfect violin? Not according to Ivry Gitlis. He plays his Stradivarius every day.

Your life, your salvation, is a gift from the Messiah, Jesus Christ. And He wants you to take the life He has given you and play it for His glory. He wants you to say, "Lord, I'm not going to put my life on the shelf. I'm not going to hide myself away. I'm going to put myself in the middle of whatever You have for me, so that You can use me for Your glory."

Reflect and Discuss

1. How does understanding Christ's character shape and transform our character as Christ-followers?
2. Many observers note that the world seems to becoming more and more wicked. Do you agree or disagree? What biblical passages confirm your answer? If wickedness is increasing, how is it expressing itself in our culture? Why?
3. How does being right with God through Christ prepare you to stand for His righteousness?

4. As a follower of Christ, what can you do where you are to make a difference for His justice?
5. What are some "big picture" opportunities to express God's righteousness? What are some "small scale" opportunities? How are both kinds of opportunities important?
6. Our passage pictures sinners as prisoners, trapped in a pit. What kinds of pits do people who need the Lord's deliverance fall into?
7. What alternatives do "pit-dwellers" choose instead of receiving God's deliverance?
8. Who in your life needs to hear the gospel message? What have you done recently to extend God's promise of deliverance to them?
9. Consider the four images in Zechariah 9:14-17 that describe God's glory revealed in Christ. Why has Jesus chosen to reveal His conquering power in your life? How has He provided a shepherd's care for you? In what ways does His word reveal that you are His treasure and delight? When has He given you spiritual strength and nourishment?
10. Because Jesus Christ is a glorious king, how can you reflect His glory in your relationships, your habits, your attitudes, your service, and your values?

Following the Right Shepherd

ZECHARIAH 10:1–11:17

Main Idea: Where God's people wind up depends on whom we follow.

I. The Work of the Faithful Shepherd (10:1-12)
II. The Wailing of the Fallen Shepherds (11:1-3)
III. The Wisdom of the Forsaken Shepherd (11:4-14)
IV. The Worthlessness of the False Shepherd (11:15-17)

I was in a high school classroom in Costa Rica on a mission trip a few years ago. Our group leader, Guillermo, had all the students hold hands to form a circle. In Spanish he told them, "No matter what, don't let go of each other's hands! Now, follow me." Guillermo took the hands of two of the students and quickly started weaving his way through the room. He would step over or go under the joined hands of different pairs of kids, as the teenagers dutifully followed behind him and each other, struggling to keep their hands together. It took him less than a minute to get the whole group tangled into one big mess. Then Guillermo released the hands of the students on either side of him, joined their hands to each another, and said, "Now, without letting go of each other's hands, make a circle again." For the next four or five minutes, the students worked together, retracing their steps, shouting out, "Go under us," or "Step over our hands here," until they successfully made their way back to a circle.

My friend Guillermo's purpose in the exercise had mainly been to teach the students the value of teamwork, but I walked away with a few other lessons:

- It's a lot easier to get tangled than it is to get untangled.
- Often, the person who gets you into the tangled mess leaves you to untangle things by yourself.
- And the biggest lesson of all: *Where* and *how* you wind up depends on *whom* you follow.

When Scripture talks about whom we're following, where we're going, and how they are leading us, the Bible often uses the image of sheep and a shepherd. It's a very common image in Scripture.

The first shepherd we meet in the Bible is also the first man who died because of his faith in God. His name was Abel, the second son born to Adam and Eve (Gen 4:4). After that, Abraham, the father of faith, was a shepherd (Gen 12:16). His grandson, Jacob, whose name later became Israel, was also a shepherd (Gen 30:31). Moses, the great lawgiver and the leader of Israel, worked for a season of his long life as a shepherd (Exod 3:1). David shepherded the sheep in the field before he became king and shepherd over Israel (1 Sam 16:18). The most beloved psalm begins with the words "the Lord is my shepherd" (Ps 23:1). It's no surprise, then, that when Jesus described Himself, He described Himself as the good shepherd who "lays down His life for the sheep" (John 10:11).

Throughout the Bible, both in the Old and New Testaments, the best-known passages of Scripture that use the image of the shepherd describe the shepherd in a positive way. But there are a number of places where the Bible talks about shepherds from a negative context, especially in the prophets. Men of God like Isaiah, Jeremiah, and Ezekiel railed against some of the shepherds of Israel—ungodly leaders, including wicked kings, corrupt priests, and even other prophets—because they were leading God's people in the wrong direction.

Zechariah 10–11 warns against following the wrong kind of shepherd and calls us to follow the right kind of shepherd. Zechariah 10:3 is pivotal in these chapters:

> *My anger burns against the shepherds, so I will punish the leaders. For the Lord of Hosts has tended His flock, the house of Judah; He will make them like His majestic steed in battle.*

Notice that the shepherds are equated with leaders. God is angry with these leaders and promises to punish them because He cares for His flock, the people of Judah.

Where God's people wind up depends on the type of leader or shepherd they follow. Zechariah 10–11 presents four pieces of evidence to prove this central truth.

The Work of the Faithful Shepherd

ZECHARIAH 10:1-12

Verse 1 of this chapter is transitional, bridging from the promise of health and welfare for God's people at the end of chapter 9. The encouragement from Zechariah to ask the Lord for rain can be seen as a rebuke to those in Judah who looked for Baal to provide favorable weather for the land. After reminding the people that it is the Lord who "makes the rain clouds" and provides "showers of rain and crops in the fields for everyone," the prophet begins contrasting the work of the Messiah as Israel's faithful shepherd and the misleading work of false shepherds who follow idols.

"The idols speak falsehood," verse 2 declares. "Falsehood" is the Hebrew *ʾawen,* which denotes vain assurances and comfort that were empty and meaningless. The idols themselves were mute and impotent. Jeremiah had written, "Like scarecrows in a cucumber patch, their idols cannot speak. They must be carried because they cannot walk" (Jer 10:5). However, the "diviners," soothsayers who served the idols by seeking omens and signs, spoke lies on their behalf. These diviners were deceiving Israel, the very people they were entrusted to care for and guide. Instead of speaking truth from God, they were relating "empty dreams" that led to "empty comfort." As a result the people were led astray, left to "wander like sheep" and to "suffer affliction," experiencing catastrophe after catastrophe because there was no faithful shepherd for them to follow.

In verse 3, following His declaration of anger at the false shepherds—also identified as "leaders," literally "he-goats," a derogatory term (Hebrew *ʿattud*)—the Lord expresses His commitment to tend His flock and to make them like His majestic horse in battle. Though the shift from sheep imagery to horse imagery may seem inconsistent, the constant factor here is the Lord's care. A shepherd watches over His sheep, as a warrior gives attention to his horse, as the Lord gives attention and care to the house of Judah. In the subsequent verses the Lord promises to provide personal care and leadership for His people through the Messiah.

In verses 4 and 5 God uses three images to describe the work of the Messiah: "cornerstone," "tent peg," and "battle bow." A cornerstone was a block placed in the intersection of two walls to establish the proper location and correct orientation of the whole building. As the cornerstone, the Messiah is faithful and reliable. Psalm 118:22 famously uses the same image to describe Christ's rejection by men but validation by God: "The stone that the builders rejected has become the cornerstone." The "tent peg" can be seen as a double image, referring both to a peg in a wall that could support frequently used items in the house (as in Isa 22:23-24), or pegs in the ground that secure a tent and support it so that it can accommodate a large family (as in Isa 54:2). In either case a tent peg created stability for a home (Stuhlmueller, *Rebuilding*, 130). The image of the "battle bow" depicts the Lord's fearlessness and conquering power. As a result of the Messiah's strength and stability, verse 5 promises that He will cause His people to fight "like warriors in battle." Because the Messiah will be present to empower them, God's people "will put horsemen to shame" and triumph over their enemies.

Zechariah 10:6-12 enumerates what God will do in Israel under the faithful leadership of the Messiah. There are 21 predictive statements in these verses, a number of which focus on the Lord's personal actions on behalf of His people. For example, the declaration, "I will strengthen the house of Judah and deliver the house of Joseph" not only assures God's power to His people, but also reemphasizes God's intention to unite the southern kingdom of Judah with the northern kingdom, represented by "the house of Joseph." The phrase "I will restore them because I have compassion on them" emphasizes God's care and provision for His flock. "I will answer them" signifies His nearness to His people and responsiveness to their needs, resulting in their strength in battle and renewed joy (v. 7).

There is prominent shepherd imagery in the promise "I will whistle and gather them because I have redeemed them." The whistle was a sharp, clear signal shepherds would use in calling sheep. Even though God's people were scattered in distant places, they would return as He called (v. 9). "I will bring them back from the land of Egypt and gather them from Assyria" uses language that may have been taken from Hosea 8:13 and 11:5, where exile to Syria was spoken of metaphorically as a return to bondage in Egypt. God's promises not only mention the places from which the Lord would deliver His people, but also the places to which He would bring them: "I will bring them to the land of Gilead and to Lebanon." Even in the promised land, the people would be so numerous that there would not be enough room for them (v. 10). After judging and disarming the powers that had captured His people, and after overcoming any obstacle that would have hindered them from returning (v. 11), the Lord promised, "I will strengthen them in Yahweh," empowering them to "march in His name."

Zechariah 10 underscores the truth that the work of the Messiah, God's faithful shepherd, is to deliver, strengthen, save, and care for God's people. His faithfulness was demonstrated in bringing back Judah from the exile. However, it is significant that this passage, written after the exile, is clearly oriented to the future. James Montgomery Boice notes,

> This passage refers to a future regathering—not the regathering of the people from Babylon following the exile. That was already history at the time of the writing of this chapter. The prophecy must concern a yet future day. The regathering may have begun with the reestablishing of the modern state of Israel. This will be a great regathering in which the scattered flock of the Messiah is returned to its own land and to great material and spiritual blessing. (*Minor Prophets*, 546)

The Wailing of Fallen Shepherds

ZECHARIAH 11:1-3

Zechariah 11:1-3 describes what happens as the city of Jerusalem is utterly destroyed. These verses are predictive prophecy, foretelling the results of the people of Israel rejecting the Messiah. There is strong reason to think that this is prophecy of what happened in AD 70, as the Roman army, under the leadership of General Titus, came into Jerusalem and completely leveled that city. Titus's armies even tore down the temple, until one stone was not left standing on top of the other.

Verses 1 and 2 talk about three different types of trees: the cedar, the cypress, and the oak. In the Old Testament, trees were often used to stand for leaders, such as kings and others among God's people. Zechariah laments, "The glorious trees are destroyed." This means that Israel's leaders are falling. The leaders are being taken down, and they are crying out before God because of their destruction.

Notice the words of verse 3. The word *wail* denotes a distress signal. It's a howl. It's a guttural sound of deep mourning because of despair. A wail was not a sound that was made voluntarily. Instead, it was an involuntary response to some great loss or terror. The shepherds are wailing because their glory has been ruined.

That word *glory* in verse 3 is a Hebrew word that literally means "cloak" or "coat" or "garment." It was used in Jonah 3:6 to describe the regal raiment of a king, symbolizing his dignity and power. These shepherds—human leaders who had depended on their own strength, their own wisdom, their own resources, their own cleverness, and their own ingenuity, at the expense of humbly following the leadership of the Lord, the true Shepherd of Israel—found their glory and their dignity ruined by defeat and destruction.

As we think about the wailing of these fallen shepherds at the destruction of Jerusalem, we see this: human leaders always fall short. Human leaders always—not sometimes, but always—fall short! That is true for political leaders, spiritual leaders, family leaders, academic leaders, business leaders—whatever category of leader you want to name. Human leaders will always fall short.

If we place faith and trust totally in a person, if we look to a person and say, "I'm placing my hopes and my dreams in you," we will be disappointed. Even at their very best, human shepherds fall short of the glory of God (Rom 3:23).

Human shepherds always fall short. And that's why they are wailing in this passage: because their glory has been ruined. The first three verses of this chapter point to our need for a greater shepherd, a shepherd not tainted with sin and selfishness, a shepherd who far surpasses the shortcomings of human shepherds, a shepherd like our Lord Jesus.

The Wisdom of the Forsaken Shepherd

ZECHARIAH 11:4-14

Beginning in verse 4 of the text, God calls the prophet Zechariah to be "shepherd of the flock intended for slaughter." In essence, God is commanding Zechariah to become a living picture of the coming Messiah, Jesus Christ. Apart from the life of the Lord Jesus, it is nearly impossible to interpret Zechariah 11:4-14. If we do not understand that this passage is pointing to Jesus, it makes no sense at all. But in light of Jesus, God's wise but forsaken Shepherd, we can understand this passage.

Notice in verse 7 how Zechariah began to shepherd this flock. He says that he "took two staffs." The shepherd's staff was used to guide the sheep, sometimes to correct the sheep, sometimes to rescue the sheep. Zechariah had two staffs. One staff he called "Favor." That means God's blessing, joy, and promise to His people. The other staff he called "Union." That speaks, first of all, of the union between God and His people, but also of the union of God's people together, bringing Israel and Judah together under one shepherd.

Zechariah says that he led God's people in such a way that he supplanted and replaced all of their other shepherds very quickly (v. 8). This phrase is very hard to interpret and to identify. Who are these "three shepherds"? Historically, more than 40 different interpretations have been offered, but the one of the oldest interpretations seems to be best: These three shepherds are the three classes of leader that God gave to Israel (Mitchell, *Haggai and Zechariah*, 306–7). He gave them kings, He gave them priests, and He gave them prophets. In every regard, the kings and the priests and the prophets of Israel failed. The kings of Israel turned away from the living God and started following after idols. The priests of Israel stopped being holy men of God and started abusing the people. The prophets of Israel stopped being God's spokesmen and started saying things just to please the people and the kings.

As a result, in a very short time the Messiah destroyed and replaced all of those inadequate shepherds. He came and ruled over God's people with favor and with union. He replaced all of the inadequate shepherds that had come before Him because He is the only wise and true shepherd, God's Messiah. As we continue in verse 8, we can see how God's people responded to this wise shepherd. Largely, the flock rejected Him: "I became impatient with them, and they also detested me." Jesus came to rule over God's people with wisdom, but they rejected the Messiah as their Shepherd.

As we think about Israel's rejection of Christ, it brings to mind the question, Why do people reject Jesus? Some people reject Jesus because they don't want to admit that He is God. Some refuse to give up control of their lives to Him. Others reject Him because they think they've heard everything about Him and they find Him to be outdated and outmoded. They want someone or something they feel is more sophisticated and intellectually challenging. Some reject Jesus because they're embarrassed to follow Him in a culture that increasingly mocks and ridicules His name. Still others don't want to follow Jesus as their Shepherd because it would mess up their religion and the pride they have in it. When Jesus walked on this earth, the people of Israel used all of those reasons to reject Him.

What did the Shepherd do when His sheep rejected Him? The wise Shepherd, though rejected and forsaken, is no pushover. When His people rejected Him and detested Him, He said He would not be their shepherd. He took the staff called "Favor" and broke it, and later did the same thing with the staff called "Union." He left them without a good and wise shepherd.

After resigning as a shepherd over his flock, Zechariah asked for his wages, which leads to one of the most striking messianic prophecies in Scripture. Zechariah11:12 was written hundreds of years before Jesus was born, but prophesies exactly how He would be rejected, in great detail: "Then I said to them, 'If it seems right to you, give me my wages; but if not, keep them.' So they weighed my wages, 30 pieces of silver." In Exodus 21:32 the same amount of silver was what someone paid for a slave who had been injured to the point that he was no longer able to work. An able-bodied slave would receive twice that amount of money. So basically, the people said to their shepherd, who had ruled over them and guided them with such wisdom and love, "You are worthless to us. We will only pay as much as we would pay an injured slave." In the life of our Lord Jesus this prophecy was fulfilled when Judas Iscariot betrayed his Lord and Master for the same amount: 30 pieces of silver.

Christ came as God's great, wise shepherd, and yet, Jesus was forsaken (John 1:11). Here's the truth we see illustrated in these verses: We must not reject Jesus, because He's the Shepherd we need the most. If we reject Jesus, He will ultimately reject us (Matt 23:37-38). Rejecting Jesus leaves us with the only alternative: following shepherds who will hurt us. When we refuse to follow the Lord as our Shepherd, we will inevitably follow someone or something that will lead us to destruction.

The Worthlessness of the False Shepherd

ZECHARIAH 11:15-17

In the final portion of this chapter God calls Zechariah to do something very unusual. Earlier he had portrayed a good shepherd, but now he is asked to portray a foolish, evil, and worthless shepherd. The word *foolish* in verse 15 indicates someone who is morally deficient and corrupt. Verse 16 shows that this kind of shepherd will not care for the sheep, will not seek them when they wander away or heal them when they are hurt. Instead, his only purpose will be to devour and destroy them totally, even to the point of tearing off their hooves.

The prophet's actions are designed to show that, despite having God's Messiah, Israel will turn to false shepherds. Jesus spoke of this when He said, "I have come in My Father's name, yet you don't accept

Me. If someone else comes in his own name, you will accept him" (John 5:43). These false shepherds would come to abuse the people of Israel. They would take advantage of them and harm them mercilessly. Many conservative interpreters (e.g., Boice, *Minor Prophets*, 542; Wiersbe, *Be Heroic*, 141) say that the ultimate expression of the foolish shepherd is the Antichrist of the end times, who will deceive and abuse not only Israel but the entire world (Rev 13:7). Verse 17 ends with a word of condemnation for this false shepherd. He would be struck in his arm, representing his strength, and his eye, representing his intelligence. Ultimately, the true Shepherd will triumph over the false (Rev 19:19-20).

A group of tourists was visiting Israel. They were on their bus, and their tour guide had his microphone in hand, describing sight after sight. As they were coming out of the city of Jerusalem, going into the Judean hills, he said, "When we get into these hillsides, you'll see Bedouin shepherds. They tend to their sheep in much the same way that shepherds did during the time of Jesus. They still wear the same type of clothing, and still do the same type of things that the shepherds did hundreds and hundreds of years ago."

The tour guide continued, "You'll notice that the Bedouin shepherds always lead their sheep. They stand out in front and call them, or they lead them with their rod and staff." Then he said, "But the shepherds will never get behind the sheep and drive them."

When the bus reached the hill country, the tourists saw a flock of sheep. They saw a man, dressed in Bedouin clothing, with the sheep. He had a whip in one hand and a stick in the other. He was beating those sheep and driving them.

One of the guys in the back of the bus asked the question that everybody on the bus was thinking: "We thought you said that the shepherd always led his sheep. Why is that shepherd driving the sheep?"

The guide said, "Ah, my friend, that is not the shepherd; that is the butcher!"

Where and how you wind up depend on whom you follow. False shepherds always wind up being butchers. They always drive God's people to destruction. Jesus, the Good Shepherd, leads us to life.

Reflect and Discuss

1. Why do you believe God often chooses to use shepherd imagery to describe Himself and His leaders?
2. Where are other places in Scripture that employ similar shepherd imagery? How would you construct a summary from Scripture of the spiritual shepherd's role and importance?
3. How has the Lord proven to be a faithful shepherd to Israel in its history? How does God promise to lead and provide faithfully for Israel in the future?
4. What implications does God's provision for Israel have for believers in the church today?
5. What dangers do human leaders face when we begin depending on our own wisdom or resources rather than God's?
6. Where do you believe you are most vulnerable as a leader?
7. How can a leader ensure that he or she is following the leadership of the true Shepherd?
8. What factors cause people to reject Jesus as their shepherd and leader?
9. How does this rejection of Christ express itself in the unsaved world? How can rejection of His leadership express itself in the church?
10. While the ultimate "false shepherd" is the coming Antichrist, there are also false leaders and false systems that people follow today. What is the appeal of these false shepherds? How can we warn people who are led by false shepherds?

There Is a Fountain

ZECHARIAH 12:1–13:1

Main Idea: What Jesus will do at His second coming reveals who He is right now.

I. **His Sovereign Position: He Created (12:1).**
II. **His Surpassing Power: He Conquers (12:2-9).**
III. **His Saving Purpose: He Cleanses (12:10–13:1).**

A preteen boy was standing on a sidewalk in a large city, waiting at a corner bus stop one evening around 6 o'clock. A man who worked in a store on that corner came out and said, "Hey, kid, you won't catch a bus here. The last one came at 5:30."

The boy said, "No, the bus will come." The man shrugged his shoulders and left the boy standing there waiting. 6:15 passed, then 6:30.

Again the man came out, a little irritated, "Son, I'm telling you, the bus isn't going to come. You've missed it. You need to go to another stop."

"I'm sure the bus is coming," the boy said. The man turned back to the store, muttering under his breath that the boy could stay out there all night for all he cared.

As the city got darker at 6:45 and 7:00 and the boy kept standing there at the bus stop, the man in the shop couldn't help coming out another time.

"Look, that bus is not coming," he said. "It's dangerous around here at night. You need to get home. There's a stop 8 blocks up from here. That bus runs until 7:30. If you run, you can make it."

The boy shook his head. "No. I need to stay here. My bus is going to come any minute."

By now, the man was almost exasperated. "Kid, I'm here every night. The last bus is always at 5:30. You've got to believe me when I say that last bus isn't . . ."

Just then, the man saw the boy smile, looking slightly past him. Then he heard the hiss of hydraulic brakes and smelled the diesel fuel as a bus pulled up beside them and opened the door right where the boy stood, The boy hopped on the bus as the man stood there amazed.

"How did you know the bus would come?" the man said.

"That's easy, mister," said the boy. "The bus driver is my dad."

The Bible promises that Jesus Christ is coming. His second coming is mentioned repeatedly in the OT. In fact, there are more prophecies about the second coming of Jesus in the OT than there are about His first coming. Go to the NT and you will discover that all nine of the authors of the NT mention the second coming of Jesus in some way. Based on Scripture, we know that Jesus Christ is coming again.

Yet, just as the man in the store questioned whether the boy's bus would come, there are people who doubt the Lord's second coming. The Bible talks about these doubters in 2 Peter 3:3-4:

> *First, be aware of this: Scoffers will come in the last days to scoff, living according to their own desires, saying, "Where is the promise of His coming? Ever since the fathers fell asleep, all things continue as they have been since the beginning of creation."*

Notice that, even by questioning His coming, those scoffers affirm that Jesus is coming again, because the Bible says their ridicule is a sign of the last days. Jesus Christ is coming.

Why does God's word keep revealing, over and over again, truth about the second coming of Christ? There are many reasons. Knowing that Jesus is coming again gives us hope. His return reminds us of the certainty of God's promise and causes us to remember His faithfulness, His justice, and our sure salvation. The reality of Christ's return encourages us to be mindful of His power that works in our lives right now. The second coming reminds us of God's love for His people and that His Lordship will prevail. Moreover, the second coming reminds us that God has a plan for the ages. Though the world may seem like it's spinning out of control, the promise of the second coming assures us that God is still ruling and reigning over time, history, and eternity. Ultimately, He has everything fully under His control. All of these things are taught to us through truth of the second coming of Jesus Christ.

In Zechariah 12:1–13:1 the prophet delivers a specific word from God about the Lord's return. Throughout this passage we can see that what Jesus will do at His second coming reveals who He is right now. Three aspects of the Lord's unchanging character emerge in Zechariah's prophecy of Christ's second coming.

His Sovereign Position: He Created
ZECHARIAH 12:1

Zechariah 12:1 begins the second oracle in this book, the first one having begun in 9:1. As noted previously, the word translated "oracle" can mean "to bear" and "to lift up." The word carries the idea of a weighty message delivered by God's messenger and laid upon the people. The oracle beginning in Zechariah 9 concerned Hadrach and other Gentile nations that had opposed Israel. The burden in Zechariah 12, however, is laid on Israel itself, foretelling particularly what will happen to the city of Jerusalem at the end of the ages.

Before Zechariah speaks of events that will happen in the future, he talks about something that happened in the past with continuing implications in the present. In verse 1 the prophet uses three phrases describing our Lord's work as "Creator." By saying that the Lord "stretched out the heavens," it means that that He flung out into space all of the stars, galaxies, and planets—everything we see when we look up in the sky. "Laying the foundations of the earth" indicates that the Lord set the earth on a firm foundation, making the solid ground upon which we plant our feet. The third thing this passage mentions about the Lord's creative work is very personal: He "formed the spirit of man within him." In other words, He breathed out His own life and gave life to men and women.

Interestingly, in the Hebrew text, all three of those verbs—*stretched out, laid the foundation,* and *formed*—are present tense participles. The form of the words remind us that God not only made everything, and us, in the past, but moment by moment He still stretches out the heavens, He still founds the earth, and He still forms the spirit of man within him. He sustains His entire universe continually, and He upholds us through His creative power.

Zechariah 12:1 raises a question: Why would God begin a prophecy concerning the future and the second coming of Christ by reminding His people that He is Creator? Here's the answer: The foundation for everything that God calls His people to be and do rests in the fact that God made us. Why are you accountable to God? Because God made you. Why will God one day judge the entire world? Because God made the world. It belongs to Him. We belong to Him. We didn't make ourselves; He made us. Therefore, He has the sovereign and absolute right to rule over us and even to judge us.

Have you ever bought a new shirt or a new pair of pants and found, tucked into one of the pockets, a slip of paper that says, "Inspected by . . ." A lot of times, the little note will say, "Inspected by 7." It seems like they use the number 7 a lot, maybe because they know it's a perfect number!

When I see one of those little "Inspected by 7" notes, it makes me think that somewhere in the shirt factory, at the end the whole process of making my shirt, Inspector 7 was sitting at her station when my shirt came across her table. She took my shirt, held it up, measured it, checked all the stitching, made sure all the seams were sewn right, looked to see if the pattern of the fabric was right, and if nothing was wrong with the shirt, took that little slip from a huge stack and put it in my shirt pocket: "Inspected by 7."

Use your imagination for just a moment. Could you picture a newly formed shirt ever saying to Inspector 7, "What right do you have to judge me? Who do you think you are? You're looking at me, you're pulling on me, and you're making sure that all these things are right with me. What gives you the right?"

I can imagine Inspector 7 saying, "Mr. Shirt, the reason I have the right to judge you is because I am your manufacturer. I made you, and because I created you, I have the right to inspect you and decide whether or not you meet my qualifications."

When the Bible tells us that our God stretches out the heavens, founds the earth, and forms the spirit of man within him, it is a reminder that we are accountable to God. He has the right to inspect us. He has the right to hold us to His righteous standard because He made us. As we think about judgment, as we think about the end of the ages, we need to understand that the judgment that will come at the end of the age will hold all of us accountable to our God.

An *atheist* believes there is no God and therefore no accountability. That's one of the great appeals of atheism: that there's no accountability. A pantheist, who believes that everything is God, believes that what is right for me may not be right for you, because all truth is relative. It's a subjective accountability because all of us relate to God in our own way. A *deist* believes that God created the earth then stepped back to leave everything in creation alone. A deist believes in limited accountability before God because he thinks that God is not engaged with His creation.

But a *biblical theist*, who believes in an active, present, Creator God, who has revealed Himself as the God of Abraham and Isaac and Jacob, holds to real responsibility on the part of human beings before God. Understanding that God made us, the theist believes we are accountable to Him. Furthermore, a *Christian theist* is someone who believes that God has stepped into history through the incarnation of His Son, and that, one day, He will judge all the earth against the standard of that same one person: His Son, Jesus Christ. Followers of Christ believe that we have a high and specific accountability to Him. That's why God begins this text about Christ's return by talking about the Lord as our Creator. That is His sovereign position.

His Surpassing Power: He Conquers

ZECHARIAH 12:2-9

In Zechariah 12:2-9 the prophet begins to describe what will happen when the whole world comes to besiege Jerusalem in the last days. A phrase is found several times in this passage, beginning in verse 3: *On that day.* In chapters 12–14 the phrase is found a total of 16 times, including eight times in Zechariah 12:1–13:1. The "day" that the Bible is talking about is a specific event: the day of the Battle of Armageddon. As it is described in Scripture, the Battle of Armageddon is not merely one military fight. Instead, it is actually a campaign that will be fought on several different fronts. The campaign will be fought in the Valley of Armageddon, of course. Many times in Israel, I have stood on the hill called Megiddo, looking across the Valley of Armageddon. It is a wide, flat valley. It is beautiful and lush. Military experts have described it as one of the earth's most perfect battlefields (Wiersbe, *Be Victorious*, 146).

One day all of the enemies of God, led by the Antichrist, will come to wage war against Jerusalem, gathering for battle at Armageddon (Zech 14:1-3; Rev 16:16; 19:19). The fight in the Valley of Armageddon is part of the battle. However, the battle is also going to be fought in the city of Jerusalem. "On that day," then, refers to the time of the Battle of Armageddon, a day that will culminate in the second coming of Christ.

The Lord uses two images to describe how He will defeat His enemies as they come against Jerusalem. In verse 2 He says, "I will make Jerusalem a cup that causes staggering for the people who surround the city." A cup that causes drunkenness is a common figure of speech among the prophets to describe God's judgment (Isa 51:17,21-22; Jer 25:15-28). Jesus used the same figure in His Gethsemane prayer when he asked the Father, "If it is possible, let this cup pass from Me" (Matt

26:39). During the Battle of Armageddon, as the city is besieged, God will cause Jerusalem to be like a drink that causes her enemies to become drunk and powerless. In verse 3 God promises to make Jerusalem "a heavy stone for all the peoples." Like an immovable stone that a man tries futilely to move, only to harm himself by doing it, Jerusalem's enemies would tear themselves apart by attempting to attack and overthrow God's people in the Holy City.

While verses 2 and 3 use poetic language and imagery to describe what will happen to Jerusalem during the Battle of Armageddon, in verses 4-9 the text employs literal language to describe the Battle of Armageddon as the conflict moves from house to house in Jerusalem. Verse 4 shows how God will confuse His enemies on that day. Horses will panic as a result of sudden blindness and their riders will become crazed and out of control. Meanwhile, God will keep the house of Judah under His "watchful eye." The Hebrew for "watchful" means an eye that is open and paying close attention. The word is meant to contrast with the blind eyes of the enemies' horses.

Verse 5 shows that the Lord will use His deliverance and protection during the battle to awaken confidence and faith on the part of the leaders of Judah and the inhabitants of Jerusalem. Many interpreters believe that at the beginning of the Battle of Armageddon the people in the surrounding area of Judah will be against the people of Jerusalem. But then, as they see God working and moving to bring victory to the city, the people will become convinced that the inhabitants of Jerusalem have strength because of the Lord. Consequently, they will turn to the Lord as well. As a result of their newly ignited faith in the Lord of Hosts, verse 6 indicates that the leaders of Judah would become like a "firepot in a woodpile" and "a flaming torch among sheaves." A firepot was used to carry hot coals to start a wood fire. A torch was used to light dry grain. The leaders of Judah will have new power to rout their enemies as they trust in the Lord for help.

Verse 7 promises that those living in tents in the Judean countryside would be delivered first, keeping the descendants of David and those living in Jerusalem from exalting themselves above the rest of Judah. In verse 8, however, the Lord promises that while the weakest inhabitant will fight with the courage and boldness of David himself, the house of David will fight like the Angel of the Lord, the preincarnate Second Person of the Trinity who had led Israel to great victory in the past (Exod 23:20; 32:34; 33:2; Josh 5:13), even slaying 185,000

Assyrian soldiers in one night (Isa 37). Verse 9 summarizes how the Lord would work on behalf of His people in the Battle of Armageddon: "On that day, I will set out to destroy all the nations that come against Jerusalem."

These verses remind us that God's side always wins. Some people foolishly reason that, since the Lord always conquers, we should work and pray to get God on our side. That is exactly backwards. You don't get God on your side; you get on God's side. Joshua the son of Nun learned that lesson. Joshua 5 tells about what happened as Joshua began to lead the children of Israel into Canaan. The promised land was not a vacant lot. People were there. Cities were there. Enemies were there. There were battles that the children of Israel had to face once they crossed the Jordan River.

The first major city they came up against was Jericho, the oldest city in the world. A fortress-like wall surrounded the city. Jericho had armaments and mighty men inside, ready to fight. This evil city had stood against God and needed to be defeated in the name of the Lord. But Joshua did not know how he was going to conquer Jericho.

As Joshua was trying to determine how to attack the city, he looked up to see a tall, strong warrior standing in front of him with a drawn sword in hand. Joshua asked the man a natural question: "Are You for us or for our enemies?" (Josh 5:13). The man gave an unexpected answer: "Neither," He replied. "I have now come as commander of the LORD's army" (Josh 5:14). Joshua bowed before the man and prepared Himself to obey the Lord's commander. That would be Joshua's key to victory. He understood the surpassing power of our Lord, so he said, "I'm not going to try to get you on my side. I just want to make sure I'm on your side." God's side always wins.

Through His surpassing power, Jesus conquers. As we think about Jesus at His second coming, conquering all of His enemies, we need to understand that, even now, God's side always wins. If you want to experience God's best for your life, your family, your business, and your ministry, line yourself up with Him. Get on His side.

Not very long ago, Michele and I were walking on the beach at Amelia Island on the east coast of Florida. The waves were coming in, we were laughing and talking, holding hands, having a great time. We had been walking for maybe 30 or 40 minutes in one direction, and then turned to go back to our hotel. The instant we turned, we realized that the wind, which had been at our backs, was now blowing in our faces. The walk back was so much harder! It's easy to walk with the wind at your back. It can be drudgery to walk with the wind in your face.

You can either go through your life with God's wind at your back, discovering, through His Word, through prayer, through worship, and through a submitted life what He wants for you and where He desires to take you. Or you can decide to turn against Him and live with His wind blowing in your face, always going opposite the direction that He has for you. God is not going to change His direction. When we are opposing Him, He wants us to change our direction.

Our tendency is to place our plan before God—whether it's a plan for our family, personal life, business, or ministry—and say, "God, here's the life I want to live. Please affirm my plans. I will serve You as long as You work on my terms."

And God says, "I don't work that way." His surpassing power requires that we adjust ourselves to Him. As we see Him conquering His enemies at the Battle of Armageddon, it reminds us that He wants to conquer our own obstinate spirits so that we can turn to Him and experience His victory.

His Saving Purpose: He Cleanses

ZECHARIAH 12:10–13:1

The final section of our text reveals the work of Christ at the Battle of Armageddon to cleanse the hearts of the people of Israel. Verse 10 says that after God brings physical deliverance to the people of Jerusalem, He will "pour out a spirit of grace and prayer" on them. Whether "spirit" here refers to the Holy Spirit or the inner attitude of the people is unclear from the text itself. Certainly, though, the results of "grace" and "prayer" are consistent with the work of God's Spirit in the lives of His people.

Realizing their sins, the people will cry out to God for forgiveness. The reason for their repentance becomes clearer at the end of verse 10: "They will look at Me whom they have pierced." This refers to nation's piercing of the Messiah. The term usually carries the idea of piercing to the point of death. The piercing of Jesus on the cross, as nails were driven into His hands and feet, thorns pierced His brow, and, most notably, a spear pierced His side (John 19:34,37), is intimated very strongly in this prophecy. The Hebrew for "look," *nabat*, means to look attentively. The nation will look at Him, not only physically as Christ returns to earth on the Mount of Olives (Zech 14:4), but also spiritually, as they turn from their sin to Him. As Israel looks at Christ, the people will realize something that had previously eluded them: their guilt in rejecting Him and their need for His forgiveness.

Suddenly, the hearts of God's people that have been hardened against Jesus, not just for decades, but for centuries and even millennia, will be softened. The rest of verse 10 as well as verse 11 describe the mourning and grief the nation will experience as they look upon Christ. The mourning is compared to that over the death of an only child or a firstborn. The mourning is also likened to "the mourning of Hadad-rimmon in the plain of Megiddo." This refers to the public display of grief when King Josiah, the only godly king between the time of Hezekiah and Nebuchadnezzar, was slain by Pharaoh Neco (2 Kgs 23:29-30; 2 Chr 35:22-27). "Hadad-rimmon," the name of a pagan god of storms and fertility, probably refers to a place in the valley of Megiddo near where King Josiah died and was mourned. Verses 12-13 describe further the extent of the mourning, which will include David's house (representing royalty), Nathan's house (representing the prophets), and Levi's and Shemei's houses (representing the priesthood). Verse 14 shows that all of Israel, including the women, will share in mourning at the sight of the pierced Messiah, indicating a comprehensive repentance on the part of Israel at Christ's second coming.

Zechariah 13:1 depicts the gracious result of Israel's repentance. God promises to cleanse His people from two things: "sin," which refers to anything that separates us from God or anything that is not right according to God; and "impurity," which is anything in our lives that is broken. William Cowper's hymn, "There Is a Fountain Filled with Blood," is based on Zechariah 13:1. While the Jews cleansed their ceremonial uncleanness by ritual washing in water, sin and impurity can only be cleansed by the blood of Jesus. First John 2:2 says, "He Himself is the propitiation for our sins, and not only for ours, but also for those of the whole world." Through His cleansing power, Jesus brings us salvation. The power of the gospel, the power of the death of Jesus Christ on the cross, reaches to every part of our brokenness and makes us right with God.

On a mission journey to India I was trying to be very careful to take my malaria pills regularly and properly. A good friend of mine had gone to Africa shortly before my trip and had contracted malaria. He wound up in the hospital for a long time and nearly died, so I wanted to make sure I followed the right directions with my medication.

One night I was eating dinner with a friend who is a medical doctor. I asked him, "How important is it that I take my malaria medicine on an empty stomach?"

He said, "It's very important. The food can absorb the medication and make it less potent." Then he continued, "We tell people, whether they're taking those pills for malaria or for acne, to make sure that they take it on an empty stomach."

I said, "Hold on, what did you just say? Taking it for what?"

He said, "Whether they're taking it for malaria or for acne."

I said, "You mean, this same medication?"

He said, "Oh, yeah. The medication you're taking is the same thing we prescribe to clear up your face. It's an anti-bacterial."

When I got home I went to the medicine cabinet to find the medicine my teenaged son was taking for his complexion. It was exactly the same medication. Same ingredients. Same dosage. It's exactly the same stuff.

Nobody ever died from acne. Many people have died from malaria. But the same medicine that will keep me from dying has other benefits in my life as well. It can make my skin clearer.

The most important reason to come to Jesus Christ is the deep need of sin in our lives. We're broken before God because of sin. The blood of Jesus Christ is the only medicine that will make us right. When you look on the One who was pierced for your transgressions and trust Him as your Savior, a river of life begins to flow that cleanses you of sin. But, praise God, His saving work also can cleanse you of uncleanness, of anything in your life that is broken, whether it's your marriage, family, or other relationships, whether it's your emotions, whether it's attitude and outlook on life. When we come to Jesus with our brokenness—whatever it is—by the power of the gospel of Jesus Christ, His medicine is able to save every part of who we are.

Reflect and Discuss

1. What are some practical spiritual benefits of understanding biblical prophecy concerning the return of Christ? Can you list some ways that His return affects the way you will live your life today?
2. How does God's past work of creation connect to His future work of judgment?
3. Does adherence to the biblical teaching of creation change a person's belief about moral and spiritual accountability? How?

4. From the perspective of this passage, why are you accountable to God?
5. How does your personal accountability to God affect the way you relate to yourself, family, friends, or even strangers?
6. Zechariah 12:5 indicates that the Lord will use His deliverance of Jerusalem during the Battle of Armageddon to awaken its residents' faith in Christ. How does that coming event affect your prayers and attitudes toward Jewish people now?
7. Recognizing the conquering power of Christ, what areas of your life do you need to surrender and submit to Him?
8. The fountain that washes away the sin and impurity of Jerusalem will be opened by God's own initiative. What are some of the activities of God in the lives of individuals to bring us salvation and cleanse sin?
9. What are some of the manifestations of spiritual brokenness in our lives?
10. How does the Gospel meet us in our brokenness to make us whole? Consider this question in the areas of spiritual, emotional, mental, and relational wholeness.

His Certain Victory, Your Greatest Hope

ZECHARIAH 13:2–14:21

Main Idea: God promises certain victory for His people through Jesus Christ.

I. Our Guaranteed Access to God (13:2-9)
II. Satan's Gruesome Attack on Jerusalem (14:1-3)
III. Christ's Glorious Appearance on Earth (14:4-9)
IV. God's Gracious Assurances to Us (14:10-21)

Two men were walking through a pasture when, in the distance, they saw an enraged bull charging toward them. The men began to run toward the nearest fence. The bull was in hot pursuit, gaining on them with each step. It became obvious that they were not going to make it to the fence before the bull made it to them.

Terrified, one shouted to the other, "John, you've got to pray for us. You've got to pray out loud! We're in for it!"

John said, "I can't pray. I've never prayed in public in my life."

The other man said, "You've got to! That bull is catching up, fast!"

John panted, "All right, but the only prayer I know to say is the one my dad said every night at dinner." So, he prayed, "Oh, Lord, for what we are about to receive, make us truly thankful."

I'm not sure what happened next, but I do know that silly story brings up a really serious question: **How can we give thanks to God when we're in trouble, when our lives are tough or even tragic?** In 1 Thessalonians 5:18 we are commanded, "Give thanks in everything, for this is God's will for you in Christ Jesus." You may have noticed that the verse doesn't say, "Give thanks *for* everything." There are times that would be impossible or disingenuous. But the truth is, it can even seem nearly impossible to give thanks *in* everything.

How do you give thanks when your doctor says, "You have cancer"? How do you hold on to hope when the person you love most walks out on you? How do you give thanks when you've been fired or when your dream has collapsed? Where does your hope go when you've gone through an economic tidal wave that's wiped out everything you've worked for? How can we hold on to hope and give thanks in everything when we face things like these? These are tough things, even tragic things.

The only way to keep our hope alive in life's tragic and tough circumstances is to live each day in light of God's eternal plan and purpose. That's why Bible prophecy is so important for followers of Jesus. Knowing what God has planned for the future gives us hope right now.

The Old and New Testaments are filled with promises of the second coming of Christ. In the OT alone, for every one prophecy of the first coming of Christ, there are eight prophecies concerning Christ's second coming. The purpose of biblical prophecy is not merely to satisfy our curiosity. For some people, the primary reason for studying prophecies seems to be to quench their inquisitiveness or to bolster arguments for their eschatological position. These are not the reasons God gave us prophecy. Instead, God spoke to His people about the future so that we can see His eternal purpose. Understanding God's unfolding plan for the future empowers us to live with hope and victory.

Zechariah 13 and 14 are all about giving God's people hope for the future. The major theme of these chapters is God's promise of certain victory for His people through Jesus Christ. These chapters divide readily into four major sections. Each section reveals to us something significant about the second coming of Jesus Christ and the victory His coming promises us.

Our Guaranteed Access to God

ZECHARIAH 13:2-9

Zechariah 13:2-9 describes the spiritual renewal of Israel as they repent and believe in Jesus as Messiah at His second coming. The passage shows how God will provide access for His people to call on Him as they turn away from idolatry and false prophets, are purified by the Lord, and then cry out to God in prayer.

In verse 2 God promises to "erase the names of the idols from the land." The Hebrew for "idols," *'atsav*, comes from a verb that means to form or to fashion, highlighting the fact that human hands formed idols. Describing the abolition of idolatry in Israel as erasing the names of the idols is significant. In ancient culture, a name reflected a person's character, reputation, and essence. To erase the name of the idols indicates the total destruction of their credibility and authority in Israel. Indeed,

God promises that, as Jesus returns to rule over His people, the false gods represented by the empty idols "will no longer be remembered."

Along with the elimination of idolatry, God promises to "remove the prophets and the unclean spirit from the land." Significantly, in this passage the Lord identifies the root of false prophecy as "the unclean spirit." The Hebrew word for uncleanness, *tum'ah,* was used in a variety of ways in the OT, referring to the sexual impurity of a woman during the menstrual cycle (Num 5:19; Lam 1:9) and any physically unclean thing in the temple that required purification (2 Chr 29:16). The meaning was extended to spiritual uncleanness and impurity, as in Leviticus 16:16 and Ezekiel 24:13. Jesus confronted unclean spirits a number of times in the Gospels and gave His disciples authority over them (Matt 10:1; Mark 1:23-27; 3:11; Luke 8:26-33). Revelation 16:13-14 mentions unclean spirits coming out of the mouth of Satan, the Antichrist, and the false prophet in the last days, identifying these unclean spirits as "demonic spirits" that go out to summon the nations to the Battle of Armageddon. Zechariah 13:2, however, is the only place in the OT that talks explicitly about "unclean spirits."

Verses 3-6 expand on how false prophets will be eliminated from God's people. The Mosaic law required that a false prophet be put to death (Deut 13:5; 18:20). As the people of Judah turn to the Lord in the last days, God makes the staggering promise that the false prophet's own parents will not only accuse him of his crime before God but actually carry out their own son's execution. As a result, those who had been prophesying falsely will suddenly claim a different line of work as their profession. Verse 4 says, "every prophet will be ashamed of his vision when he prophesies." The immediate shame at their own prophecies would seem to indicate that the false prophets are not altogether in control of the messages they deliver but are instruments of the unclean spirits they have served. No longer will these false prophets wear the "hairy cloak" that identified them as spokesmen for God and gave them authority and respect (2 Kgs 1:8; Matt 3:4). Instead, verses 5 and 6 say that a man will claim never to have been a prophet, but only a simple hired farm hand since his youth. He will deny that the cuts and scars on his chest resulted from ecstatic cutting rituals designed to gain the attention of the pagan gods (1 Kgs 18:28). Instead, he will attribute them to his friends.

All of this cleansing in Israel—of idolatry, false prophets, and the unclean spirit—can be attributed to the fountain of living waters opened for the people of Judah and Jerusalem through the coming of the Messiah, described in 13:1. James Montgomery Boice observes,

> Where does this cleansing from sin's power and defilement come from? It comes from the fountain. And what is that? Clearly, the "fountain" that will be opened to the house of David and the inhabitants of Jerusalem is the blood of the Messiah whom they have pierced. (*Minor Prophets*, 554)

Beginning in verse 7, Zechariah describes the slaying of God's shepherd and the scattering of God's sheep. A sword is personified, as the Lord addresses that deadly weapon as he would a sleeping warrior. He calls upon the sword to "awake" and "strike the shepherd." Notably, the Lord calls the shepherd "My associate." The Hebrew term is used in other places in the Old Testament to describe a neighbor, a close companion, or another person regarded as an equal (Lev 6:2; 18:20; 19:15). Jesus proclaimed His own equality with God the Father in John 10:30 and 14:9. Telling the sword to "strike the shepherd" shows that the death of Christ was not an accident, but was divinely planned. This is consistent with Isaiah 53:10: "The LORD was pleased to crush Him severely." At the end of verse 7, Zechariah prophesies that God's sheep would be scattered as a result of the Messiah's death. Jesus quoted this verse to His disciples on the night before He was crucified (Matt 26:31). The verse prophesies the disciples' abandonment of Jesus as He was crucified (Matt 26:56), and also points to the scattering of the Jews with the destruction of Jerusalem in AD 70 as well as during the tribulation (Rev 12:6,13-17). The phrase "little ones" parallels "the sheep" and may have in view first-century disciples, unbelieving Jews of all ages, or a faithful remnant of the future.

In verse 8, Zechariah reveals what will happen as a result of God's flock being scattered: they will face a time of crisis that will "cut off" or destroy two thirds of the flock. Only a third of the flock will survive. While the destruction of Jerusalem in AD 70 may have been a taste of the coming time of trouble facing Israel prophesied by Zechariah, a greater future catastrophe seems to be in view here. Evidently, during the tribulation of the end times, two thirds of the Jews will perish and one third will live through it and enter the millennium. The remnant that survives would include the 144,000 mentioned in Revelation 7:1-8 and 14:1-5 (Constable, "Notes on Zechariah," 83–84).

Verse 9 shows that the remnant will be reestablished in a covenant relationship with God. God promised to "put this third through the fire" in order to "refine them as silver is refined and test them as gold is tested." There is a slightly different shade of meaning between "refine" and "test." The Hebrew for "refine" is *tsaraph*, which refers to a process of purification. The word for "test" is *bachan*, which means to examine or to prove. Add them together, and a full picture emerges of what God will do to the Jews during the tribulation: He will *purify* them of anything that is impure in order to *prove* them to be His own redeemed people.

In the days of Zechariah, a refiner would take the raw gold or silver and place it in a ceramic container. Inside the container was the ore—not just the precious metal, but also impurities such as zinc, lead, and salt. The ceramic container was put into a fiery kiln for five days. During those five days, all of the impurities would separate to the outside edges of the container. Nothing would be left in the middle of the vessel but the pure silver or gold. Just as a refiner turns up the heat on gold and silver—first to make it malleable, moldable, and pliable and then to purify it—our God also will allow us, as His people, to go through times of testing and refining in order to make us what He wants us to be. He uses those times of testing in our lives to bring us to our knees, so that we will call on Him.

The culmination of God's work of purifying His people comes at the end of verse 9. God makes four statements to describe the access He will provide Israel to Himself after His people have been purged by the persecution in the tribulation. The words follow a chiastic pattern of "they, I, I, they." (1) "*They* will call on My name." This call is more than simply crying out to God for rescue from trouble. Instead, it indicates faith and repentance. (2) "*I* will answer them." God will respond to His people's sincere call by answering, accepting, forgiving, and saving. (3) "*I* will say: They are My people." Fulfilling His covenant promise to Israel, God will acknowledge and embrace the people as His own. (4) "*They* will say: Yahweh is our God." No more would the people be turned to idols or false prophets. Now their only allegiance will be to the Lord. Paul, quoting from Isaiah 59:20-21 and Jeremiah 31:33-34, rested in the promise that God would restore Israel in the future:

> *And in this way all Israel will be saved, as it is written: The Liberator will come from Zion; He will turn away godlessness from Jacob. And this will be My covenant with them when I take away their sins.*
> (Rom 11:26-27)

God's promise to remove impurities and restore Israel's access to Him has a powerful application for God's people today. Like Israel, believers need to repent from following after empty and useless alternatives to God, idols that we create with our own hands and hearts. Like Israel, we must turn from false messengers who pretend to speak truth while peddling deception and lies. And, like Israel, we can count on God hearing and answering when we call on Him, because we belong to Him.

If you're like I am, you have probably gotten a call on your cell phone, looked at the display to see who was calling, and then decided not to take the call. Instead of answering, you put your phone away in your pocket or your purse. Sometimes you put the cell phone away because you don't know the person who is calling. Other times you get the call and leave it unanswered because you *do* know the person and you just don't want to talk to them. There are also times when you'd like to take the call but you're busy with something else, and you simply are not available to talk.

As human beings, we're limited in our availability. We can't be available to everybody all the time, even when we want to be. But God is unlimited in His power to hear and answer when we call, and because of the work of Jesus Christ, God is always available to His people. He never sees us coming and ducks out of the way to avoid us. He loves us. He cares about us. He hears when we call. That's the guarantee of our access to Him through Christ.

Satan's Gruesome Attack on Jerusalem

ZECHARIAH 14:1-3

Zechariah 14:1-3 is a graphic description of the details of the Battle of Armageddon, specifically related to what will happen in the city of Jerusalem. Though the attack from Satan-inspired forces will be severe, God provides hope through the Messiah's victory.

In verse 2 God says, "I will gather all the nations against Jerusalem for battle." In the final days of the tribulation, all of the nations from throughout the earth will march, anticipating triumph over Israel. These attacking nations will ransack the city of Jerusalem. Verse 2 goes on to say that houses will be plundered, women will be brutalized, and half the city will be taken into exile. While attacks against Israel and Jerusalem have been common throughout history, even up to the present day, it's important to understand that the attack described here is not just a hit-and-run event. This is not a rogue nation lashing out against Israel. The intent of this worldwide attack will be to impose satanic authority on Jerusalem and to subdue God's people completely.

However, in verse 3, something momentous happens: "Then the LORD will go out to fight against those nations as He fights on a day of battle." Just when Satan and his all-nation forces seem to have gained the upper hand, the Lord Himself will enter the battle. Instantly the balance of power will shift in the favor of God's people.

Think about that scene: The attack is gruesome, merciless, and unrelenting. The enemy is satanic and extremely powerful, even employing wicked, supernatural powers. But God's people will find their victory in God Himself. He promises to fight for His people and protect them. God's faithfulness and protective power during this gruesome attack on Jerusalem remind us that our safety does not depend on our distance from danger. Our safety depends on our nearness to God. If we are with Him, He will keep us through the most dangerous times we will ever face.

One evening I was walking our little Yorkshire terrier down the sidewalk. Joey weighs, at most, six pounds, and he lives by this motto: "Love all people; hate all dogs." Every time we take him out we have to be on the lookout for other dogs because Joey goes crazy, barking and trying to attack. On this particular evening, as I was walking I heard a lady yell from her driveway, "Come back here!"

I looked to my left and saw a little white poodle running away from this lady, toward Joey and me. Joey started barking furiously. I reached down and picked up Joey in my arms. As soon as I did, that other dog ran up and nailed me right in the leg. His bite broke the skin and drew blood. Then, our attacker ran back to the lady in the driveway, who apologized profusely.

On the way back home, I looked down at my little Yorkie and said, "Always remember, Joey, I got bit for you. That could have been you, but I took the hit." Joey didn't seem to be all that impressed by my sacrifice. He just kept walking and wagging his tail. But I do think he knows, somehow, that his safety simply depends on his closeness to me. As long as he's with me, he knows I will to do everything I can do to protect him.

Here's what the Bible says about you and your God: Your safety does not depend on your distance from danger. There will be times when the path that God has for you will take you into dangerous, difficult, tragic, and even hurtful circumstances. But your safety does not depend on your distance from danger; it depends on your nearness to your God.

At the Battle of Armageddon, when danger will encircle God's people, when they will be attacked and brutalized by Satan's forces in ways that are beyond our imagination, the Lord Jesus will show up and take the hit for them. He will fight the battle for them. And, in the same way, He will fight for us today. The cross of Jesus Christ has already proved that fact conclusively. When Jesus died on the cross for our sin, He bore the brunt of every attack that Satan has to offer and He came out of the tomb on the third day victorious. We can praise the Lord because we share in His victory.

Christ's Glorious Appearance on Earth

ZECHARIAH 14:4-9

Verse 4 tells what will happen when Jesus returns physically to earth, setting His feet on the Mount of Olives. Situated to the east of the Kidron Valley, right next to Jerusalem, the Mount of Olives rises to a height of 2,710 feet, making it higher than the Temple Mount. The grey soil of the mountain is suited to the growth of olive trees (Barker, "Zechariah," 691). The Mount of Olives occupies a prominent place in the earthly ministry of Jesus. We read in the Synoptic Gospels that Jesus preached His most extensive sermon concerning the future, end times, and prophecy from the Mount of Olives. Recorded in Matthew 24, Mark 13, and Luke 21, it is often called the "Olivet Discourse." Then all four Gospels tell us that during His last night on earth before His crucifixion Jesus went to the foot of the Mount of Olives, to the Garden of Gethsemane, and offered up His soul to the Father in surrender (Matt 26:36-56; Mark 14:32-53; Luke 22:39-53; John 18:1-14).

Acts 1 says that after appearing numerous times following His resurrection, Jesus appeared to His disciples on the Mount of Olives and ascended to heaven. As the disciples gazed into heaven, two angels appeared to them with this message: "Men of Galilee, why do you stand looking up into heaven? This Jesus, who has been taken from you into heaven, will come in the same way that you have seen Him going into heaven" (Acts 1:11). The place from which Jesus ascended is identified as the Mount of Olives in Acts 1:12.

Writing over 500 years before the birth of Christ, Zechariah prophesied that at the climax of the Battle of Armageddon, the Lord will one day personally, physically, and visibly descend to earth at the Mount of Olives, just as He ascended into heaven from that place. At the instant

Christ appears on the Mount of Olives, Zechariah identifies six amazing events that will happen:

(1) The Mount of Olives will divide in two. Verse 4 promises that the mountain "will be split in half from east to west, forming a huge valley, so that half the mountain will move to the north and half to the south." A hairline fault line runs east and west through the Mount of Olives, and there a new valley will be formed on the day Jesus returns. This cleaving of the mountain may be caused by an earthquake that will accompany the Lord's return, although not necessarily. Certainly, the dramatic physical change in the landscape surrounding Jerusalem will be a sign of God's supernatural judgment.

(2) The people of Israel will flee through the newly formed valley to Azal. Verse 5 says to the people of Israel: "You will flee by My mountain valley, for the valley of the mountains will extend to Azal." Students of the Bible have offered various guesses about the exact identity of Azal. The word itself may be a preposition meaning "near to," "beside," or a noun meaning "the side." For that reason, the word could be translated "very near," implying that escape will be easy. Others have surmised that Azal may be the Valley of Jehoshaphat mentioned in Joel 3:2 and 12, or that it may be the Wadi Yasul, a tributary of the Kidron River (Barker, "Zachariah," 691). These are only guesses, however. The location of Azal remains a mystery. What is sure is that Azal is a place to which the inhabitants of Jerusalem will flee for security, and that their flight to Azal will be as urgent as when their ancestors had fled from a notable earthquake during the time of King Uzziah, also mentioned in Amos 1:1.

(3) The Lord will return, accompanied by His holy ones. Verse 5 concludes, "Then the LORD my God will come and all the holy ones with Him." God's holy ones are not only the angelic armies of heaven but also resurrected and glorified believers. In the OT "holy ones" or "saints" is used to refer to angels (Deut 33:3; Ps 89:5-7; Job 15:15) as well as to godly people (Lev 11:44-45; Ps 16:3; Dan 8:24). Jesus described His own return by promising to come with both angels and His saints:

> *And they will see the Son of Man coming on the clouds of heaven with power and great glory. He will send out His angels with a loud trumpet, and they will gather His elect from the four winds, from one end of the sky to the other.* (Matt 24:30b-31)

Along with His angels, the souls of the redeemed who have been saved, resurrected, and glorified with Jesus will come back with Him in victory.

(4) Jesus will make dramatic changes in the heavens. Verses 6 and 7 say that on the day of Christ's physical return "there will be no light; the sunlight and moonlight will diminish. It will be a day known only to the Yahweh, without day or night, but there will be light at evening." This depiction is very similar to how the new Jerusalem is described in Revelation 21:23, where John writes that the city will not need the sun or the moon to shine on it because the glory of God will give it light and Jesus, the Lamb, will illuminate it.

(5) Jesus will cause a river to flow that will refresh and restore the land. Verse 8 describes a river that will flow in two directions. Half will flow to the Dead Sea, identified as "the eastern sea." The other half will flow to the Mediterranean Sea, called the "western sea." This renewing water will never dry up or stop running. Instead, "in summer and winter alike," it will keep flowing year round. The perpetual and abundant fertility of the land of Israel during the millennial reign of Christ, described in places such as Isaiah 27:6 and 35:1-3, as well as Amos 9:13-14, may be attributed to the river.

(6) Jesus Christ will rule as King over the earth. This is the most glorious thing that will happen. Verse 9 states that Yahweh, in the person of Jesus Christ, "will become King over all the earth." The verse concludes that the ruler of the earth will be "Yahweh alone, and His name alone." This means that everyone will acknowledge Jesus as the only Lord. No longer will people claim that you can call God this name, that name, or some other name. No longer will they say, "There are many paths to God. Jesus is a good path, but not the only path." Instead, the whole world will acknowledge that there is only one Lord: Yahweh, revealed in the person of Jesus Christ. He will rule and reign over the earth.

Some words and melodies are inseparably linked to one another. When we read the words from the "Hallelujah Chorus," taken from Revelation 11:15, our minds automatically replay the striking and famous melody as well:

> The kingdom of this world
> Is become the kingdom of our Lord,
> And of His Christ, and of His Christ;
> And He shall reign for ever and ever.

Those majestic words resonate together with the prophecy of Zechariah 14:9 fulfilled here: "Yahweh will become King over all the earth." Jesus is coming to reign. Every time we repeat the words of the Lord's

Prayer—"Your kingdom come!"—we are praying for this day. Zechariah foretold a day when Jesus Christ will bring into fulfillment the victory that He has already won through His cross and His resurrection from the grave.

The story is told of a Midwestern farmer who hated God, hated the church, and hated religious people. Every Sunday morning, as he was out plowing in his field, he would shake his fist at all the people driving past on their way to church. October came, and the farmer had his finest crop ever. In fact, he had the biggest crop of anyone in the county.

When the harvest was complete, that farmer placed an advertisement in the local paper. In that advertisement, he belittled the Christians in his community for their faith in God. At the end of his letter, he wrote, "Faith in God must not mean much, if someone like me can prosper."

The response from the Christians in the community was quiet and polite. Someone placed a small ad in the next edition of the town paper, and it said simply, "God doesn't always settle His accounts in October."

God does not always settle His accounts in October, or in our lifetimes, or even in centuries of history. Injustice and great wickedness seem sometimes to go unaddressed by our holy and righteous God. But He will settle His accounts. Jesus will come to rule the world in God's justice and righteousness. The kingdoms of this world will become the kingdom of our Lord and of His Christ. And He shall reign forever and ever, hallelujah! His certain victory, in His own time, gives us reason to praise Him and to give thanks in every circumstance.

God's Gracious Assurances to Us

ZECHARIAH 14:10-21

Verses 10-21 of our text provide three assurances that God graciously promises to His people. The promises He made centuries ago to the people of Judah have real implications for us, assuring us of victory in the future and providing us with hope right now.

(1) The Bible assures us that King Jesus will establish His kingdom. Verse 10 describes a total transformation of the area surrounding Jerusalem. From the northern border at Geba to the southern border 35 miles south in Rimmon, the region will become flattened into a plain, so that the city of Jerusalem will become more prominent. Additionally, verse 10 lists a number of gates and other landmarks in the city, promising that Jerusalem will "remain on its site." With Jesus reigning from the city, Jerusalem will dominate the landscape and will be firmly established. In light of the fact that Zechariah and his contemporaries were working hard to restore the ruined city of Jerusalem, this prophecy must have been especially encouraging.

Verse 11 continues with another promise for Jerusalem: that the city will be inhabited, that it will never again be completely destroyed, and that it will dwell in security—a Hebrew phrase that carries the idea of enduring and staying. This promise was not fulfilled in the time of Zechariah, nor in the era of Jesus and the early church. But when Jesus rules and reigns at His return, the city of Jerusalem—attacked, besieged, and destroyed so many times in history—will be absolutely secure forever. Verses 12 through 15 tell us that any enemies that would dare to rise up against Jerusalem and its King will be struck with a plague and wiped out instantly.

(2) The Bible assures us that all nations will worship King Jesus. In verses 16-19 Zechariah prophesies that all of the survivors who did not die at the Battle of Armageddon will celebrate the Festival of Booths, also known as the Feast of Tabernacles, annually. Since Jesus will destroy all of the soldiers of the nations that come against Jerusalem at the Battle of Armageddon, these "survivors" are those who did not engage in the attack. Instead, they are noncombatant citizens of the nations that had attacked God's people. Along with the people of Israel, they will come to Jerusalem each year for the Festival of Booths, which was a celebration of the harvest. It was a time of giving thanks and praise to the Lord. Verses 17-19 tell us that any nation that refuses to worship King Jesus will suffer drought. Specifically, the text warns against Egypt refusing to come and to worship Jesus. Egypt depended on the overflowing of the Nile to irrigate its crops. With no rain, the river would not flood and the fields would dry up and die.

Imagine what would happen in our lives if we suffered drought every time we failed to give God thanks? What if the blessings started to dry up in our lives? We can be grateful that Jesus is gracious enough to care for us even when we neglect to give Him thanks. Still, we miss out on certain blessings when we fail to give God thanks. We can live our lives day by day giving thanks to King Jesus and worshiping Him because of the ways He has blessed us.

(3) The Bible assures us that the holiness of King Jesus will prevail. Verses 20 and 21 show how Christ's holiness will permeate the entire city of Jerusalem. The bells on the bridles of common horses will be engraved with the same words inscribed on the turban of the high priest when he served in the temple: "HOLY TO THE LORD." Further, every pot in the temple would be just as holy as the bowls used in service at the altar. Even more, verse 21 promises that common pots and vessels in the houses of Jerusalem would be so holy that they could be used for service in the sanctuary. Wicked and unholy people, described as "Canaanites" in our text, would no longer be in the house of the Lord at all. Though Jerusalem has often been called the "Holy City" in Scripture and in history, with Jesus reigning, Jerusalem will truly *be holy*. Every part of the city—to the smallest part, such as bells on horses and pots in cupboards—will be holy to the Lord because Jesus is ruling. His coming promises our certain victory.

I heard about a high school football game where the home team was losing terribly. They could not close the gap in the score, no matter what they did. The clock was about to run out, everyone was discouraged, and the coach was frustrated. Then he looked over to see all the cheerleaders for his team sitting on the grass, their pom-poms down beside them. Their heads were hung low.

Irritated, the coach ran over the cheerleaders and said, "Girls, don't you think that our team would do better if you girls would stand up on the sidelines and cheer?"

The head cheerleader looked up and as sincerely as she could, said, "Coach, I think our team would do better if we girls would go out on the field and *play*!"

Maybe you've seen a game like that, when victory becomes not just unlikely but humanly impossible. That will be the story in the last days for God's people. The whole world, led by a satanic ruler empowered by the Devil himself, will be bearing down, not only on the little sliver of land called Israel, but on one city, Jerusalem. The attack will be such that it will be humanly impossible for anything to happen other than defeat. And then Jesus will show up, He will place His feet on the Mount of Olives, and He will change the game.

The same thing that's true for Israel in its last days is true for followers of Jesus right now. When defeat is absolutely inevitable, when victory is humanly impossible, Jesus shows up. He's the game changer. For followers of Jesus, victory is on the same road as defeat. Victory's just a little further on down the road. So if you're being defeated right now, be assured, based on the Word of God, Your victory is sure in Jesus Christ. Because of His coming, we can have certain victory and the greatest hope.

Reflect and Discuss

1. Zechariah 13–14 promises certain victory for followers of Jesus Christ. How does assurance of ultimate victory change the way you view temporary failures?
2. What forms of idolatry are most present in our culture today? How does idolatry influence followers of Jesus?
3. Idols, though empty, are also associated with spiritual uncleanness. In what way does idolatry lead to demonic influences?
4. God promises to use the tribulation of the end times to purify Israel. How do trials and persecution refine believers and confirm our relationship to the Lord?
5. Is there anything that can limit your access to God as a believer? Why? How does understanding the access we have to God through Christ change the way we pray and worship?
6. At the Battle of Armageddon, the Lord promises to "go out and fight against the nations." Do you usually think of Jesus Christ as a warrior? Why or why not?
7. How does this passage's description of Christ's future activity in earth's final battle relate to His response to sin and rebellion today?
8. This passage shows that our safety depends on our closeness to God. Have you been seeking safety by fleeing from danger? Does God call His people to a risk-averse life? What adjustments do you need to make to become a more daring Christian?
9. What message does Christ's coming kingdom speak to the injustice and wickedness of the present world?
10. Zechariah ends with a dramatic picture of holiness pervading throughout Jerusalem. What about you would be different if the Lord's holiness permeated to the smallest parts of your own personal life?

Malachi

Malachi Introduction

MALACHI 1:1

Most teenagers are remarkably similar creatures. For instance, independent of each other, most implement a similar strategy when confronted with an error. It may present itself like this:

A father walks into his son's room and says, "You did not clean up your room, so you're not leaving the house tonight."

The teenager replies, "What do you mean I didn't clean up my room?"

"Your mother and I told you to clean this place up, and there are still things everywhere."

"But I organized it all. I know where everything is!"

"There are still dirty clothes piled up in the corner!"

"That's better than them being everywhere."

"I said everything had to be off the floor."

"Well, what did you mean by everything?"

Even though conversations like this can be frustrating for the parent, they are needed. Parental parameters are not enforced for cruelty, but for protection. Clothes on the floor is not the end of the world, but the act of picking things up off the floor was not the intention of the parents' mandate. More important than the room being cleaned is the son's practicing obedience, and his practice of obedience allows for more intimate parent-child fellowship. Similarly, God outlined rules and regulations for our protection as well as for intimate fellowship with Him.

When we stray from Him, He lovingly corrects us. Love is not only expressed by words of affirmation and appreciation, it can also come in the form of a rebuke.

Love is a double-sided coin.

Love is looking in your spouse's eyes and saying, "You mean the world to me. I wouldn't want to go on without you." But, love could also be a protective warning. When a friend is about to engage in adultery, the loving thing to do would be to say, "STOP! Don't do it!"—even if it means losing your friendship over it.

Throughout Malachi we will see how God, as a loving Father, confronts, corrects, and challenges the people of Israel about straying from Him. No one is excluded.

This book is a deep but short one, and it is easy to gloss over it in our study of the Bible. It contains theologically heavy material, which can be easily understood once certain frameworks are set. There are five crucial facets of Malachi that this introduction will explain:

- Its Author
- Its Audience
- Its Occasion
- Its Oracle
- Its Style and Structure

Malachi is a call for Israel to return to God before the Messiah comes to earth, for it was written to a people who lived in expectation of Him, but who had not yet seen Him. We are in a special situation, though: we have the privilege of looking in remembrance, not anticipation, of the Messiah who lived, died, and rose from the dead 2,000 years ago. Fortunately, the message of Malachi is not only for those who hadn't yet encountered the Messiah, for its message is not merely, "shape up, because the Messiah is coming"; it is, "evaluate yourself, for you are not measuring up to what is required of you." Just as the people in Malachi's day were to introspectively evaluate their walks with God, we must take an inventory of our lives as well.

The Author of the Book

The name *Malachi* can mean "My Messenger" or "My Angel." That causes a problem to the modern audience: we are forced to determine whether this is a human messenger or a heavenly one. Throughout this book, there are four mentions of "My Messenger":

- 1:1: "The word of the Lord to Israel through 'My Messenger'";
- 2:7: The Messenger to the priesthood;

- 3:1a: The forerunner to the Messiah;
- 3:1b: The Messiah Himself.

It's difficult to determine exactly who Malachi was because there is no mention in the book of his father's name or of his place of birth. Some people believe *Malachi* is a title for Ezra the Scribe. John Calvin preferred that view (*Minor Prophets*, 5:459).

We can narrow the search a little bit, though. It can be rightly inferred that he was a contemporary of Nehemiah, because both of them dealt with similar issues.

- Nehemiah addressed the defection of the priesthood in Nehemiah 13:1-9, which Malachi addresses in Malachi 1:6–2:9.
- Nehemiah addressed the people's diminishing concern for tithing in Nehemiah 13:10-13. Likewise, Malachi spoke about robbing God of the tithe in Malachi 3:8-12.
- Finally, Nehemiah warned the people about intermarriage between Jews and Gentiles in Nehemiah 13:23-28. Malachi offered the same warning in Malachi 2:11-16.

Furthermore, because Malachi seems to be a proper name rather than a title, we will operate under the premise that Malachi is a human prophet not God's angel. While this is the assumption under which this commentary will operate, it is crucial to remember that the text never emphasizes the messenger; the focus is entirely on the message. But in order to determine the message, first the recipients of the message must be determined.

The Audience of the Book

Discovering the identity of the people to whom this book's message was to be delivered will reveal important truths about the message itself. Based on Malachi's word choice, we can assume that the nation of Israel has returned from the Babylonian captivity by the time of this book's writing. By addressing the book "to Israel" rather than "to Israel and Judah," he is stating that there are no longer two separate kingdoms and that they have returned to their unified state. This has to have been after 538 BC, when Cyrus of Persia's decree that all Jews return to the land of their fathers was delivered (Ezra 1). God is declaring that those who returned are indeed the continuation of His covenant people, so the term *Israel* is used to refer to the entirety of the people.

The Occasion of the Book

The majority of scholars agree that the book was written between 450 and 430 BC. Craig Blaising provides reasons to support this date:

> (1) Malachi's rebuke of the priests' malpractice in the temple shows that the temple had been rebuilt and the priesthood reestablished. (2) The moral and spiritual conditions Malachi addressed were similar to those encountered by Ezra, who returned in 458, and Nehemiah, who returned in 444. These included intermarriages with Gentiles (2:10-11; cf. Ezra 9:1-2; Neh 13:1-3,23-28), lack of the people's support for the Levites (Mal 3:10; cf. Neh 13:10), and oppression of the poor (Mal 3:5; cf. Neh 5:4-5). Either Malachi was addressing the same generation that Ezra and Nehemiah spoke to, or Malachi spoke to a later generation some time after Ezra's and Nehemiah's corrections. ("Malachi," 1573)

During the time of Malachi's writing, the temple was fully functioning with all the rituals and sacrifices of the Mosaic law. A significant portion of the book is addressed specifically to the priesthood, which would only happen should the priesthood be functioning.

As will be demonstrated, moral degradation was at an all-time high, with adultery, divorce, falsehood, fraud, and sorcery running rampant throughout the city; the source of much of the corruption was the priests themselves. As already mentioned, intermarriage between Jew and Gentile, a practice prohibited in the Mosaic law, was commonplace. Additionally, traditionalism was beginning to trump the commands of Scripture, laying the foundation for both Pharisaism and Sadduceeism.

Malachi, like the prophets before him, looks forward to the Messiah's coming. He prophesies about the forerunner of the Messiah, John the Baptist, who will prepare the way for Jesus. In the same passage, he also predicts the coming of the Lord Christ Himself:

> *"See, I am going to send My messenger, and he will clear the way before Me. Then the Lord you seek will suddenly come to His temple, the Messenger of the covenant you desire—see, He is coming," says the Lord of Hosts.* (Mal 3:1)

The prophecies and warnings that will be exposited in this book bear a special weight also because Malachi is the final canonical work of the OT before the coming of Christ. A 400-year silence from God will be broken by Gabriel's prediction of John's and Jesus' birth in Luke, the direct fulfillment of the promise in Malachi that God will send a messenger. As readers who have already encountered the promised Messiah, we can view the unprecedented miracle represented here: that the Author entered into His ow=n story and played a role in His own providential plan.

The Oracle of the Book

The first verse of Malachi has two words that require a bit of special attention: *oracle* and *hand*. You have not misread that, nor have you missed something in your English translation—"oracle" is clearly stated, but "hand" is not. In Hebrew, verse 1 reads, "An oracle of the word of the LORD to Israel by the hand of Malachi." "By the hand of" is a Hebrew idiom that would have resonated with the hearts of Malachi's audience. Malachi claims divine inspiration as the source of his words in order to eliminate any doubts in the minds of the hearers. It was the hand of God that delivered the prophetic oracle, Malachi wrote it down, and then he handed it to the people of Israel.

The tone that this beginning sets is interesting as well: Malachi is almost threatening the people, saying, "I swear that this is going to happen. You can take this to the bank: God's punishment is imminent if you don't repent."

The Hebrew word *massa* is translated into English "oracle." Both Habakkuk and Nahum begin their books with the same word, which literally means "burden" or "load" (cf. Exod 23:5; Num 4:24,32; 11:11; 2 Sam 15:33; Isa 22:25; 46:1-2; Jer 17:21-27; 22:33-40) (Clendenen, *Haggai*, 242).

Traditionally, *massa* could be used as a judgment against a person, as in the "pronouncement" against Ahab in 1 Kings 9:25-26. In Malachi, though, *massa* signifies judgment against the nation of Israel (cf. Isa 22:1; 30:6; Ezek 12:10; Hab 1:1). However, the prevailing usage of the word was in judgment against foreign nations (Isa 13:1; 14:28; 15:1; 17:1; 19:1; 21:1,11,13; 23:1; Nah 1:1; Zech 9:1) (Clendenen, *Haggai*, 242).

If this is a word straight from God, why was it literally a "burden" for Malachi to deliver it to the nation of Israel?

We must remember that the office of prophet was not something one aspired to, like he would a political position or business role. It was a calling, much like a pastor or shepherd. The prophet had two distinct functions:

1. Instituted in Deuteronomy 18:15-18, the prophetic function in the context of the theocratic kingdom was to call the nation of Israel back to the Mosaic law. The conditional covenant of the law blessed obedience and punished disobedience.
2. The prophet would deliver predictive messages, typically about the coming Messiah.

Like a megaphone held to the mouth of an announcer, the prophet stood between God and the people, much like the expository preacher does today. At one time, God spoke directly to Adam and Eve in the garden and directly to Moses on Mount Sinai. But from then on He has used prophets: often solitary, devoted, and quite lonely individuals who lived secluded, extremely difficult lives.

People who choose the title of prophet for themselves should be taken with caution, for the life of a prophet is indescribably difficult. Think of Isaiah. God instructed him to discard his outer garments and sandals and then walk naked around the city for three years as a visual sign to the people of Israel of their coming captivity (Isa 20:1-4). Imagine God saying to your pastor, "Your people are stiff-necked and selfish. They are not getting the message. I want you to take off the suit and tie. In fact, take everything off and walk the halls of your church completely nude for three years."

Jeremiah has been labeled the weeping prophet of the Old Testament, and for good reason. Israel's slide into Babylonian captivity was too much for him to bear. He preached the very words of God—the words God told him to speak—for decades. He watched his brothers and sisters disregard God's words, disregard *God*, and give themselves over to their Babylonian captors. Throughout the course of his preaching, Jeremiah saw not one person respond to him. He preached a lifetime of sermons and nobody "came down front" even once. In his eyes and in the eyes of Israel, Jeremiah was a massive failure. But his success was measured not by his fruit, but by his faithfulness to preach God's Word.

The life of a prophet was a tough assignment to receive, but that was only half of the struggle: the words they were given were rarely easy to deliver. The words given to Malachi were extremely weighty. He was not communicating a health, wealth, and prosperity message. He didn't prescribe "10 easy steps to be the best *you* you can be." He said, "repent, or be destroyed" to his *own people*. And, as was the case with the majority of his prophetic contemporaries, his words—God's words—were brushed off.

The Style and Structure of the Book

The book radiates with rich theology, covering themes such as the nature and majesty of God, the coming Messiah, and the steadfast love of the Lord.

Six speeches and two commentaries provide a framework for Malachi:

- Speech 1: God's Love (1:2-5)
- Speech 2: Unfaithfulness of the Priests (1:6–2:9)
- Speech 3: Divorce (2:10-16)
- Speech 4: Divine Justice (2:17–3:5)
- Speech 5: Tithe (3:6-12)
- Speech 6: Day of Judgment (3:13–4:3)
- Commentary 1: Observing the Law (4:4)
- Commentary 2: Coming of Elijah (4:5-6)

Malachi was heavily influenced by the Persian world. We know this by the use of the term *governor* in 1:8. Instead of using the Hebrew word for governor, he opts for *pechah*, which is a Hebraic transliteration of a Persian word. Furthermore, Malachi uses the Socratic dialectic method of communication. Socrates was a classical Greek philosopher who cross-examined someone in order to uncover contradictions or inconsistencies in their assertions. Rather than teaching by coming right out and stating a conclusion, the dialectic style piles questions on top of each other in order to make the conclusion come from within the student—and thus, to make the lesson stick. Malachi, a relatively short book, is packed with questions:

- 10 questions in chapter 1
- 7 questions in chapter 2
- 6 questions in chapter 3

This dialectic method consists of three parts. Arnold Fruchtenbaum explains,

> First, there is a basic declarative statement. Secondly, this is followed by an objection. In the book of Malachi each of these objections begins with the same Hebrew word translated *Wherein* six times and *What* once. The third part is to give the answer to that objection. The Socratic method, then, is a statement, followed by an objection, followed by the answer. ("Malachi")

Again, the Socratic dialectic is a method of teaching that brings answers not from the mouth of the teacher to the ears of the student, but rather from the heart of the student into his mind. Rabbis used this same approach constantly, and Jesus was no different: much of His teaching was done by merely asking questions.

If a rebuke is raised against you, it is easy to brush it off as just a negative, misunderstanding opinion. However, should the accusation be raised in the form of a probing question, so that your realization of the error of your ways comes from *within* rather than from *without*, it is no longer a mere outside, misinformed opinion; it is an opportunity for reflection, self-examination, and repentance.

How a person handles correction speaks volume about their character. The author of Hebrews says,

> *My son, do not take the Lord's discipline lightly or faint when you are reproved by Him, for the Lord disciplines the one He loves and punishes every son He receives. . . . No discipline seems enjoyable at the time, but painful. Later on, however, it yields the fruit of peace and righteousness to those who have been trained by it.* (12:5-6,11)

This is why Malachi begins his book with the words, "'I have loved you,' says the Lord."

God loves you so much that He is willing to bear the difficult burden of exposing your sin. He loves you so much that He doesn't allow you to wallow in it. Malachi will demonstrate just how God goes about doing that.

Sovereign Love

MALACHI 1:2-5

Main Idea: God's covenant faithfulness to His people is manifested through sovereign love and demonstrated by His declaration, election, and rejection.

I. **Introduction: Missing the Obvious**
II. **God Substantiates His Love for His People through His Declaration (1:2a).**
III. **God Substantiates His Love for His People through His Election (1:2b).**
IV. **God Substantiates His Love for His People through His Rejection (1:3-5).**
V. **Conclusion: Christ as the Pinnacle Display of God's Sovereign Love**

Introduction: Missing the Obvious

The rather checkered history of Israel in the OT testifies to how often God's chosen people are oblivious to His obvious love for them. Israel had forgotten how God repeatedly showered His love upon them through His electing grace. In Malachi 1:2-5 God substantiates His love by protecting His people and punishing the wicked.

Although Malachi centers on only one dimension of God's covenant with Abraham, namely Jacob and Esau, the entire story stretching back to Genesis 12 serves as the backdrop for this text. God called Abram to leave Ur and to follow Him to another land. As Abram obeyed, his descendants multiplied. His progeny, the Israelites, were later enslaved in Egypt for over 400 years until God called them out under the leadership of Moses. Eventually they were allowed to enter the land God had promised them, but the book of Deuteronomy casts an ominous shadow over this achievement, predicting covenant infidelity on the part of Israel and consequent exile.

Despite a golden age under the Davidic monarchy, the positive political and spiritual situations of God's people quickly turned. After King Solomon died, Israel was split into two kingdoms—the northern kingdom (Israel) and the southern kingdom (Judah). Israel was the first to be taken into exile by the Assyrians in 722 BC, and Judah followed in 586 BC at the hands of Nebuchadnezzar, the ruler of the Babylonian Empire. Jerusalem was destroyed, the walls were knocked down, and the temple was burned. The history of God's elect had come full circle.

Many of God's prophets predicted that exile was temporary; it would eventually end, allowing the people to return to the land promised by God to their forefathers. Jeremiah 29:10, for example, states, "When 70 years for Babylon are complete, I will attend to you and will confirm My promise concerning you to restore you to this place." This return occurred in three waves. Zerubbabel led the first assembly back to the land and laid the foundations of the temple. The temple was completed during the second wave under the leadership of Ezra, the scribe. The third wave came under the leadership of Nehemiah, who led the people to rebuild the walls around Jerusalem. The last three books of the Old Testament—Haggai, Zechariah, and Malachi—were all written after this return.

One might think Israel would have learned her lesson, but following this return, pervasive corruption among the priesthood had initiated a trickle-down effect among the people of God. The book of Malachi is replete with prophetic indictments. But, as is common among God's prophets, before the bad news comes the good news. Malachi first reaffirms God's sovereign love for His people in four ways.

God Substantiates His Love for His People through His Declaration

MALACHI 1:2A

The Hebrew word translated "love" in Malachi 1:2 is in the perfect tense, signifying a completed action with continued ramifications (cf. the translation of the GNB: "I have always loved you"). The Hebrew word for "love," *ahav*, is used 32 times in the Old Testament to refer to God's covenantal love; it is used to explain God's love for Israel or individuals 23 of those times (Els, "*'āhab*," 276). Ray Clendenen states,

> Terms for "love" were common in ancient Near Eastern treaties as synonyms for covenant loyalty. In Mesopotamian texts divine love also motivated selection of a king (see also Neh 13:26). Likewise in the Hebrew Bible, especially in Deuteronomy, *'āhab*, "love," often is found in texts dealing with choosing and with faithfulness. (*Haggai*, 247)

God's love was the reason for choosing Israel (Deut 7:7), and His good pleasure is the only reason for continuing to care about them. God substantiates His love for His people by reminding them of how He redeemed their ancestors from bondage in Egypt and themselves from captivity in Babylon. He brings to mind their exclusive relationship with Him and His steadfast love toward them. And all this was manifest before He gave Israel the law. In the OT *relationship* always precedes *requirement.* As C. J. H. Wright explains, "God did not send Moses down to Egypt with the Law already tucked under his cloak" (*Eye for an Eye*, 22). Instead, He miraculously delivered them from the oppression of the Egyptians, protected them from the 10 plagues, and supernaturally parted the Red Sea *before* giving the law. That is, God showed grace to the generation under the guidance of Moses before making covenantal demands. Likewise, God, in Malachi 1:2, reminded the Jews of His grace before reminding them of His law.

God Substantiates His Love for His People through His Election

MALACHI 1:2B

Despite God's clear declaration of His love, the nation of Israel questioned God's affection by inquiring, "How have You loved us?" It seemed to them that God had not kept His promise to restore the tribes and the land. The short-sightedness of the people incited God to give a history lesson. Malachi reminded Israel of the account of God's esteeming Jacob above Esau.

The words *love* and *hate* should be understood in their covenantal sense as "chosen" and "not chosen." Since God chose Jacob to fulfill the Abrahamic covenant, *He loved him.* Since God did not choose Esau, *He hated him.* God went against the standard rules regarding the priority of the firstborn son by electing Jacob. According to the apostle Paul, this choice took place prior to the birth of the twins:

> *And not only that, but also Rebekah received a promise when she became pregnant by one man, our ancestor Isaac. For though her sons had not been born yet or done anything good or bad, so that God's purpose according to election might stand—not from works but from the One who calls—she was told: The older will serve the younger. As it is written: I have loved Jacob, but I have hated Esau.* (Rom 9:10-12)

God's election, then, is not influenced by human interaction or cooperation. He chose Abraham out of all the people of the world. He chose Abraham's son, Isaac, instead of his half-brother, Ishmael. He chose Jacob over his older brother, Esau. He chose the Israelites over all other nations. But He did not choose them based on their merit. Deuteronomy 7:7-8 states,

> *It was not because you were more in number than any other people that the Lord set His love on you and chose you, for you were the fewest of all peoples, but it is because the Lord loves you and is keeping the oath that He swore to your fathers, that the Lord has brought you out with a mighty hand and redeemed you from the house of slavery, from the hand of Pharaoh king of Egypt.*

God does not grade on a curve. If He did, Esau might have passed. Jacob, on the other hand, certainly would have failed, as he conned his father into placing the blessing on him rather than on his older brother. According to cultural traditions, Esau deserved God's blessing. Yet God does not bestow grace on those who seem to deserve it. If one's righteousness were the condition for God's grace, no one would enter the kingdom. All would experience separation from Him in a Christless place called hell if grace were based on human response to God's righteous conditions. But that is what is so amazing about grace! The point is not that God loved Jacob more than Esau, but that He desired to make a covenant with Jacob instead of Esau. Consequently, the reason why election is referred to in Malachi 1 is not to create a sense of exclusion. Instead, **election is deployed by the prophet to comfort and reassure the people of God.**

God's electing love is not based on performance, position, or power. It's based on His *prerogative*. The input you have in election is the same input you had in choosing your parents, the country you were born in, or the city in which you were raised. In the same way, the Jewish audience of Malachi had done nothing to deserve God's grace and love. But they had it!

God Substantiates His Love for His People through His Rejection

MALACHI 1:3-5

God's rejection of Edom is a response to their wickedness. There is a contrast in the text between wicked Edom and blessed Israel. Since the

Edomites demonstrated pride, arrogance, and violence, God is considered righteous by the prophet in His harsh punishment of the nation. The nations will experience two closely connected penalties for their unrighteousness: (1) The land will be destroyed and left completely uninhabited by humans. (2) The land will be possessed by the demonic (i.e., cursed) (Utley, "Study Bible Commentary"). The Edomites, descendants of Esau, were destined for destruction. One commentator expresses it this way:

> Esau's descendants would be excluded *as a nation* from that special electing love that would belong to Israel. God's choosing Jacob and his descendants meant that he established a permanent relationship with Israel as a whole, in which he would instruct them with truth, train them with righteousness, care for them with compassion, bless them with goodness, and discipline them with severity; regardless of how often they strayed from him, he would be faithful to them by his grace until his work in them was complete and "all Israel" (Rom 11:26, referring back to true Israel in Rom 9:6) would enjoy the righteousness, peace, and joy that come from knowing God (Jer 33; Ezek 36; Acts 13:16-41; Rom 9–11). (Clendenen, "Malachi," 253)

Malachi's prophecy comes to fruition when the Nabataean Arabs force the Edomites to settle in Idumea between 550 and 400 BC (Du Plessis, "Getting to Know," 209). Tensions would continue between the people of Jacob/Israel and the people of Esau/Edom. In 37 BC Herod the Great, an Idumean, began to rule the nation of Israel as a client-ruler of the Roman Empire (Josephus, *Antiquities of the Jews*, 12.8). The Romans appointed Herod over the land because they recognized the ancestral relationship between Idumea and Israel but did not understand the situation fully. The story of Jacob and Esau is played out in miniature in the interaction between Jesus and Herod. No wonder Herod, the Roman appointee, was worried when he heard of the One "*born* king of the Jews" (Matt 2:2). Like Jacob, Jesus was chosen by God. Herod was not!

God's love for Israel should not be left to speculation. He pointed the people to a historical event to prove His love: the people of God had been brought back from Babylonian captivity while the land of Edom remained in perpetual ruin.

Conclusion: Christ as the Pinnacle Display of God's Sovereign Love

Reading about the suffering and destruction of God's people, you may ask, "How do I know God loves me?" The answer to this question now, as in Malachi's day, is found in a historical and historic event, the cross of Jesus Christ. Romans 5:8 declares, "God proves His own love for us." How? "In that while we were still sinners, Christ died for us." The cross stands as a historical landmark to the bold declaration with which Malachi opens his prophecy: God has loved us. Jesus Christ *is* the pinnacle display of God's sovereign love.

Like Israel, God's love for us is an *electing* love that places the initiative with God. Scripture says that we were once wayward in sin, unable to save ourselves. We were alienated from God (Col 1:21), dead in our trespasses and sins (Eph 2:1-2), blinded by the enemy (2 Cor 4:3), morally bankrupt (Gen 8:21), and defiled in our bodies (Rom 1:24-25). Yet God saw our condition and initiated our adoption. Ephesians 1:3-6 states,

> *Praise the God and Father of our Lord Jesus Christ, who has blessed us in Christ with every spiritual blessing in the heavens. For He chose us in Him, before the foundation of the world, to be holy and blameless in His sight. In love He predestined us to be adopted through Jesus Christ for Himself, according to His favor and will, to the praise of His glorious grace that He favored us with in the Beloved.*

Election, then, is a biblical expression of God's love for us in Christ. Election is meant to humble us, remove boasting, remove entitlement, remove pride, and eradicate self-reliance.

God's love is unconditional. The nation of Israel did nothing to deserve election or salvation from slavery, and, in the same way, you did nothing to deserve His love. Even when we stray, He runs to meet us, just as the loving father did in the parable of the Prodigal Son (Luke 15). The father of the wayward son, who represents God in the story, ran to embrace his repentant son, even though the son had asked for his inheritance early (which was tantamount to telling his father, "Hurry up and die already!") and had squandered it! There was no way that the son could have paid his father back, nor did the father wish him to! He wanted nothing but reciprocal love from his son, and this is all God wants from us. We can do nothing good to persuade Him to love us more. Neither can we do anything wrong to make Him love us any less.

No one will ever love you like God loves you (1 John 4:9,19) and the only proper response is to love Him back.

Reflect and Discuss

1. Discuss ways it's easy to "go through the motions" when it comes to worship.
2. Why is mundane/routine worship such a tendency for most of us?
3. Some perceive the God of the OT as strict and harsh in His punishments. What other OT passages can you recall that show God to be a God of love?
4. What life situations might lead someone to the conclusion that God doesn't love him?
5. What evidence of God's sovereign love and grace can you point to in your life?
6. How would you respond as a parent if your child asked, "How have you loved me?"
7. Read Genesis 25:19-26. Who were Jacob and Esau? What do we know about their relationship?
8. What does it mean to be chosen by God? Why is this significant in affirming His love for us?
9. Read Hebrews 12:3-11. How do you explain the relationship between love and discipline?
10. How does this passage in Malachi communicate hope? How can the realization that God loves you affect a hopeless situation in your life?

Meaningful Worship

MALACHI 1:6-14

Main Idea: Despite God's sovereign love, Israel's priests respond with depraved actions stemming from apathetic worship.

I. Introduction: What Is Worship?
II. God's Complaint against Israel's Priests for Their Depraved Actions of Worship (1:6-12)
   A. Israel's priests despise God's name in their contribution (1:7-9).
   B. Israel's priests despise God's name in their commitment (1:10-12).
III. God's Complaint against Israel's Priests for Their Apathetic Attitudes toward Worship (1:13-14)
IV. Conclusion: Christ as the Image of God, Worthy of Spiritual Worship

---

Introduction: What Is Worship?

It is an unfortunate reality that words like *excellent, devoted,* and *committed* are almost exclusively used in our culture to describe the work ethic of athletes, career men and women, and those who take pride in their hobbies or pastimes. These same descriptors, to our shame, are often absent from our lips in describing the whole-hearted devotion of our brothers and sisters in the Lord. Indeed, if we are honest, we know that we, too, lack such devotion in our own worship and obedience.

Given the pervasiveness of human sin and the hardness of the human heart, it is not surprising that Israel likewise lacked such devotion in the time of Malachi. God had given His people the best: He had redeemed them from the Egyptians, led them through the desert, shown them the land, promised the basic necessities of life for herdsmen (i.e., milk and honey), marched them into the promised land, and conquered their enemies. But what was their response to His steadfast love for them? While one would think it would be extravagant praise and loving obedience, they instead offered Him what can only be described as *worthless worship.*

As we examine this text, we would do well to examine the current state of our own worship and our attitude toward the Lord to determine if it is meaningful—worthy of the God who has saved us in His Son Jesus Christ—or worthless.

First, it may be helpful to ask what is meant by the term *worship*. Most Christians, when they think of worship, immediately imagine singing, praying, or a certain posture. To be sure, worship will include all of these things, but it must also be more than these. **Worship is an attitude of one's heart.** It's from an old word that means "worth-ship." It's to ascribe to something or to an individual honor and respect. It is to proclaim their worth.

In Israel's case (as in ours) we are talking about God. We worship God most importantly because of who He is: the supreme creator and ruler of the universe. But we also worship Him for what He has done for us. Malachi 1:6 reminds Israel that God has loved them like a father. Furthermore, the word *Hosts* is a military term. It refers to an army. In this case it is the army of the Lord—likely the angels. Hence, Malachi is reminding the reader that God deserves respect not only like a father of a family or a master of a house; God demands honor based on His status as the divine general of the angelic armies.

So it is clear that Israel's God is calling for proper worship of who He is and what He has done for them. Because He has set His love upon Israel like a father upon a child, and because He is the commander of an army of angels, He is worthy of meaningful worship. Already in verse 6 we see that God is not receiving the worship due His name, and He holds the priests, in particular, responsible for this failure.

God's Complaint against Israel's Priests for Their Depraved Actions of Worship

MALACHI 1:6-12

God is referred to in this passage and throughout Scripture as a father. He was the Father of Israel. Why? Because He redeemed them. Like a loving father, He nurtured them. Like a loving father, He disciplined them when they were disobedient (cf. Heb 12:3-11). So God is referred to as a father, their heavenly Father. God commanded in the Ten Commandments, "You shall honor your father and mother" (Exod 20:12). Is it any wonder, then, that God as a spiritual Father expects obedience?

However, we see in the text that Israel did not obey Him as a child obeys a father. In the first place, they offered Him no honor. That word *honor* is an interesting word. It's the Hebrew word *kabod,* which is elsewhere translated "glory." They did not glory in Him. They did not revere Him. They did not respect Him.

Then the Lord issues a second indictment: Israel does not fear God. We must be careful not to take this word *fear* in the sense of being horrified or frightened. This word refers to an appropriate respect, a reverential honor for a holy God. What God is saying through the prophet Malachi is, "You have not honored Me, and you do not respect Me."

The text clearly states that the priests were to blame. These were the religious and political leaders of Israel. That is, they were the representatives of both God and His people. They were the ministerial servants in the temple, commissioned to carry out sacrifices and lead the festivals and feasts. The depth of their failure is seen in that, despite their privileged position, they despised God.

The term *despise* is significant. It is the attitude of ongoing disrespect. It also refers to the act of conveying insignificance or worthlessness upon an object, idea, or individual. It is the same word used in the Genesis story concerning Esau and Jacob, when Esau thought that his birthright was insignificant, so much so that he could trade it away for stewed meat (Gen 25:34). In the present context the priests are said to despise God's name, which is shorthand for the person, character, and work of God. They despised who God was. He wasn't important to them anymore. He wasn't breathtaking to them anymore. He wasn't significant to them anymore. Even though they gave extravagant sacrifices, they considered God to be without worth, and this estimation affected the form of their worship.

Israel's Priests Despise God's Name in Their Contribution (1:7-9)

At the end of verse 6, Malachi asks a question that God knows the answer to. God knows their hearts, and He will show them how they have despised His name. The people ask, "God, how in the world is offering unclean sacrifices polluting to You? How is our offering contaminating, Lord?" And to this God responds, "Just look at what you've done!"

What they were doing was no minor sin. The word *defiled* or *polluted* can also be translated "unclean." It is a ceremonial way of saying "unauthorized" or "unacceptable." As we know, and as the priest should have realized, God takes His sacrifices very seriously. When Aaron's two sons, Nadab and Abihu, offered unauthorized sacrifices to the Lord (Lev 10:1-3), do you remember what the Lord did? He sent down fire and consumed them! But in spite of such a stark demonstration of what kind of holiness God demands, the priests here are offering unclean sacrifices to the Lord and acting as if there is nothing wrong. In verse 8 Malachi points out that the priests were offering crippled, lame, and blind animals to the Lord, even though God expected a spotless sacrifice. He didn't want the second best. He didn't want "good enough." He wanted the very best they had.

When God asked the question "Is it not wrong?" the answer should have been obvious: Absolutely it was wrong! It is embarrassing that God would even have to point this out to the priests. God basically says, "Use common sense here, guys. Don't you see that this is wrong? You should never offer this to Me, and you *sure* wouldn't offer this to the governor!"

When He says, "Present that to your governor," He uses a Persian loan word to describe this pagan leader. One commentator says,

> The governor's table was a lavishly prepared banquet that included offerings from the people. Certainly the governor would not have been pleased with the meat of blind or crippled or diseased animals. In fact, he would not have accepted it. How much more absurd it was to expect the favor of the Lord almighty with such offerings. He did not accept such sacrifices nor did he accept the priests. (Blaising, "Malachi," 1578)

In modern times God may have reason to say something to you like this: "You offer your best to Uncle Sam, but you offer less to the work of God. You spend all your time watching college football, but you spend minimal time reading My Word. You spend all your time in your hobbies, but you devote little time to praying, seeking, memorizing, and meditating. And now you solicit the favor of God?"

This is exactly what He says in verse 9. The term *ask*, when woodenly translated, means, "to smooth over." In the vernacular of today it could be translated, "butter someone up." And as ridiculous as this sounds, we do the very same today: "God, I know I haven't attended church in a while; I know I haven't been faithful to read the Word; I know I haven't given any of my resources to the ministry; I know I haven't devoted any time to the work of sharing the gospel; and I know I haven't memorized and meditated on Your truths. But God, would You PLEASE bless this situation at this time?" Of course this is not to suggest that we ever merit God's favor by actually doing any of these things, but the inconsistency is appalling! Really?! *Now* we want to honor God and ask Him to honor us? We betray our lack of reverence, and we despise His name with such requests.

From this rebuke we can clearly see this important truth: **Before God ever accepts your gift, He inspects your heart.** The value of the offering is determined by the heart of the one who is offering it. Before you give anything to God, you must give Him yourself completely.

This truth reminds me of the young believer who had attended church shortly after being baptized in Africa. During part of the service, they were passing the plate. Because she was a new believer, this was an unfamiliar practice. She saw people taking money out of their pockets and their wallets and putting it into the offering plate. She, as a new believer and living in menial conditions, reached into her pockets and realized she had no money. As the plate was being passed down her row, the usher handed it to her. She didn't know what to do so she set it on the ground, and she stood inside the plate before speaking out loud, "God, I don't have any money but You can have all of me." Surely this was an acceptable act of worship.

The people of Israel had despised God's name. They had forgotten about His wondrous nature and His glorious works. He wasn't impressive to them anymore. Therefore, they dishonored God in their contribution, and as a result they defiled His altar. Unfortunately, their trespasses extend greater than this.

Israel's Priests Despise God's Name in Their Commitment (1:10-12)

Notice, also, that the people disgraced God's table in verses 10-11. In emphasizing how great His name will be among the nations, God is indicting Israel for her lack of esteem for His name. In essence, the Lord says, "Apparently My name is no longer great to you, Israel, but it will be great among the nations."

He moves His attention to their lack of commitment in verse 12. Their service to the Lord was monotonous. It was a job to them. The priests were merely going through the motions in the temple, and God wanted to shut them off from His presence because of it. He was sick and tired of their heartless rituals and routines. He wanted no more of their prayers and hymns. He was done with their sacrifices and feasts.

His desire was for heartfelt devotion, which, judging by their commitment to His worship, was absent.

Because of their actions, God would not accept their offerings. We know the full realization of this condemnation to be in AD 70 when the temple was utterly destroyed and not one stone was left upon another. It is very difficult for modern Christians to comprehend the force of this event in Israel's history. It would be roughly similar to God saying, "Shut the doors to every church in the world. No more church. No more meetings. It's over." But that analogy doesn't really convey the whole picture, because the Israelites were dependent upon the temple for everything—for their sacrifices, for the forgiveness of their sins, and for their festivals, feast days, and offerings. The temple was even the center of national banking and Jewish political power. Without the temple, the nation would cease to function.

Why would God call for such destruction? In the New Testament we find that the temple is no longer needed because Christ is the fulfillment of everything the temple offered in the life of the Israelites. But in Malachi 1, the reason is that the priests, the socio-religious leaders of Israel, were playing games with God. And when the leaders possess a lackadaisical attitude toward God, the people adopt the same mentality. But now, Malachi reports, the games are over.

We should resolve decisively today to cease the spiritual farces. Let's be through with casual Christianity once and for all. Let's be through with worthless worship. Let's be through with selfish service that we give in order to get, and let's come before the One who knows all. We can't hide from this God. You can fool your husband. You can fool your wife. You can fool your kids. You can fool your co-workers. You can fool your Sunday school class. You can fool your pastor. But you cannot fool God. In our offerings of worship and in our commitment to obedience, may we give to the God of Israel meaningful, heartfelt worship.

God's Complaint against Israel's Priests for Their Apathetic Attitudes toward Worship

MALACHI 1:13-14

Malachi proves that when there are listless actions, at the root is always an apathetic attitude. When your actions are tedious toward the Lord, when you're monotonous in your rituals, it's always stemming from an apathetic attitude. We have seen the actions; verses 13-14 reveal the attitude.

The priests had become tired of the sacrificial system. It was a burden to them. The word *nuisance* is used five times in the OT. It's the same word that's used to describe the weariness of the Israelites as they walked through the wilderness ("hardships" in Exod 18:8; Num 20:14). They were just burdened by the process. The priests had viewed their service as a system of checking boxes or punching cards and they just wanted to get their work done in order to return home to relax.

Up to this point, we've seen two forms of unacceptable sacrifices: the people were offering both lame and sick animals (1:8). Now God introduces a third category: those that are "defective." They were stealing animals without paying for them. They weren't offering the best animals they owned. Obtaining them in an illegitimate manner, they offered them up secretly. It didn't cost them anything. And because it cost them nothing, it was no sacrifice at all. In fact, we might say that **if there's no sacrifice in your sacrifice, it's not a sacrifice**.

Worship is more than words. It's an attitude of the heart. I believe someone's offering and actions are connected to their attitude and, in particular, to their view of God. For when you see God for who He is and what He's done, your worship will be affected.

This reminds me of the Archbishop of Paris. Many years ago he told the story of three young men who were traveling around Paris indulging in all the sensual appetites that the city had to offer. They sampled all the delicacies of sin, if you will, and at the end of their night, parading and carousing through the city, they found themselves on the steps of the cathedral, sprawled out in a drunken stupor. As the sun rose, the partygoers relived their escapades from the night before.

One of the men had the bright idea, "Why don't we go inside and find a confessional booth. We'll ask the priest to forgive us of all of our sins that we just committed by confessing them out loud." They were going to do this in a blasphemous manner, not seeking true forgiveness from God, believing this act would be the crowning glory of a night to remember.

Invigorated by the laughter of his friends, one young man volunteered to do it. He walked into the chapel and requested the attention of a priest. He sat in the confessional booth and confessed his sins loudly one after the other in lurid detail. The confession was concluded with these words, "I know all that You did for me, and I don't give a @!#!"

The priest, realizing what was happening, stopped him and said this to him: "Young man, I have heard enough. You don't need to confess anything else to me. If you would like to be forgiven of your sins, you only need to do one thing. Outside of the confessional are steps leading up to an altar. On the altar is a statue of Jesus on the cross. Simply go to the statue, kneel down at the steps, look at Christ on the cross, and say these words: 'Lord Jesus, I know all that You've done for me and I don't give a @!#!'" The boy, if you can imagine, was shocked. So the priest repeated those words again to him. "You will be forgiven if you go outside, look at the cross, and say to the Lord Jesus, 'I know all that You've done for me and I don't give a @!#!'"

At this point the boy, now surprisingly sober, stumbled out of the confessional booth and into view of his friends. Wondering how the priest had responded to the vulgar confession, his partners in crime watched their friend walk toward the steps. He knelt down on the stairs, looked up to Jesus hanging on the cross, and said, "Lord Jesus, I know all that You've done for me. Would You forgive me of my sins?"

The Archbishop of Paris said, "I know that story is true because that story is of me."

As long as the boy was playing games, his sacrifice and his worship meant nothing. When he was forced to take a serious look at Christ, he responded in worship. The same happens to us, too.

Conclusion: Christ as the Image of God, Worthy of Spiritual Worship

When you get a glimpse of the greatness of God, when you gain a proper perspective of who Christ is and what Christ has done for you, you'll never again play games with God. When we see Christ as the image of God, clearly presented to us as worthy of worship and praise, we must respond with loving worship and heartfelt obedience. And because of Christ, we are able to offer these sacrifices from a pure heart. In Romans 12:1 Paul says as much:

> *Therefore, brothers, by the mercies of God, I urge you to present your bodies as a living sacrifice, holy and pleasing to God; this is your spiritual worship.*

Malachi was talking about Aaronic priests, a class that does not exist today. Paul says that every believer in Christ is a priest, called to offer spiritual sacrifices of worship. You don't need an outfit. You don't need a white collar. You don't need a black robe. First Peter 2:5 confirms this:

> *You yourselves, as living stones, are being built into a spiritual house for a holy priesthood to offer spiritual sacrifices acceptable to God through Jesus Christ.*

So you and I, as priests, offer up sacrifices to the Lord. Living sacrifices, as opposed to dead sacrifices, regularly crawl off the altar on which they are laid. So we must continually recommit ourselves to God.

Now what do we offer up? Let me briefly list five things. First, you offer up your body (Rom 12:1-2). You also offer up your finances to the Lord as a spiritual sacrifice (Phil 4:14-18). Third, you offer up your praise to the Lord (Heb 13:15). Fourth, you offer up your good works (Heb 13:16). Finally, you even offer up those who have accepted the gospel as a result of your sharing (Rom 15:16). By God's grace, may we offer meaningful worship to the only One who is worthy of all honor and glory and praise, even among all the nations (Mal 1:11).

Reflect and Discuss

1. Who is someone you admire for their devotion to their craft? What would your worship look like if it reflected such devotion?
2. What are some characteristics of worthless worship in our own day?
3. If worship is an attitude of the heart, why did it matter what Israel brought for their sacrifices?
4. How had God shown Himself to be a father to the people of Israel? What are some other ways Israel failed to treat Him as a father?
5. What are we called to contribute in worship? How can we despise God in our contribution?
6. To what/whom are you tempted to give your highest worship—that which only belongs to God?
7. How can we often reflect the hypocrisy that Israel demonstrated in verse 9?
8. How does Matthew 22:15-22 instruct us on what we are to give God in worship?
9. How can cultural, casual Christianity resemble Israel's defective worship?
10. How does the coming of Christ empower meaningful worship greater than was possible in the OT?

The High Cost of Spiritual Leadership

MALACHI 2:1-9

Main Idea: The depraved and apathetic worship of Israel's priests causes Israel to stumble and invokes God's curse as a means of ensuring the permanence of God's covenant with Levi.

I. Introduction: God's Curse against Israel's Priests for Their Depraved and Apathetic Worship (2:1-3)

II. God Reminds Israel's Priests of Their Covenantal Role Model, Levi (2:4-7).

A. Levi was a man of godly commitment (2:4).

B. Levi was a man of godly character (2:5).

C. Levi was a man of godly communication (2:6-7).

III. Four Ways Israel's Priests Failed to Follow the Covenant Role Model of Levi (2:8-9)

IV. Conclusion: Christ as the New and Better Levi, Our Great High Priest

---

Introduction: God's Curse against Israel's Priests for Their Depraved and Apathetic Worship

MALACHI 2:1-3

God's dissatisfaction is immediately apparent in this chapter. In His confrontation with the priesthood He warns, "If you do not heed the instructions that I gave you in chapter 1, then you will suffer the curses detailed in chapter 2."

The phrase *take it to heart* in verse 2 conveys the concept of determining a course of action based on information previously received. Taking something to heart is not merely hearing from God, it is putting what was heard into action. God directs the priests to meditate on the words He has already spoken to them. We consistently read in Scripture that orthodoxy leads to orthopraxy: right belief produces right behavior. God tells the priests that if they do not "take it to heart to honor My name," they will experience God's curse. But in order to honor the name of God, the priests must realize again that God's name is worthy to be praised. The priests divulge their warped understanding of God's nature by offering polluted and inadequate sacrifices (1:6-14). Therefore, since the priests' wrong beliefs have led to improper devotion, God, as is prescribed under the covenant, must curse the Levites.

The word *curse* contains a definite article in Hebrew (literally, "*the* curse"). This is not a casual curse nor is it a commonplace one; it is intentional and particular. Perhaps it is the curse from Deuteronomy 28, in which God essentially warned the people, "If you don't obey Me, you will exchange blessings for destruction." Regardless of whether this is the specific curse to which God was referring, it is certain that "the curse" will swiftly befall the nation.

In verse 9 God declares, "So I in turn have made you despised and humiliated before all the people." This verb translated "I . . . have made" is in the perfect tense. Verbs in the perfect tense represent actions that happened in the past but have continuing consequences in the present. It is used by God to convey to the people that there is no turning back God's hand; the priests have sinned heinously, and the curse for their transgression is already upon them.

So what is the price they paid for their disobedience? The punishment is twofold. First, the descendants of the Levitical priesthood will be made to suffer (v. 3a). Here we have the first of five uses of the Hebrew word, traditionally translated "behold," in the book of Malachi ("see" twice in 3:1; "indeed" in 4:1; "look" again in 4:5). This is a word used to place emphasis upon a subject or to allude to imminence. God is emphatically telling the priesthood that He is serious. Their progeny will suffer the consequences of the current generation's actions, and they will only have themselves to blame as covenant transgressors.

Not only will the priests' offspring face judgment, but the priests themselves will be humiliated by the Lord (v. 3b). God certainly discloses how He perceives the priesthood's disobedience. God reveals to the priests how repulsive He finds their glib handling of His commands. By rubbing feces on their faces, a visual is given to them of what their worthless sacrifices look like to Him. God will embarrass them by adorning their bodies with impurities for all to see.

God Reminds Israel's Priests of their Covenantal Role Model, Levi

MALACHI 2:4-7

We have seen the priests' transgressions and have witnessed the prophecy of their demise. Next, God reminds them of the holy source and scope of the message (v. 4). God, the Lord of Hosts, reminds them of His covenant with Levi. Levi exemplified three characteristics worth noting.

Levi Was a Man of Godly Commitment (2:4)

God made a covenant with Levi, whose descendants would become the priesthood in the land of Israel, the promised land. When all the tribes eventually made it into the place they were promised, the Levites were the only ones who didn't receive a portion of the land, as explained in Joshua 18:7: "But the Levites among you do not get a portion, because their inheritance is the priesthood of the LORD." Their share of God's blessing in the promised land was when He made a covenant with them granting them the privilege and responsibility of leading His people in worship.

Although the covenant with Levi is not as prominent as those with Abraham or Moses or David, it is, nevertheless, an important covenant because of the duties they were expected to perform. Examine Deuteronomy 21:5.

> *Then the priests, the sons of Levi, will come forward, for Yahweh your God has chosen them to serve Him and pronounce blessings in His name, and they are to give a ruling in every dispute and case of assault.*

The Levites had two duties. First, they settled disputes over the law, that is, the Torah. When there were disagreements in the land, they acted as judges. Second, they insulated and protected an unholy people from a holy God. They were the "go-betweens" on behalf of the Israelites before the Lord.

Today, Levites are not necessary because we have an intercessor and mediator who fulfills their functions: Christ. First Timothy 2:5 states that He is our representative, the way an attorney is the representative of a defendant before a judge. Christ is the ultimate fulfillment of the covenant God made with the tribe of Levi, and, like Levi, Jesus was a man of godly commitment.

Levi Was a Man of Godly Character (2:5)

The word *reverence* or *fear* (ESV) is used 150 times in the OT. Here in verse 5 it is placed alongside "stood in awe." The latter means "to be shattered" or "to be dismayed." We may picture the meaning as being broken into pieces, whether physically, emotionally, or spiritually. Normally when the words *fear* and *awe* appear together, they are used in the context of horror and fright. The only time in the Bible where both these words together talk about our respect and reverence for a holy God is right here. Puzzling, then, is that on multiple occasions God says to the people, "Do not fear." Which are we to believe? Is God calling His people to fear Him or not to fear Him?

In Exodus 20:18-20 we witness a paradox in the giving of the law. There are 613 individual laws in the Torah, but this passage is specifically concerned with the presentation of the Ten Commandments to Moses. When the people witnessed the thunder, the flashes of lightning, and the smoking mountain, they were frozen in fear and trembling. Standing at a distance from the mountain, they cried out to Moses, "You speak to us, and we will listen . . . but don't let God speak to us, or we will die." Moses responded to the people, "Don't be afraid, for God has come to test you, so that you will fear Him and will not sin."

Do you want to know what I think the problem is in most Christian circles? Most people don't *fear* God anymore. Oswald Chambers said, "The remarkable thing about fearing God is that when you fear God, you fear nothing else, whereas if you do not fear God, you fear everything else" (Wiersbe, *Wiersbe Bible Commentary OT*, 767). So what is the fear of the Lord? What does it mean to have a healthy fear of the divine?

Jerry Bridges, in his book *The Joy of Fearing God*, describes the difference between "servile" fear and "filial" fear (*Joy of Fearing God*, 26–27). Servile fear is the fear that comes from the Latin word *servus*, the word for "slave." He describes it this way: "It's the kind of fear which a slave would feel towards a harsh and unyielding master. It's to be subject to someone who is harsh and unyielding." It is the same fear that is seen in the Parable of the Talents, when the third man responded to the master, "Master, I know you. You're a difficult man, reaping where you haven't sown and gathering where you haven't scattered seed. So I was afraid and went off and hid your talent in the ground. Look, you have what is yours."

Bridges refers to this type of fear as "servile" fear, which is not the type of fear portrayed in Malachi. The second kind of fear, "filial" fear, is the fear a son has in relationship to his father. "Filial" comes from the Latin word that means "son," and it is this indefinable mixture of reverence, fear, pleasure, joy, and awe that should fill a worshiper's heart when giving reverence to God.

Do you have a healthy, biblical fear of God? Do you stand in awe of His authority? His power? His strength? His goodness? His majesty? The priests of the Lord during Malachi's ministry did not, but God called them, like Levi before, to demonstrate godly commitment and character.

Levi Was a Man of Godly Communication (2:6-7)

The true servant of God preaches the Scriptures unapologetically. He does not alter the message to tickle the ears of the people. He does not shrink back from doctrinal truths. Neither does he preach man-centered messages to please the masses or draw large crowds. He is a man who stands on the infallible, inerrant Word of God, preaches the entire counsel of God, and leaves the results to God. The word translated "instruction" is the Hebrew word *torah*. Levi had the Torah on his lips, therefore what he said was found to be without fault.

Ironically, God effectively says, "Malachi, My messenger, is rebuking the priests, who are supposed to be the messengers of the Lord." The messengers of the Lord, the priests, who were supposed to delegate true instruction, are being rebuked by the messenger of the Lord.

Malachi continues, "You need to guard the message that has been given to you." But how do you guard biblical truth? You guard it, paradoxically, by giving it away. You forsake it by keeping it in. Second Timothy 1:14 states, "Guard, through the Holy Spirit who lives in us, that good thing entrusted to you." Paul, how is this done? If Paul were here, he would tell us that we guard it by giving it away! This is the basis for spiritual leadership.

So we must ask, as a disciple of Christ Jesus, "In whom are you investing what you have learned while being a believer? Who are you discipling right now?" These questions are immensely important, because if you are not discipling someone, you are abandoning the gospel message.

That is, you are not guarding it. The gospel came to you because it was heading to someone else.

Four Ways Israel's Priests Failed to Follow the Covenant Role Model of Levi

MALACHI 2:8-9

God has just reminded the priests of the covenant from which they received their charge, but only because the message He intended to deliver required it. What comes next is not an encouragement (like reminders of covenants can be), but an indictment. God points out four errors of the priestly class to reveal just how far they've strayed.

First, God rejected them because of their poor sacrifices and their inadequate understanding of the Lord's incommunicable qualities, specifically His holiness. Then God presented the people with a role model for obedience by reminding them of the righteousness of Levi. Now God makes plain the areas in which the priests have rebelled.

We see in verses 8 and 9 four actions on the part of these priests that are antithetical to the deeds of Levi. These are the four ways in which the priests have strayed and violated the law of the Lord.

The priests disobeyed the Lord. The priests "have turned from *the way*," the instruction of the Torah. The proper path was cut for them, yet they decided to stray into the underbrush instead.

The priests distracted the people. How terrible it is that the priests themselves caused the people of Israel to stumble! Those entrusted to be ministers of the gospel are not only responsible for their own faithfulness in service to the Lord, but also how they lead others to do the same. It is one thing for a person, as an individual, to fall away. It is a completely different matter should one cause another person to stumble. Each person is responsible for how he acts. Ministerial actions speak as loud as words. People are watching both your lips and your life.

Jesus cautioned against this kind of destructive behavior in Mark 9:42-43:

> *But whoever causes the downfall of one of these little ones who believe in Me—it would be better for him if a heavy millstone were hung around his neck and he were thrown into the sea. And if your hand causes your downfall, cut it off. It is better for you to enter life maimed than to have two hands and go to hell—the unquenchable fire.*

The term *little ones* here does not refer to children. He is referring to the disciples, the poor in spirit, the humble ones. The normal word for "sin" in Greek is *hamartia*. But in this case, Jesus opts for the word *scandalizen*, which can also be translated "sin," but generally refers to stumbling. Jesus says, "If you are a part of shipwrecking someone's faith, it would have been better for you to have been drowned with a millstone around your neck than to have caused them to stumble."

This passage brings to mind those who infamously led many astray from the teaching of God. Think of men like Jim Jones, who duped hundreds of people into drinking poisonous Kool-Aid laced with Valium, cyanide, and Phenergan. David Koresh, the high school dropout, rock musician, and polygamist, told his people, "If the Bible is true, then I am the messiah." He convinced 74 men, women, and children to burn in a firestorm in Waco, Texas. Marshall Applewhite and Bonnie Nettles, leaders of the Heaven's Gate movement, thought a UFO was connected to the Hale Bopp comet and, at its highest point, they convinced 39 of its members to drink a concoction of vodka, pineapple juice, and phenyl barbital before putting plastic bags over their heads and suffocating themselves. May God have mercy on the souls of these men and women, for Jesus said it would have been better for a person to be drowned by a millstone than to lead someone else astray. There is a high cost to being a spiritual leader.

Unfortunately, the priests engaged in another prohibited practice:

The priests disregarded the promise of God. They "'violated the covenant of Levi." *Violated* is the word used to portray something as damaged beyond repair. This word is used in Malachi 1:14 when God described the people's unauthorized offering of sacrifices.

The priests demonstrated partiality. The priests were supposed to decide cases based on integrity and truth, but they were ruling with bias. They were showing favoritism to some and injustice to others. A valued individual received a favorable verdict. If the priests reviled an individual, justice was withheld. God accused the leadership of Israel of prejudicial priestly favoritism. Corruption permeated the society. Their teachings and their offerings were tainted, to which God ultimately responded, "Because you have no integrity in your walk and no integrity in your talk, here are the consequences."

Look at Malachi 2:9: "So I in turn have made you despised and humiliated before all the people." It's a terrible thing to be in the crosshairs of the wrath of God. Whether God meant it metaphorically or physically, having dung spread on your faces is supremely awful. Disgusting and embarrassing though it may be, this is a fairly light sentence! When you look at Numbers 18:32, their penalty for this perversion should have been death. Is God a God of mercy? He absolutely is, because He *should have* and *could have* decimated the entire priesthood in the blink of an eye. Yet God extended mercy.

They deserved death, yet were spared. Do not forget, however, that God's silence was perhaps a worse punishment. Silence can be deafening. A few hours' silence is bad enough, but it is another category entirely to hear nothing for 400 years. Can you feel the weight of what that must have been like for the people of God? No more prophets. No more words. No more truth. Just silence.

Conclusion: Christ as the New and Better Levi, Our Great High Priest

So how do we apply what we have read in Malachi 2:1-9 to our own lives? We see that leaders are held to a higher standard than those being led. And all Christians are leaders in some aspect of our lives, whether it be as mothers and fathers, teachers, coaches, or mentors—we are a kingdom of priests. Further, I believe that every one of us repeatedly commits high treason against the Lord through disrespect in our actions and attitudes. If we really think about our lives, we, like the priests, have wandered in our character, commitment, and communication with the Lord. Instead of being vehicles of consecration, we have become facilitators of contamination.

The irony of the passage is that God appointed the priests for the purpose of purifying the people and protecting the temple, but they were the source of the pollution. The ones who were called to live a life of purity before the Lord were the ones who were actually destroying the nation. Perversion originated with and was propagated through them.

Regarding vocational ministers, without a doubt, there is perversion throughout the history of the clergy; such transgression was not isolated to the priests of the OT. Whether we look at the Roman Catholic sexual scandals, the adulterous, immoral relationships of some pastors, or the greed of many televangelists, no one is outside of the sting of sin. Sadly, many apparently get away with their sinful leadership. But God, who sees it all and certainly does not forget anything, holds church leaders to a higher standard. James 3:1 is a sobering reminder: "Not many should become teachers, my brothers, knowing that we will receive a stricter judgment."

Church leaders are examined both by the Lord and by other people. Ministers' families are constantly being scrutinized. Their finances are constantly being examined. Their material possessions are being analyzed and questioned. People from the inside and outside of the church judge their marriages, speech, actions, and attitudes all the time. Additionally, a pastor experiences the constant burden for lost family members, for backslidden church members, and of performing funerals for friends. This may be one reason why hundreds of pastors leave the ministry every single month.

Ministry is both a terrifying and a thrilling endeavor. The thought of standing before a righteous God to give an account for how His gospel was carried out is alarming. But what a privilege to be set apart for ministerial service! However, with great privilege comes great responsibility. Thankfully, One has come who carried out this responsibility perfectly. He was righteous under the law, never being led astray. Jesus stands as the quintessential priest and fulfillment of the Levitical priesthood.

Five key points can be extracted from this text as they relate to the calling of ministers:

1. Pray for their proclamation, that they would be men and women who preach and teach the gospel, the whole counsel of God.
2. Pray for their purity. The greatest gift that a minister can give is not his preaching ability, his ability to visit the sick or to comfort those who have lost loved ones, how consistently he visits hospitals, or how engaging of a counselor he is. The greatest gift a pastor can offer to his church is his personal holiness before the Lord. Pray for his purity.[1]
3. Pray for your leaders' marriages. The enemy would love nothing more than to destroy marriages. What God has brought together, Satan would delight in tearing asunder.
4. Pray for their protection. The enemy is likened to a roaring lion seeking to destroy and devour leaders in the church (1 Pet 5:8).
5. Pray for their perseverance. Ask God to empower them to stand firm to the end, looking to Jesus as their source, strength, and example of faithful service (cf. Heb 12:1-4).

---

[1] This idea is from the 19th-century Scottish pastor Robert Murray M'Cheyne.

Reflect and Discuss

1. How does our worship reveal how highly we esteem God's name?
2. Read Deuteronomy 28. How does this text resemble Malachi's message?
3. What does it mean to be a man of godly commitment like Levi, and how do we see this perfectly manifested in Jesus?
4. Discuss the divergence between "servile" fear and "filial" fear and how they inform our relationship to God.
5. How can you practice godly communication? Who are you discipling, and what does that look like?
6. Who are some other leaders who have led many people astray? What did they teach? How did they live?
7. Who are the leaders who have had the biggest impact on your life? How did they encourage you in your Christian faith?
8. Who in your life can you lead spiritually? What are some lessons from this passage that can shape your investment in those disciples?
9. Why are leaders judged more strictly?
10. Which of the above prayers can you commit to pray for your leaders? Why does this seem especially important to you?

Broken Relationships

MALACHI 2:10-16

Main Idea: The permanence of God's covenant with Israel's fathers is threatened by Israel's pervasive faithlessness, but renewal begins with faithfulness to the covenant of marriage.

I. Introduction: Depraved Leadership Leads to Faithless Followers.
II. Covenant Infidelity Manifested by Israel's Faithlessness to One Another (2:10)
III. Covenant Infidelity Manifested by Israel's Faithlessness to the Precepts of God (2:11-12)
IV. Covenant Infidelity Manifested by Israel's Faithlessness to Their Marriage Partners (2:13-14)
V. Covenant Renewal Begins with Faithfulness to the Covenant of Marriage (2:15-16).
VI. Conclusion: Christ as the Faithful Bridegroom Relentlessly Pursuing His Bride, the Church

---

Introduction: Depraved Leadership Leads to Faithless Followers

Enemies from outside Rome's gates did not cause it to crumble. It was entirely forces from within its walls. The enemy was the decay of religion and the degradation of the home, a result of rampant divorce. For those of us who live in the West today, this truth should raise a few alarms.

In Malachi 2:10-16 God, through Malachi, is chastising the Israelites, particularly the priests, for the faithlessness shown to their spouses. Modern Christians are encouraged through this passage to remain faithful to our first love, the triune God.

Covenant Infidelity Manifested by Israel's Faithlessness to One Another

MALACHI 2:10

Malachi provides three ways the Israelites can renew their commitment to the Lord. First, He calls Israel to reflect on her capricious strife between tribes. He asks that the disjointed tribes recognize that they share a common Father. Some theologians, notably Calvin and Jerome, suggest that the "one Father" is Abraham. (Lange, *Commentary*, 16). However, that view seems to be a bit limited. More appropriately, "one Father" is most likely referring to God. Look at the second part of that verse: "Didn't one God create us?" The word *create* is the key. It is the same word used in Genesis 1 when Moses wrote of God creating the heavens and the earth. God formed us and afterward chose us. It's the same idea that He tried to communicate in chapter 1 when He said, "I loved Jacob, but I hated Esau."

Malachi begins to assert the notion of God's choosing and calling His people—the ultimate unifying factor between them. "The only reason you people are created as a nation, in fact the only reason you exist as a nation is because of Me," the Lord effectively says. Every time the word *create* is used in the OT it refers to God's sovereign authority.

Malachi's message is simple: Don't forget where you came from, and don't forget who called you. Here's a point to ponder: Forgetfulness will lead to faithlessness. Look at the text. "Why then do we act treacherously against one another, profaning the covenant of our fathers?" God rebukes their ill-treatment of each other within the community of faith. That phrase translated "one another" could be translated "our brothers," signifying the community of faith, the nation of Israel.

The uniform, the badge, that testifies to one's salvation in God is unity with other believers. In the OT this community of faith was the nation of Israel. In the NT, it is the church. The badge that proves you're a believer of the Lord Jesus Christ is your love for others, particularly for the community of faith—no matter the race, nationality, or ethnicity of them.

Jesus said we would be recognized as His disciples by our love for one another. By implication, a lost world will question whether you're a disciple if you lack love for one another. Could someone say of a disciple of Christ, "He's angry with everybody. She's critical all the time. He's prejudiced about everything." Malachi's point is that the children of God must be characterized by their love for one another, not hatred. Treachery among the people of God may indicate a person doesn't belong to the community bound by God's covenant.

Covenant Infidelity Manifested by Israel's Faithlessness to the Precepts of God

MALACHI 2:11-12

Next, Malachi probes a little deeper into the tribe of Judah when he says they were faithless to the precepts of God (v. 11). Judah's faithlessness is "detestable" to the Lord. If we study OT passages like Leviticus 18:29, this "detestable thing" deserved destruction and, ultimately, death. God is saying, "You have committed the unimaginable act of profaning My sanctuary."

We don't know exactly what the act was, but if we examine Jeremiah's sermon in Jeremiah 7, we get a sense of how Israel, on another occasion, profaned the Lord. Jeremiah lists transgressions that may provide clues to the meaning. He exclaims, "Do you steal, murder, commit adultery, swear falsely, burn incense to Baal, and follow other gods that you have not known?" (Jer 7:9). The accusation is given. The people of God are on the stand and God is the prosecuting attorney. Their indictment is that they have profaned the Lord through theft, murder, adultery, and deceit. Worst of all, they have chased after false gods—the ultimate betrayal of their covenantal relationship with Him.

Israel finds herself in a compromising predicament before a holy God. They have allowed their daughters to marry foreign deities by divorcing their first love—Yahweh. "Foreign god" in Malachi 2:11 refers to any other god than the one true God of Israel.

Some believe that the offense in view is idolatry because the men worshipped foreign, pagan gods or goddesses. Idolatry is certainly an issue, but the text should be examined in the context of marriage. Whenever marriage is mentioned in similar contexts of the Bible, it is talking about the covenantal relationship between God and Israel. God is always described as the bridegroom, and Israel is always described as the bride. Here it is different: Judah is the bridegroom and the bride is a "daughter" of someone else. Therefore, Malachi is not talking about idolatry in turning to the goddess-daughters of false gods. He has in mind real marriage and real divorce here, describing how the men were divorcing their wives and marrying outside the community of faith.

Basically, the sons of God were marrying the daughters of pagans. How could they marry unbelievers when God strictly prohibited this practice in the OT? The answer could be personal gain. The people had just returned to the promised land from being exiled in Babylon for many years. One of the quickest ways to secure wealth was to marry into a prestigious family. They apparently ignored the precepts of God for personal profit and intermarried with pagan women after divorcing the wives of their youth.

God strictly forbade these actions in the OT, but not because He discriminated against ethnic groups. The issue is not racial exclusivity. It is an issue of inclusivity and protection of His covenant people from idolatry. In Deuteronomy 7:3-4 God firmly outlines this for the people:

> *Do not intermarry with them. Do not give your daughters to their sons or take their daughters for your sons, because they will turn your sons away from Me to worship other gods. Then the LORD's anger will burn against you, and He will swiftly destroy you.*

The apostle Paul probably has in mind this passage of Deuteronomy when he confronts the Corinthians with these words:

> *What agreement does Christ have with Belial? Or what does a believer have in common with an unbeliever? And what agreement does God's sanctuary have with idols?* (2 Cor 6:15-16)

The problem with marrying someone who is an unbeliever isn't merely that they belong to a different religious organization. The problem with marrying an unbeliever is the **different worldview** through which they view all things. They perceive the world differently than a believer does. Christians have a certain system, a lens through which they view the world. An unbeliever does not look through that same lens.

Christians have a framework based on Christ by which we love, give, and live. It shapes how we spend our time, our talents, and our investments. It molds the way we raise our kids. It shapes the way we participate in organizations. It shapes our discipline and our dedication. And to unite oneself in marriage with someone who has a contradictory worldview creates a tremendous temptation to abandon the one true God for worldly, unbiblical pursuits. This was true for Israel, and it is still true for Christians today.

Verse 12, while difficult to translate, speaks to the consequences of disobedience to the Lord. It brings to mind 1 Samuel 15, when Saul was chosen to be the king, and God, through the prophet Samuel, provided Saul a pretty straightforward plan. He said,

> *Now go and attack the Amalekites and completely destroy everything they have. Do not spare them. Kill men and women, children and infants, oxen and sheep, camels and donkeys.* (1 Sam 15:3)

The reason for such specificity and utter annihilation is solely because God didn't want Israel to be distracted. He didn't want them influenced by unbelieving pagans. So Saul goes in with the help of the Lord and he emerges victorious, destroying the Amalekites and following the plan, except for a few minor details. First, he takes the spoils of the land for himself. Second, he takes the Amalekite king and allows him to remain alive. Third, he takes some of the cattle or sheep, surely thinking, "We don't want to waste the livestock!"

Samuel the prophet confronts Saul for an explanation about his disobedience. Saul explains his reason for taking the cattle and the extra, negligible items was to offer them to the Lord. In response Samuel pierces Saul's heart with these words:

> *Does the LORD take pleasure in burnt offerings and sacrifices as much as in obeying the LORD? Look: to obey is better than sacrifice, to pay attention is better than the fat of rams.* (1 Sam 15:22)

Apparently, the priests in Malachi's day had not learned this lesson from Israel's history. Neglecting God's clear commands by chasing after foreign wives resulted in their offerings being rejected. What a high price to pay for selfish gain!

Covenant Infidelity Manifested by Israel's Faithlessness to Their Marriage Partners

MALACHI 2:13-14

The third citation against the people was in their faithlessness to the partner of their marriage. For the third time God offers a criticism against His people (vv. 11,12,13). To understand God's disapproval, we must first identify whose "tears" are on the altar. The tears are of the men who have divorced their wives to marry pagan women. Now they expect the Lord to acquit them of the crime by accepting their offering.

Did you notice the emotional anguish in this verse? The men are "weeping and groaning"; however, God's mind is made up. He essentially responds to them, "I have cut you off from My presence." We see in this text the covenantal nature of marriage, as we see throughout the OT (e.g., Prov 2; Ezek 16). In the garden of Eden God used identical covenantal language when He stated, "A man leaves his father and mother and bonds with his wife, and they become one flesh" (Gen 2:24). Both participants are to leave the influence of their past and create, together, a new union under the guidance of a holy God. Jesus affirms this covenant in the NT:

> *But from the beginning of creation God made them male and female. For this reason a man will leave his father and mother and be joined to his wife, and the two will become one flesh. So they are no longer two, but one flesh. Therefore what God has joined together, man must not separate.* (Mark 10:6-9)

Malachi connects the covenant of marriage to their covenant with God. Effectively, God says, "You men married your wives by way of a covenant, which is a depiction of your relationship with Me."

Surprisingly, the priests respond ignorantly: "For what reason?" They're asking why God rejects their worship. The Lord answers,

> *Because the* Lord *has been a witness between you and the wife of your youth. You have acted treacherously against her, though she was your marriage partner and your wife by covenant.*

One Puritan commentator described what's happening in this verse:

> The woman whom you have wronged was the companion of those earlier and brighter days of your life when, in the bloom of her young beauty she left her father's house and shared in your early struggles and rejoiced in your later success, who walked arm in arm with you along the pilgrimage of your life cheering you in its trials by her gentle ministry. And now when the bloom of her youth has faded and the friends of her youth have gone, when her father and mother whom she left for you are in the grave, then you cruelly cast her off as a worn out worthless thing and insult her holiest affections by putting an idolater and a heathen in her place. (Moore, *Haggai*, 134).

We live in a day when divorce is not a last resort, but the first. Tom Brokaw, several years ago, spoke about the generation of men and women who lived through World War II, saying, "it was the last generation in which, broadly speaking, marriage was a commitment and divorce was not an option" (*Greatest Generation*, 231). But now people think separation would be easier for their situation, though it often only causes more problems. What is more terrible is that the true casualties of divorce are the children. They are the bystanders of separation and they are the ones who feel it the most.

Friends, let me challenge you: before a Christian should ever divorce, he should do everything in his power to make it work. Remember that your marriage agreement is not just with your wife, it's with God. When you repeated, "I do," you spoke those words in the presence of God.

Covenant Renewal Begins with Faithfulness to the Covenant of Marriage

MALACHI 2:15-16

Finally, Malachi gives a challenge, a charge. Implicitly, he said, "Follow the instructions of God. You men have been faithless to the precepts of God. You've been faithless to people of God. You've been faithless to the partner of your marriage. But now I want you to follow the instructions of God." Look at verses 15-16:

> *Didn't the one God make us with a remnant of His life-breath?*
> *And what does the One seek? A godly offspring. So watch yourselves carefully, and do not act treacherously against the wife of your youth.*
> *"If he hates and divorces his wife," says the LORD God of Israel, "he covers his garment with injustice," says the LORD of Hosts.*
> *Therefore, watch yourselves carefully, and do not act treacherously.*

The command to "watch yourselves" is a means of protection. It is a practical command for us to monitor the negative, unspiritual information that we receive from unbelievers. We need to monitor who is speaking into our lives about our biblical commitments, particularly the covenant we have made with our spouse.

If I have a strangely shaped mole on my leg, I won't go to a salesman friend of mine and ask, "Hey Mike, can you come look at this thing?" He may bend down and say, "Wow, that growth is asymmetrical and discolored. Spider veins are shooting out from the sides. It looks fine to me. Just put some Neosporin on it. You'll be fine in the morning." Would I follow that advice? No! I probably wouldn't seek Mike's opinion in the first place! I would make an appointment to see a doctor to diagnose my problem. So why would you ever listen to unbelievers about a covenant you made with God? Wouldn't you seek godly counsel from brothers and sisters in the church to speak into your relationship?

The University of Chicago supports this advice with their study of people who stayed together and people who divorced. The researchers found that couples in the midst of struggle had a significant chance of staying together when married friends encouraged them to remain together. On the other hand, couples in turmoil had a higher risk of divorce when their divorced friends expressed bitter anger toward their own ex-husbands or ex-wives (Braverman, "Healthy, Wealthy, & Wed").

Paul says that bad company corrupts good character (1 Cor 15:33). Who makes up your closest friends? Whose advice is central in your life? If you want to know your future, take a photograph of your friends.

Verse 16 effectively states, "God hates divorce." This is the hardest verse in Malachi to translate accurately. What we can say is that emphasis is added to what is being said, with God's name framing the statement. In essence, God bookends this truth with His signature. He says, "You can take this to the bank. This is something I do not want to happen. Divorce is comparable to smearing lies and treachery on your clothes, which is a deplorable act. Don't do it." The marriage covenant is a picture of Christ, the bridegroom, and His relationship with His church, the bride (Eph 5:22-32). A divorce portrays a picture of Christ (the man) abandoning His church, which He never does, and the church (the woman) leaving Christ, something we are advised not to do.

Conclusion: Christ as the Faithful Bridegroom Relentlessly Pursuing His Bride, the Church

Edward Gibbon wrote *The Decline and Fall of the Roman Empire* in the eighteenth century. In this six-volume work he says there are five reasons why the Roman Empire fell—the great Roman Empire, the *indestructible* Roman Empire. Would you take a stab at some of the five? Let me give you two of them that I think are apropos to this text.

The first and foremost reason the Roman Empire fell was the rapid divorce within the community, which in turn undermined the dignity and sanctity of the home. Divorce was the number one reason. A second reason was the decay of religion—at that time, Christianity—allowing it to become ritualistic and lifeless. This is after the rise of Constantine, when Christianity moved from the little "c" catholic church, that is, the universal church, to the big "C" Catholic Church, led by the military leader Constantine. As he looked at history, Gibbon concluded that Rome did not fall because of enemies from without; rather, it imploded from within. Those in the West today should take heed.

It is easy to take some of these words and begin publicly flogging people who have been divorced. However, let the record show: divorce is not the unpardonable sin. God does not hate divorce any worse than He hates any other sin; all sin is deplorable to the Lord. So what do you do if you've been divorced? You repent, ask God for forgiveness, and move forward with your life because failure is not final in your life. The past is unchangeable. If God has forgiven you, forgive yourself.

Let me remind you, brother or sister who isn't divorced—before you begin to point the finger at another person who is divorced—to look at the landscape of your own life to determine ways you have failed and places you have fallen. Who can stand in the presence of a holy God? Listen to God's Word and, whether you're remarried, married for the first time, or about to be married, settle it in your heart now that you will stay together to the end. "Till death do us part" is not a line you casually repeat. Make it a mantra to live by.

Finally, we must look to the One who was faithful, Jesus Christ. Israel was seduced by other gods, but Jesus Christ remained faithful to the God of the covenant, and He relentlessly pursued His bride while on earth as an example for us. Even though people were unfaithful to Him, Christ remained faithful, all the way to the cross, so that He might purchase the redemption of His people with His own blood. This is the story of the gospel, it is the standard for faithfulness, it is the confidence of our salvation, and it is the only hope we have to mend all of our broken relationships.

Reflect and Discuss

1. Recall the story of how the Lord saved you. How do you see His "creating" work in your heart and life (see Mal 2:10; Eph 2:1-10)?
2. Compare Malachi 2:10 with Jesus' words in John 13:31-35. How are they similar? How are they different?

3. What do you think it means to profane God's sanctuary? What are some specific ways we can offend God in this way, even without a temple?
4. What are some practical difficulties to marrying someone who doesn't share your worldview? How might you be tempted to compromise or devalue the gospel?
5. Discuss God's role in the covenant relationship between a man and a woman in marriage. How should that affect our approach to marriage as Christians?
6. Discuss why divorce is contrary to the biblical idea of marriage as covenant.
7. What does divorce say about the gospel of Jesus? How does this passage relate to Ephesians 5:22-32?
8. How should we respond to divorce in the culture? In the church?
9. How can we practically guard ourselves and our marriages from imploding from within?
10. What are some of God's precepts that you tend to take lightly? What does your attitude toward these reflect about your attitude towards the Lord?

The People's Court

MALACHI 2:17–3:5

Main Idea: God's complaint against Israel includes their accusation of divine injustice, but God defends His justice, promising vindication through His appointed messenger who will purify the priests and judge Israel.

I. Introduction: God's Weariness with Israel's Complaints
II. Israel Accuses God of Injustice for Allowing the Wicked to Prosper (2:17).
III. God Defends His Justice, Promising Vindication through His Appointed Messenger (3:1).
IV. God's Promised Vindication Begins with the Purification of Israel's Priestly Leadership (3:2-3).
V. God's Promised Vindication Culminates with the Judgment of His People Israel (3:4-5).
VI. Conclusion: Christ as the Promised "Messenger of the Covenant," the One in Whom God Delights

---

Introduction: God's Weariness with Israel's Complaints

Malachi begins this section with an expression of exasperation. "You have wearied the Lord with your words." The people, once again, have complained. They have doubted God's promises. They have resisted Him for the last time. In this passage the Lord assures them He will answer them, but it may not be in the way they envisioned. His covenant promises will come to pass through judgment and the promised messenger. So the Lord takes the people to court.

Israel Accuses God of Injustice for Allowing the Wicked to Prosper

MALACHI 2:17

In Malachi 2:17 the people of God question the Lord's justice, evoking an answer. There are three stages of the interrogation. First, there is an **accusation**. God accuses the people through His servant, Malachi, when he says, "You have wearied the Lord." The word *wearied* describes exhaustion from physical labor and is interchangeable with the word *annoyed*. It also means to be agitated by something or someone; in this case, the people of Israel have aggravated God.

Second, there is a **rebuttal**. The people respond defensively to Malachi's accusation. And why would we expect anything different from them? They ignorantly respond, "How have we wearied Him?" They want to know precisely where they have wandered astray.

Finally, there's the **validation**. Malachi is explicit about their wearisome ways. The people had effectively been saying that evil people were being blessed and God was letting it happen. Basically, the people are becoming impatient with the rampant immorality and the political corruption in Israel. They say, in essence, "God, why are you making the wicked prosper? Do you find joy in their transgressions? Where is your justice?" Through reflection on the law and their ancestral history, the people of Israel should have realized that God is *always* just. Deuteronomy 28 makes it clear that the people of the covenant will receive blessings if they obey and curses if they do not. But justice comes according to God's timetable and not that of the Israelites.

Questioning how the wicked can receive blessing is found throughout the OT. In fact, five books handle the question directly: Job, Psalms, Habakkuk, Jeremiah, and Ecclesiastes. But this is still a prevalent question today. How can the wicked prosper?

In this passage, however, God is not interested in providing an explanation for why He, as they perceived, showers blessings on sinners. However, God does take the opportunity to pinpoint the hypocrisy of His people. The Israelites pointed the finger at God when they should have pointed it back at themselves. By provoking an interrogation of God, the people opened a door for God to critique their lives and lifestyles.

God Defends His Justice, Promising Vindication through His Appointed Messenger

MALACHI 3:1

God promises to send His appointed messenger to announce His coming judgment. Who is this messenger? We see in Malachi 4:5 that Elijah is this forerunner, the one who comes and prepares the way of the Lord.

But the only other place in the Bible where this Hebrew phrase means to "prepare" or "clear obstacles" is in Isaiah 40:3-5:

> *A voice of one crying out: Prepare the way of the LORD in the wilderness; make a straight highway for our God in the desert. Every valley will be lifted up, and every mountain and hill will be leveled; the uneven ground will become smooth and the rough places, a plain. And the glory of the LORD will appear, and all humanity together will see it, for the mouth of the LORD has spoken.*

Each of the four Gospel writers associate the messenger of these verses with the ministry of John the Baptist (Matt 3:1-12; Mark 1:2-8; Luke 3:2-18; John 1:6-8,19-28). The question arises, How does John the Baptist prepare the way for the coming of the Lord? In the first century, and even centuries before that, the Jews believed that a person prepared for the Lord's arrival with one's body. That is, an individual removed distractions or impediments that would hinder holiness and, in turn, would hinder intimacy with God. The Essene sect, also known as the Qumran community, typified this process.

Many scholars suggest John the Baptist was an Essene (Hutchison, "Was John?," 1). There are a number of similarities between the Essenes and John. First, like the Essenes, John the Baptist separated himself from the rest of society by living and preaching in the wilderness. The wilderness in Israel was not thick forests of bushes and trees. It was a barren desert. Living in these difficult, impoverished conditions demonstrated that John, like the Essenes, did not cling to the things of this world. Rather, he focused on preparing the way for the coming of the Lord.

Second, the Essenes were known for their ritual baptisms. To maintain their cleanliness and, therefore, their ritual holiness before the Lord, the Essenes baptized themselves in a *mikvaot*, a purification bath, which was necessary for the induction of a new member.

Although there are some similarities between John the Baptist and the Essenes, there are a number of differences that must be addressed. First, although John segregated himself from society, he eventually emerged from the desert. The Essenes, on the other hand, remained in the desert until the Roman military massacred them in AD 68. Second, John baptized people once, in response to their repentance. In this way, he prepared the way of the Lord. The Essenes, on the other hand, baptized themselves continuously, at least three times a day. Third, and most importantly, John the Baptist recognized Jesus as the Messiah, whereas the Essene community overlooked Jesus and continued to wait for the coming of their "Teacher of Righteousness."

If this messenger who prepares the way was meant to point to John the Baptist, then what is God talking about when He says, "Then the Lord you seek will suddenly come to His temple, the Messenger of the covenant you desire—see, He is coming"? The temple referred to here is the second temple, the one that was built by Zerubbabel and spoken of by Haggai and Zechariah. Also, it is the temple into which Jesus entered a week before His death. So, who is the approaching "Messenger of the covenant?" He is the Christ, Jesus of Nazareth, God incarnate. Jesus' entry into the temple precincts during the week of His passion is the fulfillment of this prophecy. John the Baptist prepares the way of the Lord by summoning the people of Israel to repentance. With the scene set, God, in the form of man, enters His temple and evaluates His people.

The connection between 3:1 and 2:17 is marked with the word *delight*. Malachi 2:17 states: "Everyone who does evil is good in the sight of the LORD, and he *delights* in them" (ESV). The people claimed that God delighted in evil. But what God explains is that the Messiah, "in whom you *delight*" (ESV), is approaching not to bless the Israelites; rather, He is coming for their condemnation "suddenly." "Suddenly" does not mean "quickly." "Suddenly" refers to the way He will come—at a moment the Israelites least expect, similarly to how He will return (1 Thess 5:2).

We see this same language in Matthew 21:12-13 (cf. Mark 11:15-18; Luke 19:45-47; John 2:14-16). The Jews are going through the routine in the temple of exchanging money. The merchants are corrupt, but perhaps of even more consequence, they are meeting in the court of the Gentiles and thereby keeping foreigners from worshiping the Lord of all. Suddenly, Jesus, with whip in hand, overturns the tables and says, "It is written, My house will be called a house of prayer. But you are making it into a den of thieves." What is Jesus saying? At least in part He's communicating, "This is my Father's house and I'm claiming ownership of it. What you see here is a foreshadowing of the cleansing that is on the horizon." The warning has been given. Although the people had heard the words of Malachi, sadly, they did not heed them. God is both the proclaimer of the messenger and purifier of His people.

God's Promised Vindication Begins with the Purification of Israel's Priestly Leadership

MALACHI 3:2-3

First, we witnessed the people's interrogation of God. Next, we were reminded of God's promise to send His messenger. Now, we see the need for purification of the priesthood. God does not commence by judging and cleansing the common Israelite; He starts by purifying the once-holy priesthood.

Malachi 3:2-3 cannot be about Jesus' first coming, since Jesus did not come to refine, but to redeem. Jesus came to give His life up as a sacrifice for all of mankind. He came to emancipate sinners and establish His kingdom. At His second coming, though, He will act as judge and purifier. Martin Luther said, "There are only two days on my calendar. This day and that day." For the Israelites, there were only two days on the calendar: today and the Day of the Lord. In the same manner, there are only two days that should matter to believers: today and the day Jesus returns to test our worth.

The passage is not a warning of destruction but a promise of purification. Malachi assures the people that the Messiah brings with Him the refiner's fire. What is a refiner's fire? It is a fire used to refine precious metals. Gold, silver, copper, and other metals are heated until they liquefy. The dross (i.e., impurities) floats to the top where the refiner can skim it off. Once the process is complete, the metal is free of impurities and, therefore, of greater worth and usefulness.

For Christians there are two forms of purification. The first takes place while we are on earth. Did you know that God's divine instrument for molding and making us into the image of Christ is pain and suffering? He disciplines those whom He loves. Hebrews 12:5-6 and 11 explain it this way:

> *And you have forgotten the exhortation that addresses you as sons: My son, do not take the Lord's discipline lightly or faint when you are reproved by Him, for the Lord disciplines the one He loves and punishes every son He receives. . . . No discipline seems enjoyable at the time, but painful. Later on, however, it yields the fruit of peace and righteousness to those who have been trained by it.*

We are being purged here on earth from impurities, but we will finally be purified at the mercy seat. Every believer will experience testing, as through fire, before glorification. Read 1 Corinthians 3:11-15:

> *For no one can lay any other foundation than what has been laid down. That foundation is Jesus Christ. If anyone builds on that foundation with gold, silver, costly stones, wood, hay, or straw, each one's work will become obvious, for the day will disclose it, because it will be revealed by fire; the fire will test the quality of each one's work. If anyone's work that he has built survives, he will receive a reward. If anyone's work is burned up, it will be lost, but he will be saved; yet it will be like an escape through fire.*

Only that which glorifies our Lord will stand the test of divine fire. The sin nature with which we have been cursed will be destroyed and we will be conformed to the image of Christ.

It is important, therefore, to examine daily the landscape of our spiritual lives. Scripture consistently reminds readers to examine themselves. **Examination of works today is better than elimination of blessings tomorrow.** So praise God for purging us through suffering. The goal of God is to conform us into the image of His Son. It is not to make us happy. It is not to keep us healthy. It is not to make us wealthy. It is to conform us into the image of His Son (Rom 8:29).

God's Promised Vindication Culminates with the Judgment of His People Israel

MALACHI 3:4-5

There is a final aspect to the text. We have seen the interrogation of God, the promise of the messenger's coming, and the purification of the priest of God, but now we see the examination of Israel by God, the Judge. When judgment comes, the people will begin offering pleasing sacrifices in Jerusalem.

God expands the purification from the priests to the Israelites as a whole. God summons a star witness: Himself. He is the only one who can be trusted to act as an honest and discerning witness to the transgressions of His people. He is charging the nation for participating in four prohibited acts, each of which stems from not fearing the Lord: sorcery, adultery, lying, and oppressing vulnerable members of society.

Sorcery refers to when the people look to other places, whether to foreign gods or simple magic, for power and might. The people desire something or someone other than God, which exposes their lack of fear toward Him. Like sorcery, both adultery and lying were explicitly prohibited in the Ten Commandments. The covenant people, marked by the fear of the Lord, were to remain faithful to their partner and honest before God. In these sins, the people's heart was revealed.

By oppressing the most vulnerable in society, Israel betrayed that they had forgotten their history. Throughout the Old Testament, God reminded Israel to care for the helpless because Israel had been a helpless nation in Egypt, yet the Lord set His heart to care for her (Exod 22:21). In oppressing the weak, the Israelites displayed conscious amnesia of the grace the Lord had extended to them.

You see, the fear of the Lord preserves us for the Day of Judgment. It teaches us to live in light of God's grace and mercy. Without this proper fear, we are prone to forget the radical nature of the good news of the gospel and to wander from our covenant God. If we lack fear, we may be judged through fire to be lacking worth, showing that we had never truly surrendered to God in the first place.

Conclusion: Christ as the Promised "Messenger of the Covenant," the One in whom God Delights

The good news of Malachi 2:17–3:5 is that there was a "Messenger of the Covenant" who would come. He upheld the covenant between God and Israel in His life, and He sealed the covenant in His blood at the cross. Every time Christians take the Lord's Supper they proclaim that the messenger has come and He will come again. We look back at His faithfulness, resting in the promise of His grace. In the courtroom of heaven, Jesus' blood will be our plea. And by His power, looking forward to His return, we live with a reverential fear of the Lord, doing good works that will be tested and approved, fully pleasing to God, just like our King Jesus.

Reflect and Discuss

1. Have you ever looked around and thought that the wicked were prospering and the righteous were being mistreated? How did you respond?
2. How have you wearied the Lord with your sin in the past? How does this text warn us against such a sinful practice?
3. How is it comforting to know that God will come to judge the world? How should we Christians anticipate this judgment?
4. There are two messengers in this text. What are the roles of each one, and how are they fulfilled in the New Testament?

5. Why do you think the Lord starts with the priests and then moves to the other people? Where else can we see this principle in Scripture?
6. What does it mean to only have two days on your calendar: this day and that day? How can this help you keep perspective in this life?
7. If Christians are in Christ and are fully accepted by God through Him, why are they still judged on their works? Is this inconsistent?
8. What is the purpose of God's purifying process in our lives? Read 1 Peter 1:6-7 for more insight.
9. What does the imagery of 3:2-3 reveal about God's work in our lives? How have you seen this process play out in your life?
10. What acts do you do that reveal a lack of "fear of the Lord"? Examine your heart and consider why you still chase after these things.

Roadmap to Reconciliation

MALACHI 3:6-12

Main Idea: God's commitment to His covenant trumps Israel's rebellious history, holding out repentance to Israel and lavishing blessing on both Israel and the nations.

I. Introduction: The Immutability of Israel's Covenant God
II. Israel's Checkered History and the Reality of Her Rebellion (3:6)
III. God's Indictment of Israel for Withholding Their Tithes and Offerings (3:7-10a)
IV. God's Challenge for Israel to Test His Immeasurable Generosity (3:10-11)
V. God's Blessing upon Israel Will Result in a Good Reputation among the Nations (3:12).
VI. Conclusion: Christ as the Climax of the Covenant, Bringing Blessing to Both Israel and the Nations

---

Introduction: The Immutability of Israel's Covenant God

Even though the people have fluctuated in their affections and devotion to God, He has not changed, which, as we will see, is the very foundation of His promise of restoration.

Israel's Checkered History and the Reality of Her Rebellion

MALACHI 3:6

The text begins by disclosing *the reality of Israel's rebellion.* The drama is heightened in 3:5 when God ends the section by speaking through His prophet Malachi, "I will come to you in judgment." That is, "The shenanigans are over. I am bringing judgment." He follows up with this phrase: "Because I, Yahweh, have not changed, you descendants of Jacob have not been destroyed." God says, in essence, "You have sinned and you deserve judgment. But I'm going to extend My mercy to you because of the promise I made to your father, Jacob."

Saying to the Israelites "you descendants of *Jacob*" is a marked departure from the normal way He has referred to them: "the children of

Israel." In place of calling them "Israelites" God labels them "Jacobites." If you remember, when God gave Jacob His promise in Genesis, He changed Jacob's name, saying, "Your name shall no longer be called Jacob, but Israel, for you have striven with God and with men, and have prevailed" (Gen 32:28).

Most of the time, when the Israelites are referred to as the children of Jacob, it's a rebuke for their disobedience. It's a reference to the name of their forefather before the divine blessing was bestowed. Yet, even though they were faithless, God would remain faithful to them, as He was to their father, Jacob. Their rebellion has led them far from God, but restoration is still possible if they desire change.

Do you feel like you are far from the Lord right now? Do you feel like maybe you have turned your back on God? The recipe for a relationship with God is always confession of sin and faith in Christ. He hears the cries of a repentant sinner calling upon His name.

God's Indictment of Israel for Withholding Their Tithes and Offerings

MALACHI 3:7-10A

In the following verses the Lord offers His **roadmap to reconciliation**. Reconciliation is offered, but the people must respond by ceasing their selfish, rebellious actions. Malachi presents the evidence in verses 7-8.

The word *how* is used six times in the book of Malachi. As in the book of Judges, where the people in their typically ignorant fashion were making a habit of interrogating God, here too in Malachi they ask, "God, how can we return to You?" This is not a question of *clarification*, but one of *disputation*. The NLT renders the people's exclamation well: "How can we return when we've never gone away? God, what are you talking about?"

The word translated *return* can also be translated as "repent." It's an "about-face" in military talk. You are walking forward and on a dime, you do a one-eighty. However, the word carries with it more than mere orientation. "Repentance" is the restoration of a relationship, a reconfirmation of commitment with someone. In this case the Israelites are invited to renew their relationship with God. When you are unaware of how you've gotten to where you are, returning to where you started is rather difficult. If you are walking through the woods and you do not record your steps, it's difficult to retrace them. How much more difficult it is when you do not realize you are lost! The children of Israel, God's chosen people, are in a precarious situation. They stand shamelessly before a holy God and respond, "God, how can we *return*? We aren't even lost!"

Before you scoff, understand how easy it is for you to fall into the same trap today. We may say, "Far from God? I am not far from God! I go to church every week, pastor! My kids are in a Christian school. How can you say I am far from God?" God may reply with the same tone: "You do not think you have strayed, but you are far from Me." It takes consistent and deep personal evaluation to determine our spiritual state before the Lord. Fortunately, NT Christians have the inner working of the Holy Spirit, something to which the Israelites were not privileged. For them, God spoke in His Spirit only through the prophets. Through Malachi, God puts His finger on the pulse of the people's rebellion. In response to their inquiry, God explains that they are suffering because they have withheld "the tenth and the contributions."

God has questioned the Israelites previously for their poor sacrifices, their lack of worship, their idolatry, and their faithlessness. But here He pinpoints the heart of the problem, which is a problem of their heart, expressed through their misappropriation of funds. The problem is not what the people possessed. Rather, it is what they did with their possessions. They were withholding the proper tithes from God, to which God responds, "You have an abundance. Why? Because I am the one who blessed you. Nonetheless, you are not giving me your *best.* You are giving me what is *left.*" Look back at Malachi 1:8. There, God said, "I want the best." But notice what they give: "When you present a blind animal for sacrifice, is it not wrong? And when you present a lame or sick animal, is it not wrong?" God said, "I deserve a perfect, unblemished, pure sacrifice. Instead, you offer those that are lame or sick."

The Israelites' lack of financial generosity itself was not the problem, but was instead an indication of something below the surface: a wicked heart. Malachi 1:13 gives us a clue to this: "'You bring stolen, lame, or sick animals. You bring this as an offering! Am I to accept that from your hands?' asks the Lord." The Israelites looked at their flock and said, "We have savings here in the form of a goat. We have a nice investment in her. She's beautiful. But this scrawny-looking animal here—let's bring this one to God." In the first half of Malachi God deals with the *quality* of their offering. In the second half He deals with the *quantity* of their offering. In both sections, though, their wicked hearts are revealed before God.

If we minimize the importance of this section by saying, "It's really not about money," then we stumble. It is unequivocally about money! God is showing that you can always determine the pulse of a believer by putting a finger on their pocket book. You can always determine where a person's heart is by evaluating their bank account statements. We may not like to talk about money, but money talks a lot about us. And both for Israel and for us, our wallets betray us.

The word *tenth* in verses 8 and 10 means "ten percent." All that God was demanding of His people was the least that was required under the law. Ultimately, though, the Jews gave above ten percent. For instance, the Israelites were expected to contribute money toward festivals and feasts, as well as to the sacrifices in the temple. By totaling every offering, the people gave roughly 23 percent for the purpose of maintaining the temple of God and the priests who served within it.

I have heard people suggest that believers are mandated to contribute a tenth of their goods, and that the local Church is considered the storehouse, a replacement for the temple. Against this assertion, there are those who claim that we are not required to give a tenth of our income; rather, we have no financial obligations since we are under grace. This reasoning states that because of the sacrifice of the Lord Jesus Christ, we are liberated from offering a tenth of anything and free to give as the Spirit leads (see MacArthur, "Thoughts on Tithing," Cappocia, "The Truth about Tithing," and Johnston, *Lie of the Tithe*). Walter Kaiser and Lloyd Ogilvie state, "Christians are not governed by any law that *commands* us to give a tenth of our earnings to God; however, it must be noted that the practice of tithing antedates any provision of the Law of Moses" (Kaiser and Ogilvie, 499, emphasis mine).

There is not enough space available here to unpack this idea fully, but it is necessary to examine two points. First, under the auspices of the covenant of grace, grace always demands more than the law. A cursory examination of the Sermon on the Mount in the Gospel of Matthew reveals this truth. Jesus instructed His audience,

> *You have heard that it was said to our ancestors, Do not murder, and whoever murders will be subject to judgment. But I tell you, everyone who is angry with his brother will be subject to judgment. And whoever says to his brother, "Fool!" will be subject to the Sanhedrin. But whoever says, "You moron!" will be subject to hellfire.* (5:21-22)

Jesus consistently raises the bar. Likewise, Jesus says,

> *You have heard that it was said, Do not commit adultery. But I tell you, everyone who looks at a woman to lust for her has already committed adultery with her in his heart.* (Matt 5:27-28)

Therefore, grace never expects less; it always demands more. If we are not required to give a tenth based on the OT law, since we are not under the law, then, should we give any less than the OT saints did now that we are under grace? The answer is No! We should give more, as a spiritual act of worship. Ten percent can be used as a guide for giving, much like training wheels on a bicycle guide those learning to ride. We should seek to show our worship to the Lord through our giving and, therefore, should never be satisfied with presenting the bare minimum. No other practice allows you to exercise your faith and trust in God on a weekly basis like giving.

The second challenge to grace-inspired giving is when to give. Yes, we should give out of the abundance God has given us, but we rarely feel like giving. When people are left to their own devices and given the freedom to determine what they can give and how often to give, few ever give as they should. We should not give to God because we are under obligation to tithe, we should give because He has already given us the inexpressible gift of His Son Jesus Christ.

We can agree on two principles related to giving. First, God has given us everything we have. Therefore, let us begin to look at what we have not as our resources—that is, not as things we have amassed ourselves—but as resources we are borrowing from God. He has commissioned us to be stewards of the gifts He has bestowed. Since we will one day give an account to Him of what we have done with His time, talents, and treasures, we should begin to ponder how well we would fare after His audit.

Second, we are all stewards of the Lord's money. We should each think about how we are stewarding that money in our relationships with other kingdom-bound people. In this light, every one of us can be placed into one of two categories. Luke 18 and 19 describe two men who were diametrically opposed to one another in character. The first one is the rich young ruler:

> *A ruler asked Him, "Good Teacher, what must I do to inherit eternal life?"*

> *"Why do you call Me good?" Jesus asked him. "No one is good but One—God. You know the commandments: Do not commit adultery; do not murder; do not steal; do not bear false witness; honor your father and mother."*
>
> *"I have kept all these from my youth," he said.*
>
> *When Jesus heard this, He told him, "You still lack one thing: Sell all that you have and distribute it to the poor, and you will have treasure in heaven. Then come, follow Me."*
>
> *After he heard this, he became extremely sad, because he was very rich.* (Luke 18:18-23)

In this story we see a man who has been entrusted with much but gave little. That is, we witness an example of a man who tried to serve two masters, with the result that he demonstrated his allegiance not to God, but to money.

It is not by accident that in the very next chapter we witness the transformation of Zacchaeus. Jesus, having seen Zacchaeus up in a tree, commands him, "Let's go to your house to fellowship." As Jesus is speaking to him, Zacchaeus becomes convicted about his greed and responds,

> *"Look, I'll give half of my possessions to the poor, Lord! And if I have extorted anything from anyone, I'll pay back four times as much!"*
>
> *"Today salvation has come to this house," Jesus told him, "because he too is a son of Abraham. For the Son of Man has come to seek and to save the lost."* (Luke 19:8-10)

What a great comparison of two sinners! One man repents; one man retreats. One man is saved; one man is separated. Something similar is taking place in the book of Malachi among the people of God. Malachi is not necessarily calling out those who have been faithfully giving, asking them to give more; Malachi is calling out those who gave nothing. He is calling out those who haphazardly gave. He is calling out those who are giving without worshiping.

God doesn't need your money. He wants your heart. He wants you to understand that a closed hand is unable to receive a blessing. With a generous, open hand, you are opening yourself up to receive God's blessings. With a rebellious, closed hand, you are hindering your ability to receive God's blessings.

God's Challenge for Israel to Test His Immeasurable Generosity

MALACHI 3:10-11

Notice how God finishes this section. God gives an amazing promise to His people that will be fulfilled if they obey His commandments. In fact, it is the only time in the Bible where God actually permits one to test Him in the area of finances. Look again at verse 10:

> *"Bring the full tenth into the storehouse so that there may be food in My house. Test Me in this way," says the* Lord *of Hosts. "See if I will not open the floodgates of heaven and pour out a blessing for you without measure."*

The temple's storehouse was made up of numerous rooms that contained grain, oil, and various other supplies for the wellbeing of the priests. It was the requirement of God that the people give money and supplies for the preservation of the Levites. God, who knows intimately the hearts of men, anticipated His people saying, "We can't give ten percent." So God said, "Test Me." They thought, "We can't afford to give." God corrects them, "No, you can't afford not to give. Test Me."

The word *test* can be used to refer to a number of potential acts. It can be used either positively or negatively to connote testing or challenging. It was used to describe God testing Israel in the desert (Ps 81:7), and elsewhere it is used to refer to men challenging other men (Gen 42:15). In this context it is difficult to determine whether the testing is positive or negative. Perhaps it is an allowance of a negative action to accomplish a positive goal: the glorification of God and the restoration of Israel. God says, in essence, "Go ahead and test Me. Be obedient to Me and I will open the floodgates of blessing upon you."

The term *floodgates* is the same word used in Genesis 7:11 to describe when God opened the sky to release the floodwaters that covered the earth. Can you picture it? God will excessively pour out His blessings upon them for their faithfulness in giving.

But the Lord promises not only to provide for them, but also to protect them (Mal 3:11). The NIV alternatively renders this verse, "I will prevent pests from devouring your crops." The word *devourer* in the HCSB could refer, as it does in Jeremiah 30:16, to the destruction of Israel at the hands of a foreign army. Further, it is used in Hosea to refer to the destructive nature of fire ("consume" in 8:14). So, regardless of whether the "devourer" is insects, fire, or an army, God appears to be saying, "No matter what happens to you, when you are financially faithful to Me, I will provide for you. I will protect you."

God's Blessing upon Israel Will Result in a Good Reputation among the Nations

MALACHI 3:12

Finally, God promises that He will make those who obey prosperous. God will give them a good reputation, as He promised Abraham in Genesis 12. If the people of Israel are willing to esteem God as the highest priority in their lives, God promises to make them a great nation. That is, if Israel exalts the name of the Lord, He will exalt their name among their neighbors. He will make their land "delightful." This means that there will be no more need, no more rampant disease or wickedness among the people, no more war, and no more civil turmoil. There will be plenty to drink and plenty to eat. He promises to restore the land and her people, to give them a golden age, but only if they obey.

Conclusion: Christ as the Climax of the Covenant, Bringing Blessing to Both Israel and the Nations

What can we learn from the actions (or inactions) of Israel and the promises of God in Malachi 3:6-12? First, as with much of Malachi, we learn that if we obey the mandates of God in humble and faithful service, we can expect reward. This does not mean that reward is immediate, or even that we will ever receive it on this side of heaven. But we are guaranteed to experience God's blessing, either here or in the coming kingdom.

Second, we learn that what defines us is not what we have or what we think we have earned. Rather, it is what we do with the resources God has provided. No one will say when standing before the judgment throne of God, "If only I had had more money to spend on myself!" The one consumed with God's glory will say, "If only I had invested more of my money in the kingdom!" Financial activity, just like all other actions, evidences whether you are a kingdom-bound or hell-bound individual. "You shall know them by their fruits."

And finally, we see in this passage and in the rest of the Bible that God is always faithful to His covenant, even when the people are not.

Israel would fail again, but in Christ we see the One who gave generously of Himself, even unto death, out of obedience to His Father. And in His sacrifice He also became the generous outpouring of heavenly blessing that God bestowed on all people.

Reflect and Discuss

1. When was a time you thought you were too sinful for God to forgive you? How has He shown Himself faithful to His covenant through Christ?
2. Sometime people assume they are in a right relationship with God when they are not. What types of things other than Christ do we often claim to be evidence that we are Christians?
3. How do our spending habits and our hearts relate?
4. What does it mean that "grace never expects less; it always expects more"? How is this grace?
5. Why do you think we rarely feel like giving, even when we have an abundance?
6. Consider the stories about the rich young ruler in Luke 18 and Zacchaeus in Luke 19. How are they similar? How are they different?
7. Where else in the Bible is God tested? How are those times similar to and different from God's command in Malachi?
8. How are New Testament Christians to understand the promise that God will bless Israel if they obey? Will they have no material lack if they give generously? How have some abused this concept?
9. How do you think New Testament Christians should think about the tithe?
10. Read Lamentations 3:19-24 and Hebrews 13:8 and compare the message with Malachi 3:6. What's the consistent message in those passages?

Treasured Possession of God

MALACHI 3:13-18

Main Idea: God's commitment to His covenant demands a response from His people, and those who fear God are set apart as His treasured possession.

I. **Introduction: The Fear of God**
II. **The Wicked Respond in a Spirit of Legalism, Expecting Reward for Obedience (3:13-15).**
III. **The Righteous Respond with a Heart of Reverent Fear, Esteeming His Name (3:16-18).**
IV. **Conclusion: Christ as God's Most Esteemed Treasure, Perfectly Fulfilling the Law on Behalf of the Believer**

Introduction: The Fear of God

The promises of God will sustain the people of God through trials and tribulations. They know whose they are, and they know whom they will serve. And because they know the promises of God, whatever pain comes their way is bearable.

Recently a group of psychologists did a study and found that the number one phobia in the world is public speaking (Statistic Brain, "Fear / Phobia"). You may relate to this finding on some level, and you'd be far from alone in that feeling. But public speaking is only one of many ways that we can be afraid. Ultimately, fear will hinder us from being all that God has called us to be.

Worldly fear should never enter into the vocabulary of a Christian. Jesus, the Prince of Peace, says repeatedly, "peace be with you," and "do not be afraid." In fact, when Jesus rose from the dead and met the terrified disciples, He walked into the room and the first thing He said to them was, "Peace to you!" (Luke 24:36). Jesus was pulling from a long tradition set forth in the OT, where the people of God were consistently met with the same theme in response to fearful situations: Do not be afraid.

In what seems like a stark contrast to this biblical exhortation, however, we also have passages that talk about being fearful of God. In the story of the thieves on the cross beside Jesus, one thief looks at the other and says with understanding, "Don't you even fear God?" So should we be fearful of God or not?

I will answer this question with both "yes" and "no." Believers should never be afraid of God, but we should always have a reverential fear of Him, a humble respect for a holy and righteous God who has given His life, who has blessed but can also take away in the blink of an eye. God is pleased with us when we fear and obey Him. But those who are adopted into His family through Christ need not cower in fear of His eternal punishment. To them, He is a loving Father.

The Wicked Respond in a Spirit of Legalism, Expecting Reward for Obedience

MALACHI 3:13-15

In Malachi 3:13-15 we see God set His heart on His treasured possession. God just finished talking about money and devotion in the previous text—how the heart of the problem was a problem of the heart. God's grievance was not primarily with the people's finances; rather, He uncovered deep-rooted sin through their lack of generosity. God called the people to trust Him. In return He would pour out His blessings if they committed themselves totally to Him.

In this passage, though, God changes His tone from leniency to seriousness and divides the people into two groups: those who are not following Him, and those who are following Him; those who are separated from Him, and those who are faithful to Him.

This first group, described in verse 13, includes those who have wandered from God. We know they have strayed by their actions. Notice their evaluation of serving the Lord: "useless." That is a bold and dangerous attitude to have, for the word translated "useless" means "vain" or "futile"—something that that is a waste of time. They claim that they gained nothing by serving the Lord, but in reality they weren't serving Him, they were merely going through the motions out of religious obligation.

Their lament deepens with the inclusion of "walking mournfully," for in this text, *mourning* implies repentance. Their complaint was that they had already repented, yet God had not responded. They walked around acting penitent, then they wondered if there was anything in it for them. They adopted a mentality of reciprocity, of deserving something in return for something they had done: "We want You to do something for us because of what we have done for You." Do we see this in the church today? Can we hear people saying, "God, because I have done this for You, now You should do this for me"?

You can do the right thing with the wrong motive and miss the point completely, which is exactly what the people of Israel were doing. They were checking boxes in the ministry. They were filling out blanks under the header "stuff we've done for God." But they missed the heart of why they were doing it for the Lord.

They adopted a mentality of reciprocity not only in their actions toward the Lord, but also in their attitudes. Look at verse 15: "So now we consider the arrogant to be fortunate. Not only do those who commit wickedness prosper, they even test God and escape." In chapter 1 the people were saying, "God, You are blessing the unrighteous while we are floundering here as Your chosen people. You are blessing the wicked, but not Your people. Why is this happening?" The first group in chapter 3 echoes this concern.

What exactly does it mean when God's law seems "useless," a waste of time? How does one even get to that point? It is certainly true that God's law wasn't inherently burdensome to His people. In fact, to the Jewish mind the law was good. They loved the law. It lit their steps; it revealed their paths. To the people of Israel, the law was *life*, similar to what Paul says in Romans 7:22: "For in my inner self I joyfully agree with God's law."

This concept is foreign to twenty-first century Americans. The law is equated with sirens and speeding tickets, with courts and condemnation. No one got up this morning, jumped out of bed, and said, "I am ready to obey the laws of my state today," or, "I cannot wait to drive the speed limit on the interstate to church this morning!" Nobody speaks this way. But the people of Israel looked at the law, which was the Torah, and lived by it.

There are essentially two invalid responses to the law: license and legalism. These responses will eventually lead a person to consider the law "useless." **License** is the idea that, since we've been saved by grace through Christ, we are free in the Spirit to do as we please and indulge whatever we want, even if it opens the door for sin. These individuals see the promise of God's forgiveness as justification to do whatever they want. The law seems useless. Paul combated this false teaching:

What should we say then? Should we continue in sin so that grace may multiply? Absolutely not! How can we who died to sin still live in it? (Rom 6:1-2)

Yes, Christians are free in the Spirit. Yes, we have liberty in Christ. But we are not free to indulge in sin. This is a misunderstanding of our relationship to the law. When closeness to God is what you want, you can't do just anything you want!

On the opposite swing of the pendulum from license is **legalism**—putting fences around the law to protect yourself from breaking it. Is it any wonder that after God speaks this passage in Malachi the Pharisaical sect is birthed? Their response to God's acknowledgment of their failure to keep the law is to insulate themselves from it ever happening again.

Interestingly, the Pharisees were not the first ones to construct legalistic insulation. It was happening all the way back in the Garden of Eden. Even Eve put fences around the law:

Now the serpent was the most cunning of all the wild animals that the LORD God had made. He said to the woman, "Did God really say, 'You can't eat from any tree in the garden'?" The woman said to the serpent, "We may eat the fruit from the trees in the garden. But about the fruit of the tree in the middle of the garden, God said, 'You must not eat it or touch it, or you will die.'" (Gen 3:1-3)

Is that what the Lord said? Not exactly. God said not to *eat* of the tree of good and evil, and Eve's response was to build a fence. Now, according to her, not only is she not to *eat* of it, but she's not even to *touch* it!

We must not be mistaken. Guarding ourselves from sin is in no way a problem; it is commendable and necessary! But it becomes a problem when we miss the reason for guarding ourselves, for then it becomes legalism. The Pharisees missed the motive entirely. They had put so many fences around the law that they obscured the law itself.

Jesus spoke against both legalism and license. He criticized the Pharisees' legalistic tendencies in Matthew 23:23-24:

Woe to you, scribes and Pharisees, hypocrites! You pay a tenth of mint, dill, and cumin, yet you have neglected the more important matters of the law—justice, mercy, and faith. These things should have been done without neglecting the others. Blind guides! You strain out a gnat, yet gulp down a camel!

And He criticized license in the Sermon on the Mount:

> *Don't assume that I came to destroy the Law or the Prophets. I did not come to destroy but to fulfill. For I assure you: Until heaven and earth pass away, not the smallest letter or one stroke of a letter will pass from the law until all things are accomplished. Therefore, whoever breaks one of the least of these commands and teaches people to do so will be called least in the kingdom of heaven. But whoever practices and teaches these commands will be called great in the kingdom of heaven. For I tell you, unless your righteousness surpasses that of the scribes and Pharisees, you will never enter the kingdom of heaven.* (Matt 5:17-20)

In the mind of the Jews, the Scribes and Pharisees were second to none in terms of righteousness under the law. So Jesus' statement left them wondering, "How in the world can we ever surpass the righteousness of the scribes and Pharisees?" And in case they somehow missed the point, Jesus goes on in verse 48: "Be perfect, therefore, as your heavenly Father is perfect." Since that is impossible, the people might conclude that the law is useless.

How can anyone ever be perfect? How can anyone ever keep the whole law? We know that is impossible on our own, but we also know that Jesus made it possible. See, the OT showed us that no one is righteous under the law, but because of the death, burial, and resurrection of the Lord Jesus Christ, we now are able to fulfill the perfect law of God. It is not because of our own righteousness in our flesh that we can do this (since we have no righteousness in the flesh), but because of the absolute righteousness of God that He gives to us when we repent of our sins and put our faith in Him.

This truth destroys both legalism and license. In Christ we no longer have to look to the law for our righteousness, and in Christ we can fulfill the law of God. The people of Israel in Malachi's day did not understand this, and therefore they saw the law as burdensome.

It is crucial to understand why we obey, because if we do not understand the heart of the commands, we can follow them and still be far from God. Alternatively, we may discard them altogether and definitely distance ourselves from God. These people had strayed away in their attitudes and they had strayed away in their actions, and God demanded a change.

The Righteous Respond with a Heart of Reverent Fear, Esteeming His Name

MALACHI 3:16-18

In verse 16 the Lord switches gears. In verses 13-15 we saw the first group, who had strayed from God by expecting a reward for their obedience. Here we are exposed to a group who served God faithfully. The most remarkable difference between this second group and the first one is their *attitude.* We see it clearly in verse 16: "At that time *those who feared the* LORD spoke to one another" (emphasis added). Their attitude outlines how one should serve: with a healthy fear of God. Malachi expects everyone to possess this fear.

The word *fear* is used throughout the OT. Three main Hebrew words are translated as "fear." The first one is the Hebrew word *pachad,* which means "to dread or fear" (Isa 33:14). The second one is *ʿarats,* which means "to be terrified" (Isa 8:12). The third one is *yareʾ*, which can mean "to fear" but also means "to show reverence or respect." This third word is the one used in here in Malachi, so "those who feared Yahweh" can be aptly translated "those who showed reverential respect for the Lord."

As believers, we should never cringe in trepidation in the presence of a holy God. We should never shrink back from Him. We should stand humbly before God because of who He is and what He has done for us. This word *yareʾ* is used in a variety of ways: First, notice Proverbs 3:7: "Fear the LORD and turn away from evil." When we fear God (when we have a respect and reverential appreciation for God), we will not be involved in evil. Second, in Deuteronomy 31:12 God says, "Gather the people—men, women, children, and foreigners living within your gates—so that they may listen and learn to fear the LORD your God and be careful to follow all the words of this law." This verse shows that when we fear God, we will obey Him. The third usage can be found in Proverbs 9:10, which says that "The fear of the LORD is the beginning of wisdom." When we fear God, we are endowed with godly wisdom.

When those who feared (*yareʾ*) the Lord understood this concept, they did what was natural to them: they began to speak about Him. Maybe they spoke about the goodness of God. Maybe they gave testimonies of God. Maybe they were appreciative of what God had done for them. Specifics of what they talked *about* aren't shared, but what is evident is that fear of God will manifest itself in the proclamation of Him.

The fear of God affects both their attitude toward Him and their actions before Him. God acts as a result of their return to this posture. He basically says, "If you fear Me, I will remember you." Look at it in the text, verse 16: "The LORD took notice and listened." When they feared the Lord, the Lord heard their cries.

Verse 16 continues, "So a book of remembrance was written before Him for those who feared Yahweh and had high regard for His name." God refers to books several times in Scripture. There are three other categories of books that are mentioned. The first one is the book about our eternal destiny. We see this in Revelation 13:8, and it expresses the idea of names that are written in the book of life that was written before the foundation of the world. The second is a scroll that records the judgment of God against sinners, an example of which can be found in Isaiah 34:16. The third kind we know about are the "books" in which our sins are recorded, mentioned in Revelation 20:12.

But Malachi's book of remembrance is quite different than those previously mentioned. Malachi's book was not written before the foundation of the world and it isn't a book that records the wicked acts of sinful individuals and God's judgments against them. It is a book for the righteous acts, deeds, and motives of God's chosen people. Scripture clearly speaks of the fact that God records everything. Kings during this time frequently recorded in books instances where people would perform favors for them with the hopes of returning the favor one day (e.g., Esth 2:21-23; 6:1-3). Malachi has this kind of book in mind.

Notice that *all* things, not just the good or the bad, are recorded for eternity. God is even recording every time you respond in righteousness. Every time a woman respects her body and rejects intimacy with another man before marriage, God sees and honors that decision. Every time a husband refuses to engage in immoral talk at work or to be seduced into looking at pornography, God recognizes it. Every time you avert gossip, every time you bear the burden of an injustice and refuse to lash out, God sees that. Every time a family opens their home to be a Christian witness to the world, God sees that. Every time you share the gospel with a lost family member or friend, God sees that, whether or not anyone else does. If we lived with this in mind, would it change the way that we act?

Verse 17 contains a magnificent allusion to the Lord Jesus. God gives two promises: You will be My treasured possession, and I will show you mercy (not giving them the punishment they deserve). God secured the possession of His people forever through the death, burial, and resurrection of His Son, a marvelous picture of God's lasting remembrance that continues to this day.

The Hebrew word translated "special possession" in verse 17 is noteworthy. It is a word one would reserve for a collection of jewels. It is used in 1 Chronicles 29:3, when David had 3,000 talents of gold and 7,000 talents of silver, but stored an additional offering which was his "personal treasures." He had a safety-deposit box in addition to his savings account. God says, "*You* are My treasured possession." Can you feel the immense promise implied in that statement? The God of the universe would look at you as His private keepsake, as the item He values highly and protects next to His heart.

Malachi says God will spare the righteous as a man spares his own son who serves him. What an amazing assurance of God! God says, "I will save you not because of what you have done, for you have strayed, but because of the promise I made to your forefathers many years ago." God's memory is limitless and the content of His book is accurate. The chapter finishes with a summary statement of these two groups—the righteous who serve God and the wicked who do not.

Conclusion: Christ as God's Most Esteemed Treasure, Perfectly Fulfilling the Law on Behalf of the Believer

The promises of God will endure always. When you know whose you are, you know whom you'll serve, and you can rest in the knowledge that God will sustain His "special possession."

A. W. Tozer asserted, "The man who has God for his treasure has all things in one" (*Pursuit of God*, 19). Is God your treasure? He assured us of His love by sending us His most esteemed treasure of all, His Son Jesus, to die on our behalf. Christ responded to His Father perfectly with the fear of the Lord, and we are called to emulate Him. The Lord's book does not forget, but through Christ we don't have to live in fear of condemnation. When we see God as our ultimate treasure we, like the psalmist, are able to taste and see that the Lord is good and His mercy endures forever.

Reflect and Discuss

1. In what sense should you fear God? What are some examples of an unhealthy fear?
2. How do you see Christians adopting a mentality of reciprocity when it comes to serving the Lord?
3. In what sense is the law not a burden to God's people? How can it be burdensome?
4. Where do you see the error of license in your own life? In the wider church culture?
5. Where do you see the error of legalism in your own life? In the wider church culture?
6. Why do you think the Israelite's fear of the Lord led them to talk about Him?
7. How would you explain the "fear of the Lord" to an unbeliever?
8. Is it comforting or troubling to you that the Lord keeps a record of all that is done in this life? Why?
9. What is the day that the Lord is preparing (v. 17), and why is it significant for Christians to understand?
10. What NT passages also talk about dividing the righteous and the wicked? How do these passages resemble Malachi 3:13-18?

A Light in the Darkness

MALACHI 4:1-6

Main Idea: The Day of the Lord will bring both judgment and vindication for God's people, whose present obedience is sustained by remembering the law and anticipating future restoration.

I. Introduction: The Day of the Lord
II. The Day of the Lord as a Day of Judgment upon the Arrogant (4:1,3)
III. The Rising of the Sun and the Vindication for God's People (4:2)
IV. Remembering the Law as a Means of Sustaining Present Obedience (4:4)
V. Looking Forward in Hope, Anticipating Restoration (4:5-6)
VI. Conclusion: The Sun of Righteousness with Healing in His Wings

---

Introduction: The Day of the Lord

With the light from the sun comes life. Yet, the sun has become something to fear over the past few years. Now we know that the sun's ultraviolet rays can cause wrinkles and skin cancer. The sun can be both a blessing and a curse—it all depends on the context. The Son of God, Jesus Christ, is the same way. For believers, Jesus is a source of comfort and assurance of one's salvation. For those who are far from God, Jesus is the basis for judgment and condemnation. The book of Malachi concludes with God the Judge rewarding the righteous and punishing the unrighteous to substantiate that He always fulfills His promises.

The Day of the Lord as a Day of Judgment upon the Arrogant

MALACHI 4:1,3

A future light shines in the midst of Israel's darkness, though it launches on a negative note. Malachi first assures the people of a coming day of judgment. Verse 1 is the response to a question that was posed earlier by the people: Why are the wicked flourishing and we, as the faithful people of God, floundering (3:14)? God responds, "The day is coming." That word *day* should remind us of the Lord's appearing. It is a day when God Himself will appear and make all the wrongs right. The excitement is short lived for Israel, though, because the Lord declares, "I am going to start with you guys."

The Israelites, expecting a blessing from God, find out God will come "like a furnace." By God's own mouth, He intends to cleanse and purify, not coddle. This will happen when the arrogant and the evildoers burn like straw. That word *arrogant* is synonymous with "prideful." Pride may run rampant now, but there will come a day when all will be humbled on level ground. In their own minds the people are self-sufficient and independent of God, caring little for Him. A modern-day example would be people who profess, "I can wait to serve the Lord later. I do not need God in my life." The Lord strikes fear in their hearts with the promise of a future day of reckoning. He will come with recompense for their evil deeds.

Malachi returns to this theme in verse 3, reassuring the people that God will fulfill His promise. Once again, God implicitly answers the question posed in 3:14, where the people questioned their need for following the Lord. He reveals that those who fear God will have victory over the unrighteous, though it previously appeared the wicked were prospering.

What does this day of reckoning mean for NT believers? A day is fast approaching when God will restore all things, for nothing can get past Him who sees everything. In the meantime, as believers, we must proclaim the gospel to a lost world. We should be *longing* and *looking* for that day, for it is promised to us. While relatively few modern Christians woke up this morning thinking, "I cannot *wait* for the second coming of Christ," this belief consumed the first-century apostles. In reading their writings we witness an intense anticipation, as if Jesus could come back at any moment. Don't let the gap between His first and second coming overshadow the significance or imminence of His return.

The people of Israel were longing for the day of His arrival, but they failed to realize it would be a day of judgment, not jubilee. We know that Christ has already come and that He is coming again. The question each one of us must ask ourselves is, "Am I prepared for His second coming?"

The Rising of the Sun and the Vindication for God's People
MALACHI 4:2

When the Lord comes, He will bring perfect, righteous judgment with Him similar to the rising of the sun. His appearance will be both a blessing and a curse. Verse 2 describes the blessing. Those who fear the Lord's name are the ones whose names are written in the Lamb's book of life or the book of remembrance. Additionally, they will be insulated from the fiery furnace: "and the sun of righteousness will rise." This is the only occurrence of this phrase in the entire Bible. It conveys images of the brilliant morning sun projecting rays and providing warmth and comfort to those privileged to find solace under it. Malachi reveals that the sun of righteousness will rise also "with healing in its wings."

In Malachi this sun is not an inanimate object, but a person. It is God Himself. It is the manifest presence of God. The Hebrew word *kanaph* is here translated "wings." It occurs elsewhere in the OT to refer to a number of different things. In Genesis 1:21 it speaks of those created, winged animals who soar around the earth. Isaiah 6:2 uses the word to define the wings of the seraphim.

It is also used to refer to the corner or the hem of a garment. In the book of 1 Samuel, after Saul is disobedient to the Lord, the Lord sends Samuel to confront Saul and strip him of the kingdom. Saul responds by approaching Samuel and grabbing the corner or the hem (*kanaph*) of his garment, the force of which rips it off.

Malachi states the sun of righteousness will appear with healing in His garments; that is, His arrival will be associated with the healing and restoring of His people. The sun of righteousness, God Himself, will possess healing in His wings. It was assumed in ancient Israel that the hem of the garment of righteous men contained healing properties. Yet the healing that Malachi refers to in this passage is not merely physical healing, but a spiritual restoration from sin and from separation from the Lord. Therefore, this sun will come with jubilation and celebration. When He comes, "you will go out and playfully jump like calves from the stall." The Israelites would take the calves in the winter and put them in stalls, and they would be locked up all winter. We can imagine the calves' excitement the moment the stalls were opened. Malachi says that the excitement of God's people over His coming will resemble this jubilation.

Remembering the Law as a Means of Sustaining Present Obedience

MALACHI 4:4

The Lord shifts to speaking with the people of Israel directly. Notice the directive in verse 4 to remember the Word of God. Israel was prohibited from separating the idea of following God from the idea of following God's law. They were one and the same. Jesus affirmed this in Matthew 5:17: "Don't assume that I came to destroy the Law or the Prophets. I did not come to destroy but to fulfill." Through His Word, particularly the OT, God has given a road map for success—not to riches and fame, but a road map to pleasing Him and living the abundant life: Meditate on My Word and do it! (see Josh 1:7-9; Ps 1:1-3).

The Hebrew Bible, what we refer to as the OT, is composed of three sections, often collectively referred to as the *Tanakh.* Each of the consonants in this word represent one of the three sections. So the "T" stands for the *Torah,* the Law. The "N" stands for the *Nevi'im,* the Prophets. And the "K" is for the *Ketuvim,* the Writings. This last section contains the wisdom literature and poetic books of the OT.

Within the Torah (Genesis through Deuteronomy), God reminds the people to hold fast to the law of God, to keep it central in their life and worship. The first books of each of the latter sections both begin with a commendation of the law for God's people. After Moses passed the baton, God outlined for Joshua a recipe for success:

> *Above all, be strong and very courageous to carefully observe the whole instruction My servant Moses commanded you. Do not turn from it to the right or the left, so that you will have success wherever you go.* (Josh 1:7)

That phrase *the whole instruction* refers to the teaching of God in the Torah. Do you want to be effective as a leader, Joshua? Do you want to be successful in your life and ministry? Then follow the law. Notice what the Lord says next:

> *This book of instruction must not depart from your mouth; you are to recite it day and night so that you may carefully observe everything written in it. For then you will prosper and succeed in whatever you do.* (Josh 1:8)

If Joshua is to be successful, he must meditate on and memorize the law.

In the first book of the Ketuvim the law of God is once again essential to fruitful living before God. Psalm 1 starts by pronouncing a blessing on the man who will set his heart on the law:

> *How happy is the man who does not follow the advice of the wicked or take the path of sinners or join a group of mockers! Instead, his delight is in the LORD's instruction, and he meditates on it day and night.* (Ps 1:1-2)

If he does that,

> *He [will be] like a tree planted beside streams of water that bears its fruit in season and whose leaf does not wither. Whatever he does prospers. The wicked are not like this; instead, they are like chaff that the wind blows away.* (Ps 1:3-4)

Psalm 1 goes so far as to contrast the man who delights in the law with the wicked, foreseeing the futility of those who dismiss God's instruction.

Looking at the prominence of God's law throughout the Old Testament, it should be no surprise that God turns to the people of Israel at the end of Malachi and commands them to remember Moses' instruction. This is perfectly consistent with what He has instructed the people to do from the very beginning of their existence!

Looking Forward in Hope, Anticipating Restoration

MALACHI 4:5-6

Malachi announced in 3:1 that the forerunner to the Messiah would come. We know from the NT that the forerunner is John the Baptist. But he says here in verses 5-6 that there would be another person, another forerunner, to come before the Day of the Lord.

We know this forerunner cannot ultimately be John the Baptist because this day ends with fathers turning their hearts to children and children turning their hearts to fathers. If this prophecy was completely fulfilled in John, we might ask why Jesus was still rejected by the Jews. So what is He talking about here? Although Jesus said in Matthew 11 that John the Baptist is the forerunner, something happens in Matthew 17 to prove that yet another Elijah will fulfill Malachi's prophecy. In Matthew 17 Jesus leads the disciples up to the Mount of Transfiguration, where both Elijah and Moses appear, talking with the Lord. Peter, of course, wants to set up rooms at the Motel 6 for all three of them, but a voice from heaven rebukes his misunderstanding.

As Jesus' face shines like the sun, the disciples are awestruck, understanding Jesus true identity. The disciples cite this verse in Malachi, to which Jesus replies,

> *"Elijah is coming and will restore everything," He replied. "But I tell you: Elijah has already come, and they didn't recognize him. On the contrary, they did whatever they pleased to him."* (Matt 11:11-12)

The key for our purposes is the future tense "will restore." At the time Jesus is speaking, John the Baptist is already dead. So we know that he cannot be the Elijah of Malachi 4:5. In addition, John the Baptist cannot be this Elijah because this Elijah is going to reestablish all things. John the Baptist was hindered from doing this because of the wickedness of the people's hearts. Thus, Jesus is stating that He is the Elijah-like figure, initiating His kingdom at His resurrection and completing it at His second coming when He will turn the hearts of fathers to their children and the hearts of children to their fathers—a time of great repentance.

Notice how the book of Malachi ends: "Otherwise, I will come and strike the land with a curse." The final words from God to the people for 400 years is a warning that utter destruction will come. The final words are a curse, which left some rabbis uncomfortable with the ending. G. Campbell Morgan noted,

> The Jew always understood this as a message of love, and the Rabbis in the Synagogue from then until the coming of Christ, and in the days of Christ, and until this day, never end Malachi with its last verse. They conclude with the fifth verse. Reading the last: "And He shall turn the heart of the fathers to the children; and the heart of the children to their fathers, lest I come and smite the earth with a curse;" they revert to the fifth: "Behold, I will send you Elijah, the prophet, before the coming of the great and dreadful day of the Lord." (Morgan, *Malachi's Message for Today*, 116)

However, this discomfort does not subside with the end of the OT. God, in a similar manner, says essentially the same thing in Revelation 22:12-13:

Look! I am coming quickly, and My reward is with Me to repay each person according to what he has done. I am the Alpha and the Omega, the First and the Last, the Beginning and the End.

The same promise of judgment is given to the people in Revelation, bringing with it either a day of rejoicing or a day of mourning, depending on whether you are among the righteous or among the wicked. On this side of the life and ministry of Jesus, the determining factor will be whether or not we have received the righteousness of Christ through repentance and faith.

Conclusion: The Sun of Righteousness with Healing in His Wings

We can imagine the destruction of life that would take place if the sun faded the way a candle burns out. Life would cease to exist, causing a shift in the functionality of our planet and solar system. Severe storms would erupt all over the world because of the climate change. Temperatures would plunge, and the land would be covered with a thick layer of snow and ice. The earth might break free from its orbital path and fly off into total darkness. Such is the fate of people who do not have Jesus as their Savior. According to Malachi, however, the sun of righteousness will come with healing in His garments.

In the NT, Jesus Christ meets a woman who reaches out to Him out of complete desperation:

Just then, a woman who had suffered from bleeding for 12 years approached from behind and touched the tassel on His robe, for she said to herself, "If I can just touch His robe, I'll be made well!" But Jesus turned and saw her. "Have courage, daughter," He said. "Your faith has made you well." And the woman was made well from that moment. (Matt 9:20-22)

She was certain that by touching the hem of His garment, she would be healed. Jesus, seeing the woman's actions, commends her faith.

The key word *tassel* or *fringe* is a reference to the hem (Gk *kraspedon*; Hb *kanaph*) of Jesus' garment. Matthew knows the audience of his Gospel is made up of Jews who know the OT. They would have known immediately why she desired to touch His garment. In doing so she was confessing that Jesus Christ was the sun of righteousness from Malachi 4. He was God Himself.

To confirm that Jesus was the rising of the sun, we may also look to Luke 1:76-79:

> *And child, you will be called a prophet of the Most High, for you will go before the Lord to prepare His ways, to give His people knowledge of salvation through the forgiveness of their sins. Because of our God's merciful compassion, the Dawn from on high will visit us to shine on those who live in darkness and the shadow of death, to guide our feet into the way of peace.*

In this passage John the Baptist's father, Zechariah, has been mute for a season. When the silence is broken, his first utterance is a prophecy. He declares that John is preparing the way for "the Dawn from on high." Not surprisingly, John's ministry would be to prepare the way for Jesus Christ.

Jesus Christ is the light to our soul, "the sun of righteousness," in the same way that the sun is light and life to the planet. Jesus Himself declared, "I am the light of the world." The question for every one of us is, Has that light shone in our hearts today?

Reflect and Discuss

1. How is the promise of judgment comforting in the midst of evil and injustice in the world? What specific injustices do you long to see corrected by God's judgment?
2. How does God's judgment work like a purifying furnace? Compare this with Hebrews 12.
3. How can you live longing for the return of Christ? What does it look like to live with the eager expectation of His return?
4. What does it mean that the sun will rise "with healing in its wings"? How do we see this demonstrated in the life of Jesus?
5. If you are a Christian, think about the day you responded to the gospel. Discuss the joy you felt upon being spiritually "healed" by Christ.
6. Why does God remind the people to remember His Word? How does this relate to the judgment and deliverance He has been talking about?
7. What was Jesus' attitude towards the law of God? How should Christians think about the specific commands of the law?
8. Discuss the identity of the forerunner of 4:5. Is he the same or different from the forerunner in 3:1?

9. Discuss the significance of Revelation ending with a similar promise of judgment as Malachi. Is this referring to the same judgment?
10. How would you instruct someone who sees the promise of judgment and responds by trying to "get his life together"? What is a more biblical response, and to what passages of Scripture would you direct him for help?

WORKS CITED

Addison, Joseph, and Richard Steele. *The Spectator, Volume 1: Eighteenth-Century Periodical Essays.* https://itun.es/us/VSwxE.l.

Augustine. *The Confessions of St. Augustine.* Pages 37–302 in vol. 1 of *A Select Library of the Nicene and Post–Nicene Fathers of the Christian Church.* Edited by Philip Schaff. Grand Rapids, MI: Eerdmans, 1974.

Barker, K. L. "Zechariah." Pages 595–700 in vol. 7 of *The Expositor's Bible Commentary: Daniel and the Minor Prophets.* Edited by F. E. Gaebelein. Grand Rapids, MI: Zondervan, 1986.

Boice, J. M. *The Minor Prophets: An Expositional Commentary.* Grand Rapids, MI: Baker, 2002.

Blaising, Craig A. "Malachi." Pages 1573–89 in vol. 1 of *The Bible Knowledge Commentary: An Exposition of the Scriptures.* Edited by J. F. Walvoord and R. B. Zuck. Wheaton, IL: Victor, 1985.

Braverman, Amy M. "Healthy, Wealthy, & Wed." University of Chicago Magazine, 2003. Accessed December 9, 2014. http://magazine.uchicago.edu/0310/features/index-print.shtml.

Bridges, Jerry. *The Joy of Fearing God.* Colorado Springs, CO: Waterbrook, 2004.

Brokaw, Tom. *The Greatest Generation.* New York: Random House, 1998.

Calvin, John. *The Twelve Minor Prophets.* Edinburgh: T & T Clark, 1849.

Cappocia, Tony. "The Truth about Tithing." Accessed January 3, 2015. http://www.biblebb.com/files/tithing.htm

Carre, E. G. *Praying Hyde, Apostle of Prayer: The Life Story of John Hyde.* Alachua, FL: Bridge-Logos, 1983.

Carson, D. A., R. T. France, J. A. Motyer, and G. J. Wenham, eds. *New Bible Commentary: 21st Century Edition.* Fourth edition. Downers Grove, IL: InterVarsity, 1994.

Chambers, Oswald. *Run This Race: The Complete Works of Oswald Chambers.* Grand Rapids, MI: Discovery House, 2000.

Chesterton, G. K. *The Common Man: Essays by G. K. Chesterton.* London: Sheed and Ward, 1950.

Clark, D. J., and H. A. Hatton. *A Handbook on Zechariah.* New York: United Bible Societies, 2002.

Clendenen, E. Ray. "Malachi." In *Haggai, Malachi* by Richard Taylor and E. Ray Clendenen. NAC 21A. Nashville: B&H, 2004.

Constable, Thomas L. "Notes on Zechariah," 2015 edition. Accessed January 8, 2015. http://www.soniclight.com/constable/notes/pdf/zechariah.pdf

Du Plessis, I. J. "Getting to Know the Geography, Topography and Archaeology of the Bible Lands in New Testament Times." In *The New Testament Milieu,* ed. A.B. du Toit, vol. 2, *Guide to the New Testament.* Halfway House: Orion Publishers, 1998.

Easton, M. G. "Azal." In *Easton's Bible Dictionary.* New York: Harper & Brothers, 1893.

Fruchtenbaum, Arnold. "The Book of Malachi." Accessed July 8, 2014. http://www.arunrajesh.com/BibleStudy/mbs096m.pdf.

Galaxie Software. *10,000 Sermon Illustrations.* Biblical Studies, 2002.

Handey, Jack. *Fuzzy Memories.* Kansas City, MO: Andres and McMeel, 1996.

Heinlen, Robert. *Time Enough for Love.* New York: Ace, 1973.

Hindson, E. E., and W. M. Kroll, editors. *KJV Bible Commentary.* Nashville, TN: Thomas Nelson, 1994.

Hutchison, John C. "Was John the Baptist an Essene from Qumran?" *Bibliotheca Sacra* 159 (April–June 2002): 1–14.

Jamieson, R., A. R. Fausset, and D. Brown. *Commentary: Critical and Explanatory on the Whole Bible.* Grand Rapids, MI: Zondervan, 1979.

Johnston, R. L. *Lie of the Tithe.* Naperville, IN: Simple Truth Inc., 1999.

Kaiser, Walter, and L. J. Ogilvie. *Micah, Nahum, Habakkuk, Zephaniah, Haggai, Zechariah, Malachi.* The Preacher's Commentary Series, vol. 21. Nashville, TN: Thomas Nelson, 1992.

Keller, Tim. *Counterfeit Gods: The Empty Promises of Money, Sex, and Power, and the Only Hope that Matters.* New York: Penguin, 2011.

Klein, G. L. *Zechariah.* NAC 21B. Nashville, TN: B&H, 2008.

Lange, John Peter. *Commentary on the Holy Scriptures.* Vol. 41. New York, NY: Charles Scribner's Sons, 1886.

Larson, C. B., and P. Ten Elshof. *1001 Illustrations That Connect: Timeless Wisdom for Preaching, Teaching, and Writing.* Grand Rapids, MI: Zondervan, 2008.

Lee, Albert. "The Tales of Two Sticks." *Our Daily Bread* (September 27, 2011).

Lewis, C. S. *The Weight of Glory*. San Francisco: Harper Collins, 1949.

Lindsey, F. D. "Zechariah." Pages 1545–72 in vol. 1 of *The Bible Knowledge Commentary: An Exposition of the Scriptures*. Edited by J. F. Walvoord & R. B. Zuck. Wheaton, IL: Victor, 1985.

MacArthur, John. "Thoughts on Tithing." Accessed January 3, 2015. http://www.biblebb.com/files/tithing.htm

Mitchell, Hinkley G. *A Critical and Exegetical Commentary on Haggai and Zechariah*. International Critical Commentary. Edinburgh: T&T Clark, 1912.

Moore, Thomas V. *Haggai and Malachi*. New York: Banner of Truth, 1960.

Morgan, G. Campbell. *Malachi's Message for Today*. Eugene, OR: Wipf and Stock Publishers, 1998.

Morgan, R. J. *From this Verse: 365 Scriptures that Changed the World*. Nashville: Thomas Nelson, 2000.

Nietzsche, Friedrich. *Thus Spoke Zarathustra*. London: MacMillan, 1896.

Palau, Luis. "Hope for Healing." Accessed December 10, 2014. http://change.palau.org/on_demand_resources/articles_for_growth/story/hope_for_healing_58.

Pelikan, Jaroslav. *The Vindication of Tradition: The 1983 Jefferson Lecture in the Humanities*. New Haven: Yale University Press, 1986.

The Pew Research Center for the People and the Press. "How Young People View Their Lives, Futures, and Politics: A Portrait of 'Generation Next.'" Washington, D.C.: Pew Research Center, 2007.

Pink, Arthur W. *The Sovereignty of God*. Grand Rapids, MI: Baker, 1970.

Piper, John. *Desiring God: Meditations of a Christian Hedonist*. Colorado Springs, CO: Multnomah, 1986.

Putman, Jim, and Bobby Harrington, with Robert E. Coleman. *DiscipleShift: Five Steps That Help Your Church to Make Disciples Who Make Disciples*. Grand Rapids, MI: Zondervan, 2013.

Sproul, R. C. *Five Things Every Christian Needs to Grow*. Lake Mary, FL: Reformation Trust, 2002.

Statistic Brain. "Fear / Phobia Statistics." Accessed December 9, 2014. http://www.statisticbrain.com/fear-phobia-statistics/

Stuhlmueller, C. *Rebuilding with Hope: A Commentary on the Books of Haggai and Zechariah*. Grand Rapids, MI: Eerdmans/Edinburgh: Handsel, 1988.

Tozer, A. W. *Born after Midnight.* Camp Hill, PA: WingSpread, 1989.

———. *The Pursuit of God.* Camp Hill, PA: WingSpread, 2006.

Utley, Bob. "The Study Bible Commentary Series, Old Testament." Accessed December 9, 2014. http://bible.org/seriespage/malachi-1.

Wallace, David Foster. "This Is Water." Lecture given at Kenyon College, Gambier, OH, May, 2005.

Wiersbe, W. W. *Be Heroic: Demonstrating Bravery by Your Walk.* Colorado Springs, CO: Chariot Victor, 1997.

———. *Be Victorious: In Christ You Are an Overcomer.* Colorado Springs, CO: David C. Cook, 2010.

———. *Wiersbe Bible Commentary OT.* Colorado Springs, CO: David C. Cook, 2007.

Wright, C. J. H. *An Eye for an Eye: The Place of Old Testament Ethics Today.* Downers Grove, IL: InterVarsity, 1983.

Zacharias, Ravi. *The Grand Weaver: How God Shapes Us through the Events of Our Lives.* Grand Rapids, MI: Zondervan, 2007.

SCRIPTURE INDEX